The Marching Chiefs
of Florida State
University

The Marching Chiefs of Florida State University
The Band That Never Lost a Halftime Show

BILL F. FAUCETT

McFarland & Company, Inc., Publishers
Jefferson, North Carolina

LIBRARY OF CONGRESS CATALOGUING-IN-PUBLICATION DATA

Names: Faucett, Bill F., author.
Title: The Marching Chiefs of Florida State University : the band that never lost a halftime show / Bill F. Faucett.
Description: Jefferson, North Carolina : McFarland & Company, 2018 | Includes bibliographical references and index.
Identifiers: LCCN 2017048453 | ISBN 9781476668321 (softcover : acid free paper) ∞
Subjects: LCSH: Marching Chiefs—History. | Marching bands—Florida—Tallahassee—History.
Classification: LCC ML28.T22 M374 2018 | DDC 784.8/30975988—dc23
LC record available at https://lccn.loc.gov/2017048453

BRITISH LIBRARY CATALOGUING DATA ARE AVAILABLE

ISBN (print) 978-1-4766-6832-1
ISBN (ebook) 978-1-4766-3049-6

© 2018 Bill F. Faucett. All rights reserved

No part of this book may be reproduced or transmitted in any form or by any means, electronic or mechanical, including photocopying or recording, or by any information storage and retrieval system, without permission in writing from the publisher.

On the cover: 2010 Marching Chiefs © 2018 Melina's Photography

Printed in the United States of America

McFarland & Company, Inc., Publishers
Box 611, Jefferson, North Carolina 28640
www.mcfarlandpub.com

To all Marching Chiefs,
but especially to those in my family

Colleen Vaverek Faucett, flag corps
Adam Faucett (2nd generation), trombone
Julie Greenwood Faucett (in memoriam), majorette
Kevin Vaverek, Big 8
Kerry Vaverek Israel, majorette
Katy Vaverek Shisler, flute
Carter Vaverek, saxophone
Jenna Vaverek (2nd generation), flute
Caroline Vaverek (2nd generation), flute

And to my favorite non–Chief, Billy Faucett

The Chiefs undoubtedly stand as one of the finest marching bands in America.
—*The Florida Flambeau* (September 24, 1957)

If there is one thing about the Marching Chiefs, we love our traditions.
   We love what we do, and we love how we do it.
—David Westberry, The Voice of the Marching Chiefs (2016)

Table of Contents

Acknowledgments   ix
Preface   1
Introduction: FSU vs. East Carolina, September 20, 1980   4

Part I. Marching Chiefs One Time!

1. College Town (to 1937)   9
    Higher Education in Tallahassee   9
    "Femina Perfecta": The Florida State College for Women (1909)   16

2. Picture and Sound (1938–1946)   21
    The Tally Troopers   21
    Two Cellists   24
    "Band Pageantry" and War   30
    The Remarkable Frank Sykora   35
    Sellers Returns   39

3. Becoming the Chiefs (1947–1953)   42
    A Coed University ... Again   42
    Halftime Hijinks   48
    Robert Braunagel (1949–1953)   52
    October 1950   55
    Football Gets Serious   59

Part II. Marching Chiefs Two Times!

4. Whit (1953–1962)   65
    Manley R. Whitcomb   65
    "Music, Music, Music"   69

Table of Contents

    "Hell-Raisers" 74
    Small Scandals 84
    Damned Gators 85
    Whit Retires 89

5. The Art of the Marching Band (1963–1970)   91
    Charlie Carter 91
    "Brownie" 97
    "Never lost a halftime show" 101
    Forging an Art Form 109
    "Ghosts of FSCW" 113
    The Chiefs Go Bowling 116

6. World Renowned (1971–1976)   121
    "With an ever present flair" 121
    "Anti-Football Views" 130
    Syria and Jordan (1974) 135
    Dis-Spirited '76 138

Part III. Marching Chiefs Three Times!

7. Football Rising: Bowden, Bernie and Bentley (1976–1990)   146
    Tradition Returns 146
    "Where our traditions come from": FSU at Ohio State, October 3, 1981 152
    The Voice 159
    Shellahamer Returns 161
    "We played the 'War Chant' non-stop" 164

8. A Marching Band for a New Era (1991 to Today)   168
    Dunnagin and Plack 168
    "Zero tolerance" 172
    Exit Charlie 177
    World Renowned ... Still 182

Post-Game: "Here's a hymn..."   189

Chapter Notes   197

Bibliography   212

Index   215

Acknowledgments

Writing this book has been a pure pleasure, one significantly enhanced by the fact that so many people were willing and eager to assist. First, I would like to extend my sincerest thanks to the many Marching Chiefs directors and alums who were willing to share with me their experiences and memories. If not all are quoted here, all significantly impacted the story and enlivened the narrative. Their voices are a crucial and often fascinating part of this story. The names of all interviewees and correspondents may be found in the bibliography.

Special thanks to Sandra Varry, Heritage Protocol & University Archivist at the Special Collections and Archives of Florida State University and her staff, especially Hannah Davis, Heritage Protocol & University Archives Assistant. They provided much helpful information, as well as access to the collection, photograph scans, and permissions. Their timely and friendly support has been much appreciated.

Several others gave important archival assistance. LeEtta Schmidt, Resource Sharing and Copyright Librarian at the University of South Florida, provided invaluable aid in locating and acquiring books and microfilms. Florence Ashby, in her capacity as FSU Marching Chiefs Alumni archivist, kindly provided access to the treasures at the College of Music Band Archives. And Dr. Bentley Shellahamer loaned me his six imposing photograph albums/scrapbooks, which provide a wonderful retrospective of his term as director of the Chiefs. Hearty thanks to Paul Ort for providing copies of a number of his 1950s-era recordings and DVDs, especially the documentaries *Marching Chiefs at the Sun Bowl* (1955) and Dick Mayo's *FSU Bands: Proud Heritage, Bright Future* (1993). All of these have been invaluable resources.

Acknowledgments

Many thanks as always to Douglass Seaton, the Warren D. Allen Professor of Musicology at FSU, for his encouragement to pursue this project and for his careful reading of the manuscript. Several other readers—Pat Dunnigan, Jon Gilbert, Bill Haggard, Chris Haughee, Bentley Shellahamer, Mike Pate, David Plack, David Westberry, and Tim Wise—made helpful comments, corrections, and clarifications to various chapters and sections. I am deeply indebted to them.

I would like to give special acknowledgment to Bob Thurston, percussion expert and arranger extraordinaire, who was extremely helpful, supportive, and generous during the course of my research and writing. Bob read most of the manuscript, asked many questions, and shared significant insights, especially on the topics of Charlie Carter, Big 8, and the art of arranging music. I also sincerely appreciate Bob's permission to quote extensively from his master's degree thesis and from his emails, and I am grateful for the invaluable information, good ideas, and gentle criticism that he offered throughout the process.

There are many stray artifacts related to the Marching Chiefs, materials forgotten by most but retained by a few. I am indebted to those who directed me to important bits of Chiefs history. Sara Carter Pankaskie supplied the Syria/Jordan itinerary; Leslie Ray Zebrowitz provided the London itinerary; Bennett Shelfer answered myriad questions and directed me to a number of interesting photos; Steve Sparkman sent me record label listings; Lil Classen, George Corradino, and John Garrett graciously shared written memories; and Heather Ambrose Trkovsky provided copies of *The Legacy*, the Marching Chiefs 1998 and 1999 yearbooks. Sincere thanks to Curtis Falany, moderator of the online chat group called the "60s list," for granting me access to conversations and for inviting me to ask questions. When many small details proved elusive, I could always count on the 60s list for guidance (and opinions!).

I am indebted to the professional and amateur photographers who gave me permission to include their images. My thanks to Steve Chase (Chase-photography.com), John F. Ervin, Kim Hadley, Melina Myers (Melinasphotography.com), Bob O'Lary (Olary.com), and Bennett Shelfer.

My family—Colleen, Billy, and Adam—has been patient, supportive, and always willing to listen to me tell yet another Marching Chiefs story. You are loved and appreciated!

Acknowledgments

Finally, everyone mentioned here, and many others not mentioned, played a role in the creation and shaping of this history, but I happily accept the customary responsibility for accuracy and interpretation. Although I hope they are few, any errors contained within are mine.

Bill F. Faucett, PhD
Flush, 1980 and 1981
Assistant Drum Major, 1982
Drum Major, 1983 and 1984

Preface

This volume explores the history and traditions of Florida State University's world-renowned Marching Chiefs. It presents many facts and details and also plumbs the myths, the lore, and even a few of the rumors. It provides a glimpse into the inner workings of the band by chronicling its leaders, discussing its shows and music, and probing the origins of some of its cherished traditions. At the same time, the book attempts to give a sense of the rise of a great university and its Department (later School, now College) of Music, the evolution in Tallahassee of Big Football, and changes in American society that impacted all of these.

The history of the Chiefs may be partitioned neatly into three broad periods. The first considers musical development at FSU's predecessor institutions through 1952, just two years after the band was named the Marching Chiefs. Tallahassee's appetite for music—and its belief that it could foster good morals—mirrored that of the nation, and was assiduously cultivated with the goal of building character and school spirit. In chapters one through three I examine the ever-growing influence of music, especially band music, on campus.

The 1953 arrival of the revered Manley R. Whitcomb inaugurates the second era of the Chiefs. He brought with him from Ohio State University many of the traditions that resonate to this day, as well as a talented young arranger. Whitcomb's influence was especially felt by the two directors who succeeded him, Robert Braunagel and Richard Mayo. Their stories are conveyed in chapters four, five, and six.

Finally, following a rough patch in the mid–1970s, a third epoch begins in 1977. Bentley Shellahamer resurrected traditions that had been briefly jettisoned, yet he astutely maintained a few that gave the band a modern look and appeal. Robert Sheldon, and especially Patrick Dunnigan and David Plack, continued those traditions even through times of trial. This period in Chiefs history is investigated in chapters seven and eight.

My examination has taken into account records available in FSU's Heritage Protocol & University Archives and ephemera from the College of Music Band Archive. I have also relied on a variety of news reports, including those found in the campus newspaper, the *Florida Flambeau* (later strangely re-titled *FSView & Florida Flambeau*). The *Flambeau* is an extraordinary resource I have used extensively, especially for the information and photographs it contained about music and marching in the early years of both the Florida State College for Women (FSCW) and Florida State University. Its remarkable value comes as no surprise; a 1916 *Flambeau* editorialist predicted that the newspaper would one day be an important resource for research related to the university. "And our history?" the writer asked rhetorically:

> We are now having a most illuminating history published weekly, the *Flambeau*. We imagine that this real live history of school, bound yearly and placed conspicuously in the library, would be of much interest and like old wine grow better with age.[1]

As far as the Marching Chiefs and its musical predecessors are concerned, the writer was certainly correct.

No small part of what makes up this book are the recollections of some of the Marching Chiefs themselves, whose combined memories and experiences span eight decades. This part of my inquiry—the chance to meet and talk to so many people whose love for the Chiefs is palpable—has been one of the greatest joys of preparing this book.

Of course, a pitfall of writing a book that relies in part on human memory is that sometimes multiple memories do not neatly align. I tend to agree with author Jodi Picoult, who wrote that "Recollections are in the eye of the beholder. No two held side by side can ever quite match." Because many of my interviewees recalled events from as many as seven decades ago, there are naturally inconsistencies. When confronted with such dissonances, I consulted with several parties and searched elsewhere for corroborating evidence. I have presented in this book the story that holds up best to historical scrutiny, although the gist of alternative narratives is supplied in the text and in footnotes.

Naturally, this is *a* history—not *the* history—of the Marching

Preface

Chiefs. The collected stories and recollections of current and alumni Chiefs would fill a large repository. Nevertheless, I hope that this modest attempt will convey impressions of what it has been like to be in the band; impart a good idea of where the Chiefs come from; convey how its leaders thought and acted; chronicle how the band has changed over the years; and demonstrate that gridiron excellence—in music, marching, and entertainment—has been its unwavering goal since its very inception.

Introduction
FSU vs. East Carolina, September 20, 1980

If you are an alumnus of the Marching Chiefs, you own innumerable memories. Many of them are indelible: the first days of freshman (later "gunkie" and now "rookie") week. Sweaty, dusty, hot, miserable practices. Sectionals. Skull Sessions. The first home game. The first away game. Your last half-time show. The Come-On and Go. Hairy Buffalo. Bowl games. The *Hymn.* Your director. Charlie Carter. Lifelong friends. Frenzied cheers from the bleachers following a magnificent performance. And many, many more.

If you are among the legions of Marching Chiefs fans there is also much to appreciate and admire. Entertaining, sometimes even stirring, pre-game and half-time shows; often ceaseless playing in the stands to invigorate the football team; the tremendous spirit and spectacle that the Chiefs bring to football games; and pride in a stellar and historical FSU organization.

My own memories of the Marching Chiefs began on the first day of 1980, before I was even a member. On a comfortable, slightly humid New Year's Day evening, I went to "the strip" on Fort Lauderdale Beach, not too far from my Pompano Beach hometown. The Chiefs, including a handful of my Coconut Creek High School band friends—Daryl Verhoeven, Amanda Monroe, and others—were staying at a beachfront hotel there following their appearance at the Orange Bowl, one of the most important bowl games in FSU's then relatively short football history. In a contest of national import, the team lost to Barry Switzer's

Oklahoma Sooners, but to judge by the excitement of the band you would not have guessed it. There was an air of jubilance all around. Half-time had apparently gone well for the Chiefs, and the strip offered lots of things to see and do. For my part, I renewed acquaintances with my old high school friends, who were nothing less than ecstatic, even if tired and soaked in sweat. A few oddities caught my eye: I remember being surprised to see no chaperones—there was not a "real" adult in sight; the young men in the band sported lots of facial hair; and I seem to recall the presence of girls.

My high school band directors—Robert Spradling, a talented and charismatic musician and teacher; Kathleen Murphy, an amazingly patient and dedicated soul; and Scott Smith, a positive and enthusiastic newbie to the band-directing profession—had all been Chiefs. Given these facts—as well as my previous three summers spent at FSU's celebrated band camps—there was little chance that I would be anything other than a Nole and a Marching Chief. I eventually applied to two universities: the University of Hawaii (a natural for a kid from greater Fort Lauderdale) and FSU. But given that Hawaii was an impossibly long and expensive haul, and that I had already developed a strong affection for FSU, the decision was easy.

I cannot honestly say that I remember much about my gunkie week, the often grueling pre-season practice sessions that act as both auditions and intensive trainings. It was beastly hot, of course. And the university-owned metal sousaphone that I now shouldered weighed considerably more than my high school fiberglass instrument. First up was a playing audition. I might have been asked to render a few scales and to sight-read the "Victory Song" or some other beloved FSU tune. An on-field audition no doubt required 8-to-5 high-stepping while playing the "Fight Song." For much of that first band camp we resided at the off-campus private Cash Hall until, sometime during the week, we migrated to our on-campus residences. I was one of five or six band members—Dawn Lockhart, Carrie Belton, Joanne Haigh, and others—living in Landis Hall (I was in room 407), and I remember other gunkies being jealous that, following the long rehearsals on Chiefs Field, I could go home to air-conditioning when so many of them were forced to brave the stagnant August heat trapped within an ill-equipped dorm room.

But if some aspects of those first gunkie days are lost in the fog, one early game experience remains unforgettable. Although my appetite for serious college football was only just developing, I knew that FSU held a 1980 preseason ranking of no. 13; we jumped to no. 10 following a beatdown of LSU in Tiger Stadium—a steep and treacherous arena, especially if you're carrying a tuba—just a week before. Our first home opponent, the University of Louisville Cardinals, was not expected to accomplish much that season, and indeed, they were crushed by the Noles in a 52–0 sleeper on September 13. The highlight of that game may well have been the christening of a new scoreboard. A week later, on September 20, we played the Pirates of East Carolina; the team was up and coming, but, like Louisville, the Pirates were not expected to present a problem for the home team. And they didn't; we walloped them, 63–7. The game failed to captivate, but the half-time show promised to be something special. My band director, the incredible Bentley Shellahamer, the man widely known to have restored the Marching Chiefs to their historical glory, had big plans in store.

I did not take too much notice of the football activities of the day, but I nevertheless got a tremendous jolt from our pre-game show. For tuba players—members of the "Royal Flush"—the thing is really remarkable. In what can only be described as the most awesome tuba display in the history of the marching band—with no apologies to Ohio State's "I" dotters—the Royal Flush at the end of pre-game was performed flawlessly. One giant circle of magnificent tubidity rounded the centerfield Seminole head in precise coordination. Our instruments were gleaming. Bodies were equidistant. All were totally in step. And the PYFEs? Perfect. The whole had been expertly choreographed by my section leader Mike Kuperberg, the very model of competence, dedication, and cheerfulness.

Our East Carolina half-time show theme was patriotic, rendered amidst the contentious 1980 presidential election and the emotionally-charged Iranian hostage crisis. A special surprise was planned for our audience, and the Chiefs were looking forward to the spectacle no less. As a tuba player, I was naturally in the back of the band. The noise made the whole experience a bit surreal; I've never heard a louder crowd. I could not even hear myself playing, and I was really blowing. But I could see much of what was going on thanks to the bell of my tuba, which, like a mirror, reflected the student side of Doak Campbell Stadium behind me. As we reached peak intensity in a gorgeous Charlie Carter arrangement of "America the Beautiful," fireworks—several minutes of riveting spectacle—were ignited.

FSU vs. East Carolina, September 20, 1980

For the most part, I intently watched my drum major, Kenny Williams, who was by far the most dynamic drum major who ever led me. But for a few seconds, my eyes drifted away from him. From the bell of my horn—my shiny and somewhat dented silver tuba—I could see the fireworks exploding in the distant dark sky behind me. They were distorted, of course, bent oddly in some kind of parabolic way I am sure I learned about in a class.

But this experience, for me, was unlike any before it. Here was color; here was energy; here was pageantry; and here was music that was totally awesome. The throng of fans—50,000? maybe more?—roared unlike any I had ever seen, heard, or imagined. If it was the first time I had been around such thrill and excitement, it would not be the last. I was a Marching Chief. In my five seasons, that rush would visit me many more times.

PART I.
MARCHING CHIEFS ONE TIME!

∰ 1 ∰

College Town (to 1937)

Higher Education in Tallahassee

Florida Institute (1851)

It is impossible to know how many people were executed on "Gallows Hill," but we can imagine that few citizens wanted Tallahassee's new city school to be located at such an unseemly locale. Not only had it been the site of hangings since the 1820s—which made it something of a ghastly choice—but it was also hugely inconvenient. Well outside the city center, Gallows Hill was a mile-long westward trek from downtown Tallahassee. It was a journey made more difficult because the low ground that had to be traversed to get to Gallows Hill was virtually impassable following a hard rain. But, as is often the case, governmental convenience trumped common sense. The city already owned the land, and, although other more suitable locations had been identified and recommended, in 1854 officials declared that the Florida Institute would be built atop Gallows Hill.

Tallahassee's city fathers were motivated to move quickly on the construction of a building for the Florida Institute. Three years earlier, in 1851—the year its successor institution now claims as its founding—state legislators voted on and approved the establishment of two state-run educational seminaries, one that would lay to the east of the Suwanee River, the other to the west.[1] The former, East Florida Seminary, would be formally located at Ocala in 1853, but the latter's location was yet to be determined. Several cities indicated an interest in hosting the site, and their leaders could substantially enhance their prospects by chipping in financially to ensure the new school's success: donations of land, structures, and operating cash could go a long way toward securing the blessings of the legislature. Besides Tallahassee, the towns of Quincy and Marianna also vied to provide a home for the new western seminary.

Before the legislature determined where it would locate the seminary, however, the all-male Florida Institute—known variously as City School, Tallahassee Institute, Tallahassee Seminary, and other names—opened in April 1855. It was divided into two sections, a preparatory school and a collegiate department. Total enrollment included about a hundred students, many of them from prominent Tallahassee families.[2] One of the more recognizable names on the Florida Institute roster was collegiate department student, James D. Westcott.

The Florida Institute would not be a long-lived endeavor.[3] Following several years of jockeying by Tallahassee leaders to win the distinction of becoming home to the western seminary—and less than two years after the opening of the Florida Institute—Governor James E. Broome signed into law on January 1, 1857, the legislation that designated Tallahassee as the site of the new West Florida Seminary (also called the Seminary West of the Suwanee).

West Florida Seminary (1857)

Tallahassee had more to offer the state legislature than just the original Florida Institute building. The city was also willing to throw in a second, recently-built schoolhouse, as well as a good deal of cash that would sweeten the deal.[4] Those were not Tallahassee's only attractions. Relative to its competitors, at nearly 2,000 residents it was a positively bustling city. Its position as the territorial capital since 1824 undoubtedly induced many legislators—many of whose own children would likely attend the new seminary—to vote in the affirmative.

Although begun as a school for boys, girls from the financially faltering Leon Female Academy were admitted to the seminary in the fall of 1858.[5] Of course, the times mandated separation between the boys and girls, and the seminary essentially existed as two institutions, each with its own building and its own faculty. The curriculum—including classes in farming and agriculture, the mechanical arts, and teacher education—had not changed drastically since its Florida Institute days, but, in an eerie foreshadowing of the travails that would soon engulf the nation, the seminary added military instruction to the men's

1. College Town (to 1937)

curriculum in 1859.[6] Just eight years following its legislative establishment, West Florida Seminary was granted the authority to confer degrees on January 1, 1860.

Tallahassee was not, of course, unaffected by the Civil War. The seminary's name was changed to the Florida Military and Collegiate Institute in 1863, and its teachers, most of whom were men, were in short supply, as were operational funds and instructional materials. The seminary struggled through these unwelcome years, and the unavoidable results were the cancellation of classes and periods of closure. The military instruction proved handy, though; some of the young men enrolled in them had a chance to test their mettle in Tallahassee's Battle of Natural Bridge, a day-long skirmish that prevented the city from being taken by Union forces. Occurring on March 6, 1865, it was one of the last battlefield salvos before Confederate forces surrendered at Appomattox.

Novelist Maurice Thompson gave an impression of the war-time condition in Tallahassee in his 1882 novel, *A Tallahassee Girl*:

> When the war came, it did not reach Tallahassee. Atlanta, Nashville, Savannah, Augusta, Charleston, Richmond, each a social and commercial centre peculiarly Southern, fell in the way of armies, and lay at the mercy of a triumphant soldiery; but the fair queen of Florida, beautiful, embowered, aristocratic Tallahassee, escaped such a fate. When the blare and thunder and crash of those four cataclysmal years had sunk into silence, she sat upon her high green hill, wrapped in her mantle of orange, fig, and live-oak trees, without a scar or a hurt visible.[7]

Once the war was over, Tallahassee experienced something of a boom. It was partly reflected in the jump in Florida's population, from about 140,000 just before the war to more than 400,000 in 1890. The increase naturally ignited economic prosperity, which in turn led to a period of growth for the school, known again as the West Florida Seminary.

A leading light of the seminary was Albert Alexander Murphree, who arrived in Tallahassee as a math instructor in 1895. Respected by the faculty and beloved by students, just two years later he was named the seminary's president. By 1902, Murphree's attributes bordered on the legendary. Wrote one yearbook editorialist:

> A man of untiring energy, of constant sympathy with the aspirations of all his students, of sound judgment, of high integrity and rugged honesty, [Murphree] has, by his interest in the students, and the example set before them of his pure, noble life, won their love and esteem forever.[8]

The same year he arrived in Tallahassee he married Jennie Henderson, the daughter of a distinguished Tallahassee family and an 1895 seminary graduate.

The seminary was organized into three sections: a high school, a normal (or teachers) school, and a college. Degrees offered included the bachelor of arts (emphasizing Greek and Latin); the bachelor of science (modern languages and physical sciences); and the bachelor of letters (English, German, and Romance languages).

Although from nearly the school's founding young ladies with an interest in music were provided with piano lessons, President Murphree was the first to give the subject serious attention. It helped that Murphree himself was a talented singer, a tenor whose skills were recognized and sought after.[9] His organization of the seminary's first music department in 1902 was not only an acknowledgment of his own intense devotion, but also a clear signal of the subject's surging popularity as a course of study. Early class offerings included lessons in piano and voice, as well as sight-singing instruction. Students who sought performance opportunities could join the newly-organized Glee Club.

Murphree's leadership made a positive impact on the institution and on the city, and its pupils could not help but notice the progress. One hopeful student-poet conveyed pride in the seminary with the lines, "It has made its mark in years two score, and will be the best in that many more."[10]

Florida State College (1901)

In 1901, the school's name was changed yet again. Florida State College (FSC), many thought, was more representative of the growing population of students—some 300 enrolled in the 1901–1902 academic year—from throughout Florida and the South. One yearbook historian noted that "It has been our pleasure to witness the growth of the institution from an almost local patronage to an attendance extending to almost every county in Florida."[11] Part of the college's appeal rested with its numerous comforts. Students were enticed to attend in part because "These buildings are furnished with steam heat, baths, and the latest and most approved sanitary plumbing, rendering them as complete and comfortable as first-class hotels."[12]

FSC strongly encouraged physical activity through sports. Teams included football, baseball, track, tennis, basketball, and golf. The college fielded a football team in 1900 and 1901, although the only play seems to have been intra-squad. In 1902, Francis B. Winthrop, FSC's team manager, began discussions with city fathers in Bainbridge, Georgia; it was hoped that those negotiations would lead to a football game.[13] Bainbridge was at a distinct disadvantage, as they had not yet formed a team. The FSC challenge—one which fostered both local enthusiasm and civic pride— led to the organization of a Bainbridge football club. A contest was scheduled for November 21, 1902, and, although FSC won the game in a 5–0 battle, the proud citizens of Bainbridge were not disappointed: "The Tallahasseeans scored only once against our men," wrote the editor of the Bainbridge newspaper, *Search Light*, "and we consider this a splendid showing for the home boys, for they went into the game without ever having had any team against [which to] practice."[14]

There was by this time already plenty of school spirit at FSC. The game, played in Tallahassee, was acknowledged as an important step for the college. It was memorialized in "The Bainbridge Game," a poem that appeared in the FSC yearbook, *Argo*:

> No; ne'er was such a tumult heard
> At F. S. C. again
> As Freshmen, Preps, and Seniors raised
> The evening of the game;
> It kept old Bainbridge long awake,
> Her team at last got rattled,
> And Georgia sympathizers quaked,
> For those who with us battled.[15]

Then as now, football was recognized as a dangerous sport. It was reported that through Thanksgiving 1902, ten Americans had been killed playing the sport; another seventy were seriously injured.[16] One scribe noted that "quite a hue and cry" was being made over the situation, although Princeton president and future U.S. President Woodrow Wilson insisted that the injuries were occurring mostly at "smaller towns and schools where the boys have not been thoroughly trained."[17] Certainly, no one could claim that the FSC or Bainbridge boys had been "thoroughly trained."

Despite its perils, football had proven a passionate avocation for the men and women at FSC. But, as they often had, the times were about to change; they were in part precipitated by a wholesale reorganization of higher education in Florida.

Florida Female College (1905)

Although Florida State College and its earlier iterations had been coeducational, that was about to end.[18] The State of Florida had long supported, fully or partially, the operations of eight institutions of higher learning, and the burden of financial support was increasingly unsustainable. In 1905, State Representative H. H. Buckman, of Duval County, laid out a plan to reorganize the State's college system, eliminate some of its duplicative efforts, and rein in spending. The Buckman Bill proposed state ownership of just four schools. Two of the existing ones would be retained—the Florida Normal and Industrial College for Negroes in Tallahassee and the Institute for the Blind, Deaf, and Dumb in St. Augustine. One new school would be the males-only University of the State of Florida, forged from the remnants of the East Florida Seminary and opened in Gainesville in 1906. Tallahassee's Florida State College would henceforth be known as Florida Female College (FFC), its fifth name in fifty years.

Still under the leadership of President Murphree, music remained a curricular focus at FFC. Unlike other state-operated institutions in the South, which tended to concentrate on the sciences of industry, agriculture, technology, and teacher training, FFC was a traditional liberal arts college.[19] Its programs emphasized six main areas: liberal arts (including languages and literature), industrial arts (i.e., home economics and related pursuits), music, art, expression, and the normal school.

Murphree was not entirely sure that FFC's curriculum would attract students in the numbers required to make the college an educational and financial success. Although the separation of the sexes at college was not unknown to Floridians, co-education had long been the rule in Florida. Nevertheless, the state's new model created no small amount of consternation as many, including Murphree, feared that dividing the sexes would be unpopular. His fears proved unfounded, however, and school enrollment grew steadily; by the start of FFC's second semester he was already scouting locations on which to build new residences and classrooms.[20]

The crowded conditions that were experienced by nearly all FFC academic programs were equally inconducive to the progress of music. Students required areas for private practice—whether voice, piano, or other instruments—and dedicating precious space to accommodate a single student or a small ensemble was simply not deemed efficient. As quarters grew increasingly cramped, students were found practicing in stairwells, hallways, and all manner of unsuitable places.[21]

But if space was at a premium, Murphree nevertheless insisted on well qualified staff. Madeleine Keipp was appointed in 1905 to a three-year term as director of the music department. A graduate of the Cincinnati Conservatory, she had spent several years of additional study in Germany, after which she taught in the South—Alabama, Virginia, and Georgia. Keipp added the study of organ to the curriculum; it was a bold move, considering that the college did not own an instrument. Local churches helpfully provided students with access to their organs until the school acquired a Lyon and Healy model in 1907.[22] Keipp did not last beyond her initial contract. She was replaced as director in 1909 by Martha May Cline, another Cincinnati Conservatory graduate who had also studied in Chicago at the reputable Sherwood Conservatory.

✤ ✤ ✤

Music was not unknown in Tallahassee before it became part of the college's curriculum, of course. Fenton Garnett Davis Avant, who began at Florida State College in 1902 and graduated from Florida Female College in 1908, reported on a number of musical encounters in her memoir, *My Tallahassee*. Among the most notable were the regular appearances of the circus and the awe-inspiring parade that routinely greeted its arrival. "Music for the parade," Avant reminisced, "was furnished by a brass band riding in a huge gilded bandwagon drawn by several pairs of well-matched horses wearing elaborate trappings."[23]

The musically knowledgeable had also been entranced by the piano recital appearance in Tallahassee by "Blind Tom" Wiggins, a former slave whose musical abilities were nothing less than spectacular. "He was totally blind and had a defective mind," Avant reported, "but [he] was a musical genius."[24] Wiggins crafted a number of original compositions and played them for adoring crowds, but his special gift was his ability to re-play perfectly anything he heard. "I thought his talents for original composition were greatly overrated," Avant wrote, "but he could reproduce anything played once in his presence." Besides that stupendous talent, "I remember that for one number he played simultaneously 'Dixie' with one hand and 'Suwannee River' with the other. It was quite a sight."[25]

Other musical sustenance was available in the city. Trinity Church possessed a fine, if small, hand-pumped pipe organ.[26] And Mrs. McMahon, "a lady of culture and refinement" who lived on North Monroe Street, owned a piano. A timid performer, she apparently practiced only at night when no one would hear her. It is not known if she ever awakened anyone.[27]

"Femina Perfecta": The Florida State College for Women (1909)

Florida Female College became the Florida State College for Women (FSCW) in 1909. The change occurred for no other reason than many disliked the former name, and the new one seemed to be better English usage.[28] The school's educational aims remained much as they had been:

> Its highest mission was felt to be the infusion of the young women of the Commonwealth with such light and warmth that they should become lamps, trimmed and burning with perennial flame, radiating the spirit of helpfulness, usefulness, and good will in every neighborhood of this State; to be a place where young women might come for intellectual light and spiritual quickening and warmth, a place where all noble ambitions should be awakened, where the best that is in human character should be brought to the light, and where love to God, love to humanity, and love to country should be made a ruling passion.[29]

FSCW took as its motto, "Femina Perfecta," a term that conveys that it was the institution's goal to turn out the "perfect woman"; that is, one informed to all the possibilities of her gender—wife, mother, professional, intellectual. FSCW admitted no limits; the college would stand for achievement, uprightness, excellence. The Florida State College for Women "is a name we should all cherish," proclaimed the 1910 yearbook, "for it is a symbol of the 'finest in the land.'"[30]

President Murphree resigned in 1909 to take the helm at the recently re-named University of Florida. FSCW's new president would be Edward Conradi, an Ohio man, who received his bachelor's and master's degrees at Indiana University before proceeding to Clark University (Worcester, Massachusetts) for his doctoral degree. Conradi studied philosophy and psychology and made a name for himself by co-translating Ludwig Kotelmann's book titled *School Hygiene*.[31] At the time, that topic was not an insignificant one, and Conradi was an expert in sanitary architecture (the design and placement of heating elements, ventilation, and the like), preventive medicine, and, of course, psychology, all of which could be useful at a growing college. Not only that, but his dissertation explored speech development in children, and he had written an article on bird song; those interests perhaps made him sympathetic toward the pursuit of singing.

Conradi's more than three decades of service at FSCW included a remarkable record of construction. He built the Administration Building (1910); Reynolds Hall (1913); the Dining Hall (1914); Broward Hall (1918); and others. He did not do it alone, of course; the raising of many of these structures was overseen by the college business manager and Conradi's right-hand man, J. G. Kellum. Conradi remained at the school until 1941, making him by far the longest-serving president in the history of the institution.

Besides merely running and improving a college, Conradi had to deal with the times. He and his students were forced to grapple with many of the major social concerns of the day: the labor movement, questions of socialism versus capitalism, women's suffrage, the Great War (World War I), temperance ("the fight against John Barleycorn," as it was put in a 1915 issue of the campus newspaper, the *Flambeau*[32]), and the Great Depression. It was not all bad news, of course; the telephone, first installed on Bryan Hall's second floor in 1916, was a herald of future technology on campus and was much appreciated by the residents.[33] But Conradi may have been surprised by the increasing disdain toward faculty and other adults among those whom he was charged with educating. By the 1920s, the paternalism that had long accompanied life at a college for women was facing heightened resistance, and everybody knew it.

※ ※ ※

Yet another music school director was necessary in 1911. Conradi hired Ella Scoble Opperman, an excellent musician who was selected from a pool of over 500 applicants. Her credentials impressed; after earning a bachelor's degree at the age of sixteen, she then received a master's degree from the Cincinnati Conservatory.[34] Following that, Opperman studied piano and organ in Paris and Berlin with leading instructors. But it was her possession of an academic degree, in addition to a music degree, that set her well apart from the other applicants.[35] Opperman's background in two worlds virtually ensured that she would develop FSCW's School of Music into a magnificent conservatory that understood its role in a liberal arts college setting; that is, music would be its students' passionate pursuit, but a solid general education would also be demanded of them.

Opperman had her hands full at FSCW. Five of the school's six faculty members had recently resigned; low salaries probably accounted for the departures, although the music department's lack of vision, leadership continuity, and rehearsal space cannot be discounted as contributing factors. Nevertheless, she managed to staff up in her first year; besides Opperman, who was an accomplished organist and pianist, her faculty included two additional pianists, a violinist, and two singers, one a soprano and the other an alto.

Ella Scoble Opperman began her tenure as head of FSCW's music department in 1911. She became the first Dean of the School of Music in 1920 and remained there until her retirement in 1944. Opperman transformed a small, provincial music department into a nationally-respected institution (photograph from *Flastocowo*, 1941. Courtesy of Heritage Protocol & University Archives, Florida State University Libraries).

Opperman seems to have been just as ambitious and effective as her president. The first FSCW bachelor's degree in music was conferred in 1912, a full decade after the curriculum had been established, but just a year after she joined the college.[36] Graduate degrees were issued the following year. Over the next decade, FSCW's music curriculum would expand to include instruction on various wind and string instruments, as well as ensemble participation. A course in the "appreciation of music"—an offering that had gained popularity throughout America in the past decade—commenced in 1921; its appearance in the class bulletin signaled the enormous thirst on campus for a deeper understanding of music. As students from around the South began to enroll at FSCW, many of those whose experiences in high school had included participation in robust music programs yearned for similar ones in college. As FSCW's musical scheme began to develop, it is little wonder that Opperman would be recognized as "a musician of great ability, whose genius for administration was largely responsible for the growth of a small, struggling Department of Music to a thoroughly creditable School of Music."[37]

As plans were implemented and as FSCW grew, good things followed. For her dedicated work, Opperman was made Dean in 1920, just as her department of music was officially upgraded to a School of Music. Not only did she and her faculty give regular recitals for students and the public, but the important FSCW Artist Series, which featured eminent guest artists from around the world, was founded in 1923. And following years of effort, the school finally acquired a four-manual Skinner organ, which Opperman inaugurated at a public performance in 1924.

The College Orchestra, an enormously important addition to FSCW's cultural life, was founded in 1925, although attempts to start a permanent one had been made off and on since at least 1917.[38] The orchestra was no small contributor to the establishment of an advanced wind program. "Through the untiring efforts of Helen L. Ladd," reported the *Flambeau*, "the String and Wind Ensemble Classes under her direction have reached the degree of efficiency to be united into one organization under the name of the Florida State College Orchestra."[39] The ensemble's debut, under Ladd's "painstaking and magnetic leadership," was considered "an epoch in the artistic growth of the College."[40]

Ethel M. Tripp replaced Ladd as the director of the orchestra in the 1926 academic year. "In addition to the full orchestra," it was reported, "Miss Tripp has organized a College band. This is an enthusiastic group of young women. Plans are being made for their appearance later in the season."[41] Tripp's twenty-nine-member band, led by drum major Mildred Billock, had impressive forces: one piccolo, one oboe, six clarinets, two saxophones, seven cornets, one alto horn, one French horn, one baritone, four trombones, one tuba, two string basses, and two percussionists.

FSCW's new band debuted in November 1926 on the basketball court during the annual Thanksgiving athletic games; it offered "a varied and peppy repertoire" of miscellaneous school songs. It was also reported that "The band was organized last year [possibly under Ladd's direction]," and "under the capable directorship of Miss Tripp is making rapid progress in both classical and lighter music. Their music added zest to the high spirits of Odds and Evens, and filled a place which other colleges have realized long ago."[42] Promises to appear later in the academic year went unfulfilled, and FSCW's band folded that fall.

The School of Music was not without other headaches. Enrollment increases exacerbated the space limitations, which began to take a serious toll on faculty and students. Opperman—sounding themes that had been voiced for nearly two decades—lamented that young musicians could be found practicing in elevator shafts, and pianos were permanently stowed in corridors throughout the Administration Building.[43]

But despite these challenges, the future was beginning to look rather rosy. The national respect Opperman's School of Music long sought finally received an official imprimatur when, in December 1930, it was granted membership in the auspicious National Association of Schools of Music. From nearly every vantage point, FSCW's music enterprise seemed poised for greatness: it had a top-notch leader, an increasingly impressive faculty, a surging cadre of talented and dedicated students, a good orchestra, and escalating national renown. The fine and growing School of Music at FSCW had everything.

Except a band.

2

Picture and Sound
(1938–1946)

The Tally Troopers

Although FSCW could not lay claim to having a band of its own, the genre itself was no stranger to the campus. By the 1920s, bands from the University of Florida had begun making regular trips to Tallahassee, often as part of annual tours that took them throughout the state. The band's appearances were very popular; following one 1922 performance, a writer for the *Flambeau* gushed, "There is only one thing the F.S.C. girls can say to the University Band, and that is that they are so glad the boys did come, and, above all, 'come again!'"[1] And while perhaps a distasteful thought today, the Gators were once supported rather strongly by FSCW students, as "backing her brother University to the best of her ability."[2] On the eve of the 1926 football season, a headline in the *Flambeau* read "Go Get 'Em, 'Gators"; the writer then asked rhetorically, "Who in Florida hasn't heard that slogan? It is everywhere in the thoughts of the University and Florida State."[3]

The Gator Band's activities in Tallahassee were varied; often they presented sit-down concerts, but over time the events became more comprehensive. In the early part of 1939, for example, the band gave a concert, paraded through downtown, and executed "precision drilling, [the formation of] letters, and trick formations."[4] Gator Band visits also afforded the opportunity for anticipated social interactions between the schools; dances were often hosted during the stayovers and were reciprocated on occasions when FSCW's choral ensembles performed in Gainesville.

The presence of the Florida bands at FSCW was not without impact. They may have in part inspired the formation of the Tally Troopers, a group organized in the autumn of 1938. Their purpose was precise: "The Troopers," reported the *Flambeau*, "will give marching demonstrations throughout the year at special occasions." It was expected that they would march to the beat of drums "and perhaps band music."[5] The Tally Troopers was founded by FSCW sophomore Betty Mayer, who was inspired to start a drill corps similar to the one she enjoyed at her Miami high school. At its formation, the Troopers were "believed to be the only all girl cadet corps in the country."[6]

The Tally Troopers were not without precedent, although it is unlikely that any member of the new drill team ever heard of FSCW's older "Broomstick Brigade" (also known as the "Broom Brigade"). Participants in the Brigade engaged in quasi-military precision marching and drills for a variety of reasons, usually related to exercise and camaraderie, but sometimes also for sheer artistry. The Broomstick Brigade was an activity that had existed for decades. Mark Twain, in his marvelous 1883 memoir-travelogue titled *Life on the Mississippi*, observed such a brigade first-hand:

> In the West and South, they have a new institution—the Broom Brigade. It is composed of young ladies who dress in a uniform costume, and go through the infantry drill, with broom in place of musket. It is a very pretty sight, on private view. When they perform on the stage of a theater, in the blaze of colored fires,

The "Broomstick Brigade" was a popular activity for ladies in the nineteenth century. Participation promoted exercise, teamwork, and camaraderie. This photograph shows FSCW's Broomstick Brigade Company "A" in 1915 (courtesy of State Archives of Florida/Florida Memory. Image no. RC01206).

2. Picture and Sound (1938–1946) 23

it must be a fine and fascinating spectacle. I saw them go through their complex manual [i.e., repertoire] with grace, spirit, and admirable precision. I saw them do everything which a human being can possibly do with a broom, except sweep. I did not see them sweep.[7]

The ladies of FSCW and its predecessor organizations had formed Broom Brigades since at least the middle of the second decade of the twentieth century.[8]

The Troopers' faculty sponsor was Claudia Moore, a new member of FSCW's physical education department. The Troopers fit well into the department's mission to "give all students an opportunity to increase health and physical efficiency and to find joy and satisfaction in activity and at the same time to enrich their repertoire of recreational activities."[9] Moore's role is not entirely clear, but the Troopers, which numbered five officers and thirty-nine members in its first season, seem to have been well-organized and efficient from the start.[10] During the October try-outs, those who auditioned were expected to learn three routines: one fifteen-minute field drill, one six-minute stage drill, and a six-minute parade drill. These were no elementary requirements for newcomers to military marching.

In its first year, the group was a sensation as a part of the campus's traditional Thanksgiving sports competitions called the "Odd-Even Games." Wrote an enthusiastic observer: "The Troopers, looking brisk and efficient in their outfits, led the way out to the athletic field with some fancy marching.... In the intervals between the games the Troopers entertained the guests by drills."[11] The Troopers had already paraded around the college grounds; they were led by drum major Sue Robinson, "followed by the color squad, [two] drummers, and the [drill] corps just behind."[12] The group really shined during a performance in the gym: "Between halves of the basketball game, the girls performed a nine-minute drill, consisting of 11 maneuvers which completed [i.e., formed] an 'O' [for Odd], and 'E' [for Even], and two 'F. S.' [for Florida State]. The pep club ended its performance with the singing of 'Garnet and Gold' and marching single file to the sidelines."[13]

Despite the popularity of the Tally Troopers, which added fifty additional members in the fall of 1939, the organization would not last.[14] According to a later account, Opperman "believed parading to be an unladylike activity and insisted that they disband."[15] She seems not to have been alone; apparently the spectacle of young ladies participating in military-style undertakings also rankled some of the locals.

FSCW student Jean Steffen wrote an angry letter to the *Flambeau* to protest the imposition of "righteousness" upon students by politicians and the community. "We cannot smoke on campus because a few articulate [i.e., noisy] townspeople would be offended," Steffen groaned; further, "We have to be careful about convocation speakers and liberal organizations, or militant minorities will label us 'red' [i.e., communist]; the Tally Troopers may not parade in town because of outside objections."[16]

Given that the School of Music did not sponsor the Troopers and that the group did have a number of ardent supporters, it is not clear that Opperman could actually have exerted enough influence to halt their activities. But she may have thought that the group could benefit from the musical leadership and resources available at the School of Music. Or perhaps Opperman simply thought the Troopers could use some healthy competition. In either case, just a month after the Troopers began their 1939 auditions, the formation of a new band was announced.[17]

Two Cellists

By all accounts, Owen F. Sellers was a remarkable young cellist. Hired by Opperman in 1931, Sellers's resume was singular, as he (like Opperman) had received a bachelor's degree from Cincinnati's famous College-Conservatory. At FSCW, he was expected to teach not only cello, but all wind, string, and percussion instruments; theory; "most of the music education classes"; to conduct the activities of the orchestra at the College's "demonstration school"; and to perform as a soloist and in faculty ensembles.[18] One student, a clarinetist who also studied string bass with Sellers, relates that his teacher was "a very mild mannered person; if he had to correct me, or when he was directing the orchestra, there was almost an apologetic tone. Like 'I hate to tell you, but you played the wrong note,' you know."[19] Sellers was "very gentle ... an extremely nice guy, and a good teacher."[20] He was also a fine performer. It did not take long for Sellers to become a coveted musical commodity throughout the South; as a cellist, he was in demand in musical locales such as Tampa, Jacksonville, New Orleans, and elsewhere.

Sellers's name is commonly associated with the founding of the

2. Picture and Sound (1938–1946)

band program at FSCW, and it is true that he was a crucial figure in its early years. But in fact, Sellers was the second cellist to lead the FSCW band. The first director was Frances M. Hughes, an assistant professor of cello about whom we know very little. Hughes was probably contracted to provide string instrument lessons during the 1939–1940 academic year, during which time Sellers had removed to Rochester, New York, to pursue graduate studies at the Eastman School of Music.[21] Hughes is mentioned in a *Flambeau* article titled "New Band to Play at Holiday Games," in which it is stipulated that the fifteen-piece "symphonic band"—comprising a piccolo, a flute, six clarinets, three trombones, a tuba, and three percussion—"will accompany college songs and yells for the first time at the Odd-Even games on Thanksgiving morning."[22] There was no mention yet of marching. Although Hughes and the School of Music were important forces behind the band's formation, later news reports often credit several enthusiastic students for the group's founding. Charlotte Cooper, Alice Ludlum, Jean Hitchcolk, and Patty Palmer were among the early organizers, who "worked together without the help of a director," although they were undoubtedly aided by the band's drum major, Marian Swanson.[23]

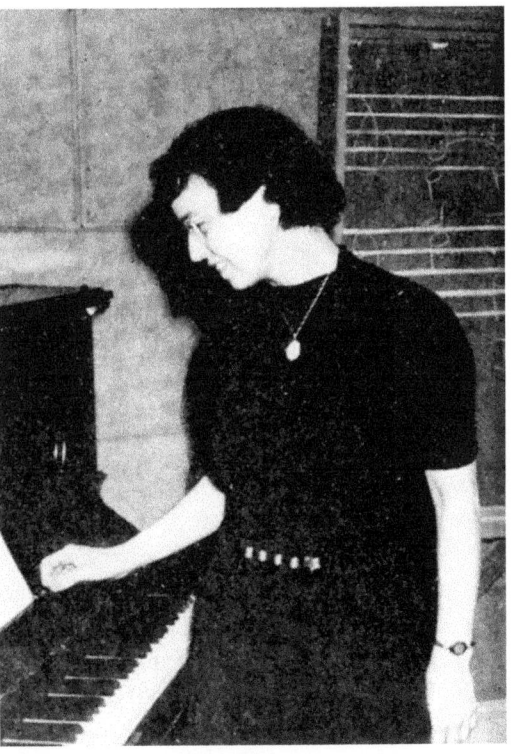

Cellist Frances M. Hughes, an instructor at the School of Music, was FSCW's first band director. The band was formed in 1939 by enthusiastic students who wished to perform school songs at the annual Odd-Even Thanksgiving games (photograph from *Flastocowo*, 1941. Courtesy of Heritage Protocol & University Archives, Florida State University Libraries).

✣ ✣ ✣

The Tally Troopers performed at the Odd-Even contests, a revered annual tradition in Tallahassee; the games also provided a perfect spectacle for the inclusion of a band. They pitted students who would graduate in odd-numbered years against those who would graduate in even-numbered years. Humorous skits were later added to the menu, as reported in a 1939 *Flambeau*:

> The first simple beginnings of the present highly developed demonstrations [i.e., games] occurred in 1910, when the freshman and junior classes linked against the sophomore and senior classes and presented skits in convocation deriding the opposite faction. In 1914 the production began to assume the form which we know today, but it was not until after the [First] World War that the idea of elaborate musical comedies was adopted.[24]

As exercises in friendly competition, the Odd-Even games included, in addition to skits, a healthy number of athletic events—basketball at first, and then volleyball, swimming, and golf. Over time, other sports were added. The Odd-Even games were also an occasion for family and alums to gather in Tallahassee and enjoy exhibitions of sports, theatricals, and healthy doses of school spirit.

All manner of one-upsmanship accompanied the games. "Until the games were played indoors," wrote one reporter, "the teams tried to out-do each other by making an unusual entrance onto the field. The teams always rode in. Mules, horses, wagons and other means of transportation were used."[25] Another important component of the Odd-Even competition was "Color Rush." It started as a tournament to raise class colors as high as possible—on top of buildings, light poles, and elsewhere—but soon became an all-out effort to display colors across the campus. These competitions, although intense, were undertaken with sportsmanship and camaraderie in mind: "Year after year the Odds and Evens contend for first places. But with all the rivalry and the high feeling and spirit for the two sides, there is underlying all this a oneness of feeling, that of the garnet and the gold. After the game is over and time has softened the hurt of losing there remains that feeling of loyalty to the alma mater, which after all is what we desire."[26]

By the late 1940s, the Odd-Even games were waning. A writer for the *Flambeau* waxed nostalgic about the old ways, which were quickly becoming superseded by the new "Pow Wow":

> Football, a name [i.e., famous] band, and a dance until 1 a.m., plus a queen and decorations galore fill the place of Odd-Even soccer and hockey games, color rush, Odd and Even demonstrations [i.e., skits], fountain decorations by the Odds and gate decorations by the Evens.[27]

2. Picture and Sound (1938–1946)

Vestiges of the Odd-Even rivalries retain a presence on campus. The Odds of 1915 and 1917 contributed the funds that built the beloved Westcott Fountain. And in the late 1920s and early 1930s, the Evens raised money to build Westcott Gate, one of the university's most iconic structures. Not to be outdone, the Odds then purchased the four bronze "memory doors" that are presently attached to the Administration Building (now the Westcott Building).[28]

❉ ❉ ❉

Sellers returned to Tallahassee from his graduate studies in the fall of 1940. Picking up where Hughes had left off a year before, audition announcements began in early December; it was indicated that the new group would form both a symphonic band and a marching band. Rehearsals occurred on Tuesdays and Thursdays beginning at 4:30 p.m.[29] "The band," it was reported, "has been organized for those people who, although 'musically minded,' do not participate in any of the musical activities sponsored by the music department, as well as for any music major who might be interested."[30] It is worth noting that the band was conceived principally for non-music majors.

The band's first rehearsal under Sellers occurred on December 10, 1940. Between that date and its first public appearance at a convocation in April—about which we know only that the band was "enthusiastically received"[31]—Sellers kept busy organizing and recruiting, and had become an advisor to the resurrected (again) Tally Troopers, whose faculty sponsor was botany professor, William Carlton.[32] The Troopers now numbered just thirty-four women.

Although the band was at first small—Seller's group numbered just twenty-eight members—the diverse instrumentation allowed them to play Schubert's *March Militaire* and Frank (Pop) G. Sturchio's *Everglades Sugar March*, "a fast, catchy march written for a Florida sugar plantation."[33] Sellers wasted no time in his effort to expand the band library, as "new music has been ordered, including several snappy marches by well-known composers."[34] The director could also report that the new band found easy acceptance by FSCW's students; almost as soon as it was formed it was considered "the picture and sound of school spirit."[35]

Sellers, along with the band president, Charlotte Cooper, worked closely with another student organization, the newly-formed Music Club. The club was organized to gather the words and music to FSCW's various school songs and arrange them "in booklet form."[36] Sellers and others then arranged them for the band. Traditional Odd-Even songs and cheers were also part of the collection. At one gathering the Music Club members sang "With Spirits So Light" and "We Are the Girls from Old Florida," two campus favorites. "Campfire songs and school songs" were requested from the FSCW population for an anticipated fall song-book printing.[37]

Despite hardy efforts, there was still no guarantee that the band enterprise at FSCW would succeed. At this time, it was just another campus club, not an officially-sanctioned class. To ensure its longevity, in the spring of 1941 Sellers and Cooper petitioned the College's Organizations Committee for official recognition of the band beginning in the next academic year. "If this goes through," the *Flambeau* noted, "there is no longer any doubt that this group will be firmly established on the campus."[38]

The size of the band has always been a concern, and its growth has long been a central imperative. After it was clear that it was growing in popularity, Sellers took steps to entice possible recruits and increase its ranks. In the fall of 1941, the FSCW band mounted a campaign to bring the membership in the band to fifty.[39] The band paraded on campus in an effort to make students aware that the group was still accepting players to fill its ranks. The ensemble was further enhanced when it absorbed the Tally Troopers. Following a lapse of activity by the Tally Troopers in much of 1940, a reorganization was announced in January 1941. "This group is not a revival of the Tally Troopers of previous years. It is an entirely new unit under the same name. The girls organizing the Troopers feel that now there is a more definite need on campus for a drill corps to work in cooperation with the newly formed FSCW band."[40]

School spirit was a high priority at FSCW, and the look of the band could naturally add to the energy. Sellers may be credited with the acquisition of the band's first uniforms—white shirts, white skirts, and garnet jerkins—which gave the unit an enormous sense of pride and cohesion. They were purchased for the winter inauguration of FSCW's new president, Doak S. Campbell, following President Conradi's retirement the previous October. The ceremony would be presided over by Florida Governor Spessard I. Holling on February 21, 1942. This grand affair called for equally grand uniforms: "Garnet and Gold, brass buttons, gold braid ... and caps or hats as yet not here ...

were the surprise for the band this week, and the uniforms will be on parade this weekend for inauguration," Virginia Dunn reported for the *Flambeau*. "So don't miss it. Just follow your ears until you trace the strains of band music.... The uniforms are really lovely; worth getting out of bed for on a classless Saturday morning."[41]

In 1942, FSCW's band was small, but there was good spirit. The members wore white shirts, white skirts, and garnet jerkins. Band director Owen Sellers is not pictured (photograph from *Flastocowo*, 1942. Courtesy of Heritage Protocol & University Archives, Florida State University Libraries).

By 1943, the FSCW marching band was embracing "band pageantry," with the adoption of distinctly military-style uniforms. This photograph shows a majorette, two auxiliaries, and drum major Marion Swanson with whistle and mace. Band director Frank Sykora is not pictured (photograph from *Flastocowo*, 1943. Courtesy of Heritage Protocol & University Archives, Florida State University Libraries).

Sellers had just gotten the band on a solid footing when, in 1943, he was called to military service like so many other young men. An aviator, Sellers served as a U.S. Army flight instructor in Macon, Georgia, not too far from Tallahassee. For the foreseeable future, it would be up to yet another cellist to carry on the work of the band at FSCW.

"Band Pageantry" and War

The whole point of the recent rise of interest in the marching band at FSCW was to amplify school spirit, but in a more advanced and organized manner than had been accomplished previously. Charles B. Righter, the director of bands at the University of Iowa from 1937 until

2. Picture and Sound (1938–1946)   31

1954, referred to the nation's burgeoning band movement as "band pageantry," and declared it a trend that not only emphasized music, but also spectacle. In his fascinating 1941 manual titled *Gridiron Pageantry*, Righter lays out the state of marching bands prior to the onset of band pageantry:

> In the very early days of the college bands their function was fulfilled to the apparent satisfaction of all by having a nondescript aggregation of drummers and horn tooters assembled on the sideline to encourage the crowd by playing school songs. Few of these bands had uniforms, and the idea of presenting formal half-time pageantry had never occurred to even the most advanced of their proponents.[42]

But for the gridiron reference, Righter's description relates perfectly to the situation at FSCW, although the notion that it would apply at a women's school probably would not have occurred to him. Righter further noted that, as the popularity of football increased, "bands became better organized and began to receive administrative support commensurate with their contribution to the athletic program."[43] As band activities became more serious, so did the approach to their management. Student leaders were replaced by adults with musical—and often military—experience, although the widespread availability of professional training for the marching band director was still years away.

Band pageantry in its early days was not especially complicated. Righter explained that "The simplest pattern is that formed by band members only, without any special movement or change, and without use of properties." Among the formations favored by early bands were: "shield, square, circle, diamond, heart, any single word, monogram, or fixed pattern. Of particular interest and varying degrees of success are the following: lyre, harp, liberty bell, four-leaf clover, horseshoe, wishbone, trees, characteristic features of campus buildings such as domes and spires, [and] map outlines with or without letters or words."[44] Righter also noted that "Simple parades on the field were followed by the formation of single letters and later by the spelling of short words. For many years the standard repertory of even the large university bands consisted of the spelling of the names of the schools. This limited plan and program was seldom varied."[45]

Later the same decade, another writer had a grander vision for what he called the "Pageant Idea." Al G. Wright, commenting in the popular music education periodical *The Instrumentalist* in 1949, believed that pageantry "provides an opportunity for more groups in the school to participate."[46] Wright, who was particularly considering pageantry in the high school setting, advocated for making the majorettes a more important part of the show, and for inviting orchestra and chorus members to take their place on the gridiron for choreographed routines and the management of props.

Band pageantry developed in part because of the small stadiums of the day. The low sightlines and the resulting impact on perspective often did not permit the comprehension of intricate drill. Overly complicated pictures formed on the field risked being lost on observers entirely. Pageantry—which effectively turned the entire field into a stage for displays of music, dance, and the accouterments of theater—entertained in a manner that was both simple and effective.

※ ※ ※

Following the attack on Pearl Harbor on December 7, 1941, President Campbell organized a convocation to alert FSCW students to the coming trials, as he foresaw them. "Dr. Campbell's timely address," a reporter noted, "concerned the place of our college in the present national crisis."[47] Campbell urged his students to do three things: first, they must remain calm. He well understood that the women now enrolled at FSCW had not lived through the excruciating experience of World War I, and there was a general (and paternalistic) fear that local hysteria might accompany the current distresses. Second, Campbell warned the girls to prepare for hardships that often accompany war, especially shortages of material goods and food. The difficulty of acquiring a product was most often related to its components. For example, pencils were hard to come by because their erasers comprised the valuable commodities of rubber affixed to the wood by steel; Coca-Cola and other beverages required glass bottles and metal caps; and candies were rare, as sugar and chocolate became virtually impossible to secure. Lastly, Campbell urged the girls "to keep alive culture and idealism in the United States."[48] Of course, one way to keep culture and idealism alive was to maintain a marching band. Righter had already pointed out that "one of the prized possessions of this type of organization," that is, the university marching band, was "the spirit of unselfish service to the school."[49] The marching band not only entertained its audience, but it also gave members a chance to contribute to the war effort.

2. Picture and Sound (1938–1946)

In many cases, maintaining a marching band would not be easy. Band historian Lamar K. McCarrell observed that the outbreak of World War II "marked the beginning of a period of dramatic changes in the college band movement."[50] As men went off to war, their enrollment at colleges and universities plummeted; at the same time, in certain coeducational situations, the enrollment of women swelled. But women were not always welcome in college marching bands, many of which stubbornly remained men-only organizations. High schools started the trend of allowing girls to participate in marching bands largely because it was the only solution to keeping up membership and providing for full band instrumentation.

College was a different matter, however. Some felt that female involvement would impede the military appearance that was standard in bands of the day. Many also believed that the mixing of the sexes would lead inevitably to a breakdown in discipline, as thoughts on the field turned to matters other than music and marching. There were also a few practical concerns: some feared that smaller women would not be able to march in the uniform step size. Additionally, women predominantly played woodwind instruments, which were less desirable than brass ones in marching bands. Bandmasters in that era were generally more interested in projection than roundness of sound.[51]

Righter's *Gridiron Pageantry* provides insights on the role of women in bands during the 1930s. "Some of the smaller colleges," he observed, "make a place for women students in their marching bands and a very few institutions have even organized complete women's bands. It is quite generally felt that the inclusion of women in the marching band, in whatever capacity, tends to lessen the effectiveness of the organization in playing and marching."[52] As we have already seen, some—Opperman among them—thought that participation in drills was not exactly a lady-like pursuit, and Righter felt similarly: "It would seem that other and more suitable outlets might be provided for those college women who play instruments."[53]

As World War II approached, many thought that bands could improve the nation's morale. University of Michigan band director William Revelli was one of the most prolific writers on the topic of bands and band music during the war era. In an article titled "How Music Can Help Win the War," he pointed out that the War Department encouraged a "singing soldiery," and reminded his readers that "much more can be done with mass singing at our football and basketball games." Revelli recommended that, as marching bands played, sports fans should be encouraged to sing to the tops of their voices. He also thought that two letter formations could galvanize the crowd: "V" for Victory and "A" for America. Revelli's own patriotism and enthusiasm were boundless, and he insisted that bands could and should be at the forefront of a patriotic movement. "Our school bands should parade through the streets of their city at least once a week, and the music on such occasions should consist of good patriotic military music."[54] He steadfastly believed that "music, as no other force, can develop unity, morale, spirit and confidence," in the hearts of the American citizenry.[55]

As the war dragged on, Campbell's warnings to his FSCW charges about war-time scarcities were proving prescient. Sugar, fuel, coffee, and rubber pencil erasers were difficult to find in Tallahassee. One instance of the pervasive shortages was brought home to the FSCW band when, in 1942, they performed in place of the absent Alabama Technical High School band, which was unable to attend the football contest versus Leon High School. "This appearance," by the FSCW band, "is purely a courtesy performance designed to raise the morale of Alabama Tech which, owing to transportation difficulties, has been forced to come to Tallahassee minus their own band and cheerleaders."[56]

The circumstances facing high school and collegiate bands in America was dire in 1943, as band leaders were being called into military service. According to Revelli, the loss of band directors—teachers who could instruct students in the technique and aesthetic of what, after all, was a reasonably recent art and entertainment form—was "a serious reality." He was also deeply concerned about student band enrollments. "Should our bands continue to decrease by number and quality in the next year as they have in the past twelve months," Revelli opined, "then the diligent and effective efforts of thousands of music educators ... will have been in vain."[57]

Revelli had good reason to be worried. He himself was forced to deal with the hazards and current unpredictability of the all-male ensemble in a time of war. These concerns failed to impact Tallahassee, however; FSCW's organization was that rarest of flowers, a marching band comprised completely of women.

2. Picture and Sound (1938–1946)

The Remarkable Frank Sykora

Frank Sykora may have been one of the unlikeliest personalities ever to run a college marching band. A superb Ukraine-born, Russian-trained cellist, he immigrated to the U.S. in 1920. Sykora arrived at FSCW in early 1943 bringing with him an astonishing array of experiences. He was not only a graduate of the Prague Conservatory, and two Imperial Conservatories, those of Kiev and St. Petersburg, but, by the time he arrived in Tallahassee, he was also a well-traveled musician, having given "performances in Europe, Russia, the Malay States, Indo-China, China, Japan, the Philippines, Hawaii, and the Western hemisphere, including such dreamed-about places as Hong Kong, Singapore, Tokyo, Moscow and Vienna."[58]

Frank Sykora, FSCW band director from 1943 to 1945, was a world-class cellist with a background as a bandmaster. He brought to his duties at FSCW imagination and energy (photograph from *Florida Flambeau*, 1946. Courtesy of Heritage Protocol & University Archives, Florida State University Libraries).

Sykora was an extremely competent professional cellist; in the U.S. he had been a member of the Kansas City Philharmonic, the Cincinnati Symphony, and the Chicago Philharmonic.[59] While in Kansas, he made the national press when it was learned that he had smuggled out of Stalin's Russia music by composer Reinhold Glière, with whom Sykora had studied. Stalin ordered Russia's composers to write pleasing music; after all, works that might remind Russians of their hardships, might also foment trouble for his regime. But Sykora did not abscond with one of these, as Glière's composition was "engagingly tuneful, richly orchestrated, satisfactorily old-fashioned."[60]

Sykora's band experience was equally substantial. His father had been a renowned bandmaster in the Russian Imperial Army—the *Flambeau* reported that "For fifty years, the name of Sykora has been famous in Russia"—and for a time his son, all of fourteen years of age, served as his assistant.[61] Later the younger Sykora served as Lieutenant Bandmaster in a sharpshooter regiment; for his service he earned decorations in the orders of St. Anne and St. Vladimir.[62]

At FSCW Sykora taught cello and presented his own frequent recitals; he also proved to be a tireless interim band director. Just months into his tenure he was leading the band in on-campus concerts and at Tallahassee's Dale Mabry Air Field, where the combination of good music and the fifty-eight young ladies who comprised the band was expected to lift the morale of the enlisted men during wartime. By October 1943, the band had instituted a series of monthly performances at the base.[63]

Sykora's FSCW band took to the field for myriad occasions. Although he was a thorough military man, he seems also to have been a fan of pageantry. In spring 1944, as the band celebrated its fourth anniversary (dating from the 1940–1941 academic year), members drilled on Landis Green and played "Garnet and Gold" at a memorial ceremony for President-Emeritus Edward Conradi. Later they performed, in concert and in parade, for the inauguration of Governor Millard F. Caldwell.[64] Additionally, two concerts—one in the theater and one in the camp hospital—were given at Camp Gordon Johnston, located forty miles south of Tallahassee; several others were planned.[65]

Among the most important performances during Sykora's tenure was the Victory in Europe (V-E) concert, which occurred on the terrace of the Westcott building.[66] "Ann Richardson, drum major, led the band members, who marched from the back of Westcott and took their places on the terrace of Westcott." Adding to the dramatic entrance, three majorettes "twirled their batons to the marching rhythm of the band music."[67]

Sykora, "a small-statured, straight little man," took the marching band to Leon High School at least once, where members performed alongside his newly-formed College Swing Band.[68] The Swing Band was intended to perform for various college events, as well as at Greek functions, which were accepted "on a paying basis."[69] Sykora valued the results that could be achieved by the use of combined musical forces at FSCW. During his years, the Swing Band joined the marching band, and sometimes even the orchestra and the Glee Club.

In keeping with the traditional emphasis on the college marching

2. Picture and Sound (1938–1946)

The FSCW band, under the leadership of drum major Ann Richardson, is ready to parade. By 1945, the ensemble was growing substantially in both instrumentalists (although nearly half of them were clarinetists) and auxiliaries. Band director Frank Sykora is pictured on the left (photograph from *Flastocowo*, 1945. Courtesy of Heritage Protocol & University Archives, Florida State University Libraries).

band's relationship to the military, and with his own background and training, Sykora introduced a distinctly military feature in the fall of 1944. "A new innovation in this year's band," it was reported, "will be the establishment of rank. Sleeve stripes and chevrons will be awarded for length and quality of service."[70]

Sykora's tenure was not without controversy. Some students apparently thought his methods too militaristic, and they rebelled by slacking. The matter was concerning enough for Dean Opperman to chime in via a letter she wrote to officers and members of the band. Opperman made it clear that the director was in charge, and that his instruction must be taken to heart. "There can be no organization without discipline," Opperman insisted,

> ... and a Band approaches Military Precision requirements more than that of any other college organization. Rehearsals must be conducted with a consciousness of responsibility approaching that of other military groups.

FSCW marching band gathered for a group portrait in 1944. Instrumentation that year included a bassoon (courtesy of State Archives of Florida/Florida Memory. Image no. RC01326).

> This College Band has the opportunity to make a name for itself amongst the Bands of other large colleges. Every opportunity is at hand with probably the largest School of Music in the South to back them. To reach this goal requires determination and denials [of personal concerns] by those taking part. No student who does not work with this effort is worthy of wearing the uniform of the Garnet and Gold.[71]

Although we cannot be certain how Opperman's missive was received, we do know that Sykora's talents did not go unappreciated. Dr. Christian P. Heinlein, an FSCW professor of experimental psychology, lauded Sykora's talents publicly, and he knew what he was talking about. Heinlein's expertise in psychology extended to music and the brain, and he had gained no small amount of notice by publishing articles, including "The Functional Role of Finger Touch and Damper Pedaling in the Appreciation of Pianoforte Music" (*Journal of General Psychology*, 1929) and "The Affective Character of Music" (*Proceedings of the Music Teachers National Association*, 1939).

2. Picture and Sound (1938–1946)

Heinlein wrote a letter to Sykora that found its way into the pages of the *Flambeau*. "The college will continue to have bands in long years to come," cheered Heinlein following one especially thrilling performance, "but no band will be just like this Band of 1945. It is unique. The reasons are obvious."[72] Heinlein attributed the growth and excellence of the band—which the previous term had numbered seventy—directly to its leader and referred to the ensemble as Sykora's band: "I say *your* band without apology in this connection," Heinlein proclaimed, "because I know that the FSCW Band could not have achieved such unity of tonal effect nor could it have reached such heights of musical excellence without the admiration and respect which your magnetic and inspiring leadership commands."[73] Heinlein waxed on:

> To me, it was a glorious evening that ended much too soon. The presentation of colors by the color guard was most impressive. The Majorettes twirled their batons with amazing rhythmic skill. The colorful uniforms of the Band provided a beautiful symbolic background which I shall long remember.[74]

"In my judgement," Heinlein concluded, "the FSC[W] Band is an institution within an institution."[75]

Sykora's tenure at FSCW ended following the fall of 1945, but fond memories of the fascinating Russian lingered. The *Flambeau* published a warm reminiscence of Sykora when he visited the campus in the early months of 1946 as a member of the touring Baltimore Symphony Orchestra.

Sellers Returns

If Sykora left FSCW quietly, Sellers returned just as quietly. The first band notice in the *Flambeau* announced performances at Camp Gordon Johnston, led by Sellers and his assistant director and former band member, Charlotte Cooper.[76] A later article, the nearest in the newspaper's pages that resembles a welcome home to Sellers, notes only that an upcoming performance will be his first "at FSC[W] since the spring of 1942."[77] The brevity of this notice perhaps portended the noticeable fall off in marching band coverage that occurred upon Sellers's return.

Sellers would soon be a very busy band leader. To accommodate the anticipated post-war influx of students in the fall of 1946, President Campbell added a huge number of new of employees to FSCW's ranks.

Besides appointing 101 new faculty members, he hired staff—including physicians and dietitians—to deal with anticipated needs in the campus infirmary and the cafeteria. Karl Kuersteiner, who was named the second Dean of the School of Music following Opperman's retirement in 1944, also benefitted from the college's expansion.[78] Kuersteiner was himself a serious musician, a violinist, and a University of Kansas graduate; he also received tutelage under conductors Felix Weingartner and Bruno Walter at the Salzburg Mozarteum.[79] One of Kuersteiner's new recruits was Robert G. Smith, who was appointed assistant professor of public school music for the 1946–1947 academic year. Smith was among the seven new School of Music faculty and would play an important role in the continued development of the FSCW marching band.[80]

Owen Sellers, pictured here in 1955, provided steady, level-headed leadership to the FSCW band in its formative years. Increasingly pulled toward administration, Sellers eventually was named assistant dean, a post he held until he retired in 1973 (from *Tally Ho*, 1955. Courtesy of Heritage Protocol & University Archives, Florida State University Libraries).

Sellers had probably had enough of military life and its cultural apparatus. He did not see fit to maintain Sykora's military officer ranks, and by early 1946 he had dispensed with them entirely and installed a President, Vice President, and other civilian-style officers.[81] And while Sykora had evidently recruited well—in his last year there were sixty-three girls in the band—the instrumentation was not ideal. With seven flutes, twenty-four clarinets, five saxophones, and even one bassoon player, the ensemble, populated with instruments which at that time were favored by females, was both woodwind- and treble-heavy. Enrollment was aided when the college started to grant credit for band participation for the first time in the 1945-1946 academic year; the *Bulletin* of classes also notes that rehearsals occurred on Tuesdays from 5:00 to 6:30 p.m. and Thursdays from 7:30 to 10:00 p.m.[82] Now that band was an academic course, with rules, expectations, and grades, there was every reason to think that it would flourish.

The end of World War II foreshadowed many changes, and among them would be a seismic shift in FSCW's musical fortunes. With a devastating war in the rearview mirror, a new era of optimism in America was at hand. And, as men returned home from the battlefront, many made it a point to seek an education and to participate in activities—including marching bands—they had missed out on in the first part of the decade. What better place for a war-weary veteran to learn, to have fun, and to pursue the opposite sex than at a college for women?

Band director Owen Sellers (right) appears in this formal photograph of the FSCW Band. Next to him is drum major Ann Richardson (photograph from *Flastacowo*, 1946. Courtesy of Heritage Protocol & University Archives, Florida State University Libraries).

◆ 3 ◆

Becoming the Chiefs (1947–1953)

A Coed University ... Again

FSCW became Florida State University on July 1, 1947, two months after Governor Caldwell signed legislation that made both major educational institutions in Florida—FSU and UF—coeducational. It was not a universally applauded development; besides the unwillingness of the legislature to provide additional funding to aid the transitions, some feared that the duplication of academic courses would prove costly. One may add that many still believed that the separation of the sexes led to better educational, moral, and societal results.

But in fact, the music school at FSCW—as well as many other areas of campus—had gone coed nearly a year earlier in the fall of 1946. The *Flambeau* reported a total college enrollment of over 3,000 students that semester, including 500 men who were the "overflow of the crowded Gainesville campus."[1] One editorialist quipped that the changes "caused us to become 'Florida State College for Women and Men,' at least temporarily."[2] Music ensembles, including choruses—with the notable exception of the Glee Club—and several instrumental groups, had already begun admitting men.[3] Many of them were veterans.

The return of men to the college campus was, of course, a national phenomenon. William Revelli well understood the issue. "The average returning veteran," he wrote, "is a serious, ambitious young man with a keen desire for knowledge. He is enthusiastic, tireless, and aware of the work confronting him.... He is grateful to be alive and back home and is deeply appreciative of the opportunity the Government is affording him [via the G. I. Bill] by making it possible for him to begin or renew his college education."[4] Revelli knew their characteristics firsthand—thirty-two members of his University of Michigan Band were veterans.

✤ ✤ ✤

In its transition from FSCW to FSU, a number of positive changes were realized at the School of Music. As Marilyn Ruth Swingle put it in her fine history of the school, "Inherent in the new status of the institution [as a coed university] was the obligation to provide university calibre service."[5] The School of Music was now positioned to expand graduate programs, which in turn, of course, would attract grad students, and to enlarge its choral and instrumental programs. In short order, recommendations to offer master's degrees in well established areas—theory and composition, voice, piano, violin, cello, and organ—were endorsed.

FSU's post-war growth in enrollment, largely due to the onslaught of male students, quickly made the campus seem even more crowded. Plans were immediately laid to add structures, and a top consideration was a new School of Music, "the first large educational building to be projected after the war."[6] The process had begun in 1945, but, as music was considered a "frill" by some legislators, the required approvals took several years to obtain. As President Doak Campbell wrote, "At first they [the Board of Control] saw no need for another classroom building with some special equipment designed to take care of the needs of music. However, they finally decided upon this building as the first major educational unit to be constructed after the war and agreed that it should be thoroughly functional."[7] It was the logical choice, for the School of Music was "in the most dire need of physical space."[8]

The new School of Music was completed in 1950. The construction costs came in at $1.65 million dollars—an enormous sum at the time—but there were several reasons for the expense: the building included practice rooms, faculty studios, administrative space, large ensemble rehearsal rooms, and a performance hall, which was named for retired Dean Ella Scoble Opperman in March 1952. It was also the first air-conditioned major facility on campus.[9] Dean Karl Kuersteiner proudly proclaimed that, "the building will have a high plane of functional architecture."[10]

Not only did the new facilities provide physical comfort and good acoustics, but they also allowed the School's ambitions to blossom. The promise of professional-quality facilities in part enabled the introduction in 1948 of the doctoral program in music education. The PhD and DMus degrees were introduced in 1953 and 1954, respectively.[11]

※ ※ ※

FSCW's new male students were housed in the former officer's quarters at Tallahassee's Dale Mabry Army Air Force Field, which until very recently had been a pilot training ground. The men took classes on the base, as well as on the FSCW campus. Twenty barracks at Dale Mabry had been converted into classrooms, and the former officers' club became a student lounge, complete with a jukebox, a dance floor, and a soda fountain. Of course, sports were not neglected:

> Extramural sports are to be worked out [i.e., organized] for the men, featuring a basketball team which may play neighboring high school teams. Only the touch variety of football will be played this year, but a number of sports are to be offered, including tennis, golf, softball, and a horseshoe team.[12]

Going co-ed changed the character of the campus in important ways. The Odd-Even rivalries were discontinued as students sought the establishment of new college traditions. There was also an observable decline in the paternalism that almost naturally attended a women's college in those days. A perceptive writer noted that the paternalistic administrative oversight of the university's young ladies was nearing its end: "In the last stages of dissolution is the old grownup-child relationship, and in its place has appeared the realization of a far more sturdy bond of cooperation and mutual respect."[13] While young ladies—and certainly their parents—may have rested easier with assurances of supervision and protection from a doting administration, there was little interest in that on the part of male war veterans, many of whom were in their mid-twenties or older.

Once FSCW became co-ed, there was very little chance that the beloved sport of football—which had not been sanctioned on campus since the school was called Florida State College more than four decades earlier—and a marching band would not become a central part of the school's cultural landscape. That a marching band had in fact developed nearly a decade earlier is nothing short of remarkable.

※ ※ ※

3. Becoming the Chiefs (1947–1953)   45

Becoming Florida State University necessitated a number of name changes elsewhere. The college yearbook *Flastacowo* (a contraction of Florida State College for Women) became the more encompassing *Tally Ho*. The FSCW quarterly literary journal *Distaff*—named for a component of the spinning wheel and intended to conjure the domestic life of women—became *The Talaria*, a word related to wings, much like those on the shoes of the ancient god, Mercury.

Of course, another campus element would require new thinking: FSU's sports teams needed a nickname and a mascot. Given that the university anticipated engaging in athletic league play with other institutions, both of these would now be mandatory. The *Flambeau*, which was growing accustomed to issuing challenges to students for naming and re-naming various groups and activities around campus, now offered up another opportunity.

The effort to provide a new nickname for the athletic teams began in the fall of 1947 with a call to students for ideas. By early November the *Flambeau* had collected over one hundred entries, which were pared down to a five-name list that would be voted on by students. Among the finalists: the Statesmen, the Fighting Warriors, the Seminoles, the Crackers, and the Tarpons.[14] A few other entries—the Swamp Rats, the Polly-Wogs, the Raindrops, the Sunshiners—were offered tongue-in-cheek. The results of the student voting were not reported by the *Flambeau*; with an unusual lack of fanfare, a headline in the sports section a week later declared simply that, "Seminoles Clash with Cumberland Tonight."[15]

※ ※ ※

Reported in only slightly more detail was the commissioning of a new school song. An alma mater (a Latin phrase meaning "fostering mother," which now commonly refers to an institution from which one graduates or, in this case, a school song), was deemed essential for school identity, unity, and spirit. And given the new co-educational status of the university, maintaining FSCW's alma mater, titled "Femina Perfecta," clearly would not do.

To rectify the problem, the *Flambeau* launched an alma mater contest in Spring 1947. Entries were to be submitted for judging in June, but summer came and went without a winner. Finally, in November, an announcement was made that John (Johnny) C. Lawrence had won the *Flambeau*'s competition.[16] Lawrence was a music student; he

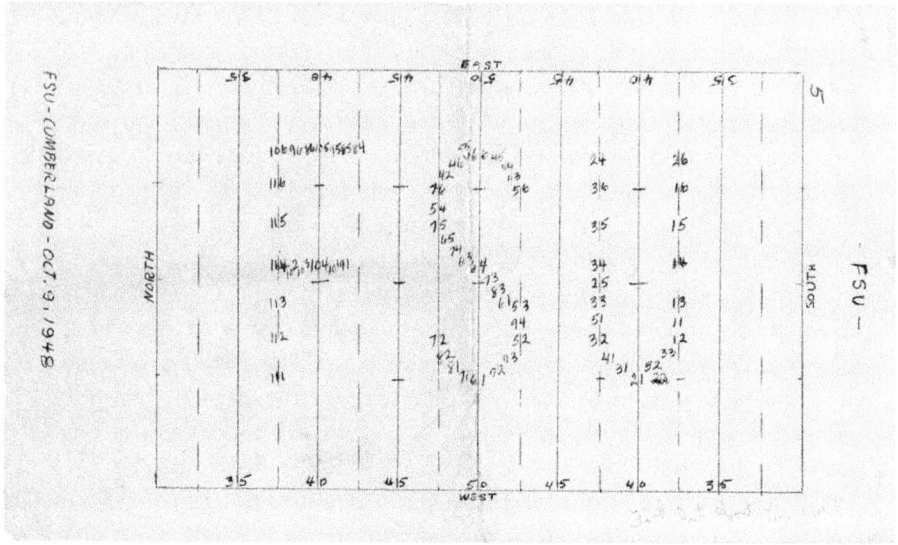

This formation was utilized for the 1948 home game vs. Cumberland, the first contest in FSU's second season of football. Having gone winless the year before, there was general jubilation when FSU smacked Tennessee's Cumberland University, 30–0. It marked the first win in the new era of football in Tallahassee (courtesy of Heritage Protocol & University Archives, Florida State University Libraries).

described himself as a "rank sentimentalist."[17] He later recounted how the alma mater came about: "We were having fun at the piano in the Student-Alumni basement. The subject of writing an Alma Mater came up, and I said, 'It ought to be something like this,' and I played the melody for the first time exactly as it is today." Words were added to the song only after the tune was invented.[18]

Lawrence's noble effort to give the university a school song that could be loved and shared brought him widespread acclaim. During the halftime of the upcoming contest between the Noles and Tennessee Polytechnic Institute (now Tennessee Tech), "Johnny will be honored by the band ... and saluted as the official winner of the contest."[19]

Although Lawrence had won the *Flambeau*'s competition, his creation, titled "High O'er the Towering Pines," was not immediately sanctioned as the university's official school song. It had been recommended by President Campbell, but the University Executive Council—a body that had the power to ratify such changes and additions to campus traditions—elected to continue to accept entries through the end of

3. Becoming the Chiefs (1947–1953)

1947.[20] Dean Kuersteiner was a member of the council; when asked why the ratification was delayed, he said, "choosing an alma mater is like choosing a wife [in] that it demands much consideration."[21] He also related that the council was still considering about twenty other song submissions that had been made by music faculty and students.

As had occurred with the contest that named the sports teams, the official selection by the university of Lawrence's song as FSU's alma mater was greeted by the *Flambeau* with near silence. Nevertheless, by the following autumn the tune was already in use by the marching band.[22]

Johnny Lawrence was a music student at FSU. His sentimental "High O'er the Towering Pines" became FSU's alma mater in 1947 (photograph from *Florida Flambeau*, 1958. Courtesy of Heritage Protocol & University Archives, Florida State University Libraries).

Lawrence's text takes advantage of imagery that is characteristic of FSU's environs:

> High o'er the towering pines
> Our voices swell
> Praising those Gothic spires we
> Love so well
> Here sons and daughters stand
> Faithful and true
> Hailing our alma mater
> FSU

Towering scrub pine trees, so common in northern Florida, and the Gothic spires that soar over the campus, remain sights to which everyone connected to the university can relate. Other elements—references to "sons and daughters" and faithfulness—are standard school-song tropes.

Lawrence proved generous to FSU. Although he personally owned the copyright to the alma mater, he ensured that the university he loved received any royalties it earned. And in 1958, FSU returned his affection. The composer returned to Tallahassee to attend several lavish Homecoming gatherings that would celebrate him and his song. During that weekend Lawrence heard for the first time his alma mater sung live.

Halftime Hijinks

By the university's first fall term as an officially co-ed school, the 54-piece marching band "will make its first public appearance between halves of the FSU-Stetson football game."[23] Wrote one reporter, "The band's performance will be made up of several drills and formations," although one band member recalled, "We did not do any fancy drilling ... it was mostly, you played the tune, and it was appropriate to the formation you were doing."[24] While corralled within one of the formations at the Stetson game, Jack and Dubby Langley, a husband and wife twirling duo, offered an "exhibition."[25] The response to this show was rousing; when the twirlers "performed their baton routine, during the half, the crowd applauded almost as much as it did for that first history-making touchdown, and the response to the band can be summed up in the statement of one sophomore girl who said between cheers as the band came off the field, 'They're so good!'"[26]

Half-time shows of the day often mixed serious and not-so-serious elements, and FSU's marching band routinely featured shtick. Later in the 1947 season, for example, FSU played Troy State Teachers College. Following the formation of a T (for Troy State), and F (for FSU), the band "moved into the center of the field to form a cross and played 'A Mighty Fortress Is Our God.'"[27] At this point, a student who "having arrived late and without [a] band uniform, was 'shot,'" by both the director and Carl Beeler, the sophomore who owns the distinction of having been the first male drum major at FSU.[28] These sorts of hijinks were not atypical, but they nevertheless drew attention away from picture and sound.

A similar brand of shenanigans was deployed in the fall of 1948 at the FSU versus Cumberland University (Lebanon, Tennessee) contest:

3. Becoming the Chiefs (1947–1953)   49

Shaking his head vigorously, [band director Robert] Smith insisted that the band had absolutely refused to march unless they had uniforms. About this time a fight, secretly incited by the band, broke out at the north end of the football field. All attention was turned toward this new spectacle when the field lights suddenly went out, plunging the field into darkness. Gun shots, yells to protect, and whistle blasts—a state of general confusion ran rampant over the stadium.

When the lights came on again, a sudden roar of applause thundered over the field as the spectators' eyes caught sight of the band. Gone were the raincoats, the overcoats, and the hairy, bare legs. In their place were uniforms of gold, trimmed in garnet and white. Brass glittered on the short coats.[29]

If the evening's entertainment included a skit to introduce the new uniforms, it also featured several more serious components: musical selections included Walter A. Finlayson's "Storm King March," John V. Eppel's "The Missouri Waltz," and William T. Purdy's enormously popular and beloved "Men of Wisconsin" (better known as "On Wisconsin"). And, because election day was nearing, "America, the Beautiful" was played while the words VOTE, DEM (for "Democrat"), and GOP (for "Grand Old Party") were formed. Another formation, FSU, was created as the new alma mater closed the show.

Marjorie Fogarty Lee in her FSU band uniform in 1949. First used in 1948, the uniforms dispensed with skirts and jerkins, although their gold color—highlighted by garnet accents and a white belt—conveys pageantry more than militarism (Marjorie Fogarty Lee Collection, 1948–1952. Courtesy of Heritage Protocol & University Archives, Florida State University Libraries).

Other examples of shtick continued throughout 1948. Below the *Flambeau* headline, "Band Members Try, Music Sheets Fly, Drum Major Cries," the reporter asks rhetorically, "Did you ever see a drum major sit down in the middle of a football field and cry?"[30] The drum major's antics occurred after an intentionally bad performance of "Men of Wisconsin," after which the drum major "ran up and down in front of the band giving vent to his displeasure, the members of the band calmly looked at each other and proceeded to tear up the music sheets." Again, there were serious elements in this show. J. H. Williams's "Blue Ribbon March" was performed, as was the Civil War ballad "Listen to the Mockingbird," which was played while the band stood in a mockingbird formation. The performance ended with "High O'er the Towering Pines," which had already become the band's expected closer.

Mary Tarver Willis holds her euphonium in this 1949 photograph. Although it was typical around the nation for most women in marching bands to play woodwind instruments, FSU inherited from FSCW a tradition of women brass players (Mary Tarver Willis Photograph Collection, 1948–1951. Courtesy of Heritage Protocol & University Archives, Florida State University Libraries).

Although FSU was new at the marching band half-time show—indeed, the genre itself was of a fairly recent vintage—it is difficult to believe that the conservatory-trained leaders of FSU's already well-regarded School of Music could look upon some of the band's antics

3. Becoming the Chiefs (1947–1953) 51

Above: The band on parade in 1948. Although the majorettes are in uniform, the rest of the band is dressed informally (photograph from *Tally-Ho*, 1948. Courtesy of Heritage Protocol & University Archives, Florida State University Libraries). *Below:* This Liberty Bell formation demonstrates that men are now an important part of the FSU band, although gender of the members may be difficult to differentiate because all of them are wearing pants. Drum major Johnny Mercer stands at the center of the field. Note the Seminole profile on the bass drum (photograph from *Tally Ho*, 1950. Courtesy of Heritage Protocol & University Archives, Florida State University Libraries).

with much pride. Sellers was now only nominally in charge; he had remained the director of the marching band through the transition from FSCW to FSU, but his role beginning in 1947 seems to have receded to director of the "concert unit." Robert Smith, director of the "marching unit," was given much of the press coverage at this time and was regularly credited as the man in charge.[31] In fact, George Corradino, who was in the marching band the very first year the institution was co-ed, reports that "Sellers never directed the band—Robert Smith was the band director."[32]

Corradino was impressed with Smith, a clarinetist and saxophonist, who had recently played in the infamous Spike Jones band. Jones was known for comical songs, satire, and an irreverence that was a bit unusual for the time. It is completely possible that some of these aspects of Smith's experience seeped into his entertainment stylings on the gridiron. Nevertheless, says Corradino, "He was a good teacher and a good role model"; Smith could also be described by other adjectives: energetic, aggressive, ambitious, and hyperactive, although "he had a good reputation" among the students.[33]

Smith wrote the drill and presumably was the creative force behind the band; in the 1948 season, he ran three practices per week and planned different shows for each home game.[34] But his duties were not to last. Following the 1948 football season, there is no further mention of Smith in the pages of the *Flambeau*, and he did not receive a listing in the *Tally-Ho* yearbook. Sellers, on the other hand, remained a beloved figure who eventually became assistant dean and continued to influence musical activities at the university until his retirement in 1973. In 1987, FSU named its outdoor performance venue, situated at the School of Music, the Owen F. Sellers Music Amphitheatre.

Robert Braunagel (1949–1953)

With Smith gone and Sellers pulled toward administration, another band director was warranted. The School of Music turned to an employee already in place. Robert Braunagel, who had joined FSU's faculty in the fall of 1947, replaced Smith as director of the marching band in the fall of 1949. A graduate of the renowned Cincinnati Conservatory of Music—where one of his classmates had been another trumpeter named Al Hirt—Braunagel had been a high school band

3. Becoming the Chiefs (1947–1953) 53

director in Antwerp, Ohio. He later served in the 315th Infantry Band and toiled for three years as an army bandleader, which included a stint as head of the 24th Corps Band in Seoul, Korea.[35] Following his discharge in 1946, Braunagel was principal trumpet in the Austin (Texas) Symphony Orchestra; during that time, he completed a master's degree at the University of Texas.[36] By all accounts, he was a remarkable performer.

Braunagel can be said to be the first director of the FSU band to enter the job with serious bandmaster credentials, although he had never been a college band director. Nevertheless, he brought some important innovations to FSU's marching enterprise. In his first season as director, the band returned to campus a week before the beginning of the fall term to prepare for the first football game. He also kept the band busy throughout the year. The group played not only for football games, but also for basketball games, pep rallies, all manner of school and community parades, and the Flying High Circus, founded in 1947. In addition, there were sit-down concerts and out-of-town performances.[37]

Like Sellers, and presumably like Smith, Braunagel fostered student involvement and leadership in the creative process. Corradino reports that "He let us do a lot of things. He'd have us over at his house, poppin' popcorn and [drinking] cokes, and we'd work up the shows and think of the music ... that was his style." Corradino further recalls that Braunagel "had a mild mannered personality, but he expected perfection, and he worked in that direction at everything we did."[38]

Apparently that perfection could only be achieved by a heightened student commitment, for the 1950 *Bulletin* shows that band activities had substantially increased from just a few years before. Membership in the symphonic band was compulsory for marching band students; rehearsals occurred on Tuesday from 7:30 p.m. to 10:00 p.m. and Wednesday through Friday beginning at 4:00 p.m. For these many hours of rehearsal students received one-and-a-half credits.[39]

Braunagel emphasized entertainment, but he did not condone the shtick favored by Smith, nor did he allow any aspect of the entertainment to interfere with the band's sound. Not that he neglected pageantry; on the contrary, by Braunagel's first year as director he had already recruited nine majorettes, "the very maximum that he wishes to use."[40] Braunagel thought that majorettes were getting a

Seven majorettes high-step at the School of Music amphitheater in 1950 (courtesy of Heritage Protocol & University Archives, Florida State University Libraries).

bit too popular; he stipulated with disapproval, "twirlers are being used as the show, and the band is being neglected, all over the nation.... It is a sad day when the band becomes only a back-drop for the twirlers." Not that he didn't appreciate their role in band pageantry, of course; majorettes, Braunagel admitted, were "a necessary part of the show."[41]

The acquisition of music was naturally a top concern. In the days before FSU had a paid arranger on the staff, the band "did mostly canned arrangements"[42]; that is, mass-produced ones purchased from a music publisher. Although these types of arrangements had—and still have—an enormous usefulness and convenience, they tended not to be very distinguished and were often adapted to the skills of the average high school band. To remedy the situation, FSU students were encouraged to create tunes the band could play. "In our band arranging classes," says Corradino, "I can remember doing a couple of things for the band myself, and I can remember that some other students did that as well."[43]

3. Becoming the Chiefs (1947–1953)

October 1950

Braunagel's term as director was marked by several football-related milestones, but none more important than those that occurred in October 1950. FSU was starting to experience a good deal of success in football; the 1949 season culminated in the winning of the Dixie Conference—whose other members included Mississippi College, Millsaps College, Stetson, Tampa, Howard, Oglethorpe, Mercer, and Florida Southern—and a trip to the Cigar Bowl on January 2, 1950. FSU unexpectedly prevailed over opponent Wofford, 19–6.

The Cigar Bowl, at first declined by FSU, was the first bowl bid it ever accepted. But it was not the first offer extended to the school. The Refrigerator Bowl (Evansville, Indiana), the Pythian Bowl (Salisbury, North Carolina), and the Tangerine Bowl (Orlando) had each recently asked FSU to appear, but the administration cordially refused them all. Although inconceivable today, those bowls were rejected because the team's appearance would have come at the expense of the holidays spent at home.[44]

The Cigar Bowl contest, held in Tampa in front of 14,000 spectators, featured the now 70-member FSU band, supplemented by Bay-area high school musicians, the local Shrine Band, and the MacDill Air Force Base band. Together the ensembles "formed a colorful mass formation and serenaded the Cigar Bowl queen ... as she was brought on the field in a large replica of a cigar box."[45]

※ ※ ※

By far the most significant act of Braunagel's tenure as director was the effort to name the marching band. A "Name the Band" contest was advertised in the fall of 1950. The deadline for entries—October 24—ensured that the new band name could be announced at the annual Homecoming celebration three days later.

The contest was co-sponsored by the marching band and the *Flambeau*. Among the judges were Ed Santana, the band president; Rube Askew, president of the University Government Association and future governor of Florida; Earl Dobert, the editor of the *Flambeau*; and School of Music percussion instructor Robert Briggs. Contest organizers sought "short catchy names ... with an Indian theme."[46] Within a week of the contest deadline, only nineteen entries had been received. Many more had been expected, especially since the winning

The Marching Chiefs in a formal 1952 portrait. Band director Robert Braunagel stands in the center of a group that is becoming increasingly male (photograph from *Tally Ho*, 1952. Courtesy of Heritage Protocol & University Archives, Florida State University Libraries).

entry would receive "a great deal of merchandise to be given away by Tallahassee merchants."[47]

The new name—selected from among the sixty that were eventually submitted—was announced at the Pow Wow at the football stadium on October 27, 1950. Suggested by Tallahassee native Pat Gunnoe, a junior at FSU, the band would henceforth be known as the "Marching Chiefs." The name was apropos, for the university was increasingly embracing its relationship to the Seminole tribe. In its premiere performance under the new moniker, "The half-time program featured music by the FSU Marching Chiefs, and a war-dance by the FSU majorettes in Seminole costumes and headdresses."[48]

The occasion also celebrated the official dedication of new stadium. Although the 15,000-seat Doak Campbell Stadium had been first utilized in early October 1949, it had not been officially named.

※ ※ ※

The lack of its own "fight song" was a widespread FSU concern. "Every good football team has a fight song," observed FSU graduate

3. Becoming the Chiefs (1947–1953)

student Doug Alley in 1950. "Every good team, that is, except Florida State University."[49] Although FSCW had inspired the writing of a number of college songs, they tended not to have a campus-wide appeal; the most popular songs in the 1920s were those composed for the Odd-Even rivalries, which "have taken the lead and forced the [more general] college songs into unpopularity."[50] That is, as long as the Odd-Even rivalries existed there seemed to be little need for a song that would unite the campus. After all, there was no inter-collegiate competition—the rivalries were entirely among FSCW's own students.

Other than a university's mascot, there is perhaps no feature more crucial to its identity than its fight song. Although things had been going very well for the Noles on the gridiron, the cheers and songs emanating from the stands were lacking. One bewildered reporter noted that "Cheerleaders and students were singing song steals and innovations [i.e., adaptations] of fight songs from other colleges."[51] Corradino recalls playing the Notre Dame victory march and others on more than one occasion; "The school had just started the marching band, and we didn't have any traditions to work from."[52] Not only was the lack of a fight song a growing embarrassment to FSU, but the pilfering of the fight songs of other schools could only have been considered silly, perhaps even slightly demoralizing. "To remedy this situation," Alley wrote, "the following words are submitted in hopes that some interested person can create an original musical theme for them. In this way, FSU can sing the praises of our Fighting Seminoles."[53] The lyrics to the "FSU Fight Song" had been born:

> You've got to fight, fight, fight for
> FSU
> You've got to scalp 'em, Seminoles;
> You've got to win, win, win, win,
> [Win] This game
> And roll on down and make
> those goals.
> For FSU is on the warpath now,
> And at the battle's end she's great!
> So fight! fight! fight! [fight!] and win
> this game, [Later: to victory]
> Our Seminoles of [Later: from] Florida
> State![54]

Alley was no writing novice. As the poetry editor for the *Flambeau*, he was a well-known FSU wordsmith; Alley had already contributed lyrics to a number of campus entertainment productions, composed the poem for his senior graduating class, and written three plays for which he was receiving royalties.[55] According to one report, the "Fight Song," which appeared in Alley's regular "Poetically Yours" column on October 6, 1950, was seen by School of Music assistant professor Thomas (Tommie) Wright, who heeded Alley's call. He immediately set about crafting a tune, and by 3 o'clock that afternoon the music to Alley's text had been completed.[56]

Wright was the perfect man to compose a tune that would reflect not only strong school spirit, but also a sound and captivating musical structure. A superb musician who was also a genial and good-humored person, Wright, a Hoosier, was experienced in this field; he had composed two other fight songs, those for Indiana University (Bloomington) and Butler University (Indianapolis).[57] He made only minor tweaks to Alley's poem, ones that would make it more suitable to musical phrasing.

Tommie Wright amplified school spirit through his music, especially the "Fight Song." But another legacy is perhaps more important: over the course of 59 years at FSU, he educated thousands of students (courtesy of Heritage Protocol & University Archives, Florida State University Libraries).

Alley and Wright wasted no time in publishing the song for the benefit of FSU students. Just three weeks after its creation, on October 27, 1950, the "FSU Fight Song" made its public debut in music manuscript (piano-vocal version) in the pages of the *Flambeau*.[58] Naturally it would have to be set for the band. Braunagel would be the first—but not the last—to arrange the "FSU Fight Song" for the Marching Chiefs.[59]

For his efforts, the Florida Legislature declared April 14, 2003, "Professor Tommie Wright Day," an honor that not only recognized Wright's contribution of the music to the beloved "Fight Song," but also his dedication to the scores of thousands of FSU students he had taught since 1949.

Football Gets Serious

Football at FSU started to heat up in the early 1950s; the enterprise had been buoyed by the unexpected Cigar Bowl win over Wofford. But the Noles really wanted to face the team just down the road. The Gators were naturally in the sites of FSU fans, and the clamoring to play them was steadily increasing. FSU's Student Senate issued a challenge to the Gator football team—one which was practically ignored—in 1950. Following a similar issuance in 1951, some thought that a game was imminent. "Sentiment for a game with the Gainesville college," enthused one editorialist, "has been running high here for two years."[60] The *Flambeau* even suggested that the two teams should take the field and donate any ticket proceeds to a charitable cause.[61] But the Gators would

Members of the 1952 Marching Chiefs brass section pose with the majorettes (courtesy of Heritage Protocol & University Archives, Florida State University Libraries).

not relent, and with no hope of a contest anytime soon, the Noles opted to play the University of Miami for the first time in the 1951 season. Miami won, 35–13.

FSU had to contend with a ten-game schedule beginning in 1952. Having played some comparatively easy schedules in the previous five years, the new season would include—besides the fearsome Southeast Conference reigning champ, Georgia Tech—two other powerhouses from the Southern Conference, North Carolina State and the Virginia Military Institute (VMI).

The increased football activity naturally resulted in heightened attention to the band. Beginning in 1952, Braunagel put the Marching Chiefs schedule into overdrive "for what promises to be their most successful season so far."[62] This year the band, "complete with a bevy of beautiful majorettes," would perform at every one of the six home games and at the Georgia Tech and Stetson games, two despised FSU rivals. In addition to those performances, Braunagel proposed to send a small pep band to the remaining away games.

On-campus pep rallies were de rigeur; at the first pep rally of the 1951 season, at the music school amphitheater, the Marching Chiefs "accompanied the songs and set the atmosphere for the pep meeting."[63] Head Coach Dr. Don Veller spoke to the 300 in attendance, after which the head cheerleader introduced three new cheers.

Also in 1951, Braunagel—with the crucial assistance of beloved School of Music chorus leader, J. Dayton Smith, who additionally served as Braunagel's assistant and the band announcer—inaugurated FSU's first Band Day. This was a project that would not only appeal to the audiences, but would also have a positive impact on band recruiting.[64] Twenty bands—eighteen from Florida and two from Georgia—featured 1,100 students during half-time of the FSU versus Wofford game. Preceded by a parade through the Tallahassee business district, the show promised to be "one of the most spectacular exhibitions to be seen on any gridiron in Florida this year."[65] President Campbell introduced the guest bands at half-time. Because the team was looking rather lackluster, "the high school bands were a challenge to the dispirited crowd and a comfort to the hoarse cheerleaders."[66] FSU ultimately prevailed.

If that first Band Day had been a success, the 1952 event was even more noteworthy. Audiences cheered the inclusion of 2,000 high school musicians and nearly 200 majorettes who took to the field "in

3. Becoming the Chiefs (1947–1953)   61

The band's reed section poses for this 1950 portrait at the School of Music amphitheater. Note the inclusion of a bassoon. It was not the first time that instrument could be found in the marching band (courtesy of Heritage Protocol & University Archives, Florida State University Libraries).

a blazing panorama of color and rousing march music"; also included were the University of Louisville "Marching Cardinal" Band and its acclaimed majorette, Hilda Gay Mayberry, who had recently been named "Miss Majorette of 1952" in a national competition.[67] There was tremendous energy at half-time that day: "The whole picture took on the aspect of a three-ring circus and, as in a circus, it was difficult to keep your eyes on one thing with so much going on."[68]

After two good years of Band Day shows, one *Flambeau* reporter predicted that these annual sonic spectaculars "will become a staple"

FSU's Band Days were becoming successful publicity and band recruitment events. This Florida-shaped formation was created with the help of 1,700 high school band students from around the South (photograph from *Florida Flambeau*, 1953. Courtesy of Heritage Protocol & University Archives, Florida State University Libraries).

of FSU's football season.[69] Indeed, their value as a recruiting tool and a publicity agent for the university was already apparent.

※ ※ ※

If football and marching band enthusiasts began the 1952 season with high hopes—it was noted in October that school spirit seemed to be at an all-time high[70]—by December those hopes were almost completely dashed. The team had gone 1–8–1. The final humiliation occurred when arch-rival University of Tampa trounced the Noles, 39–6, the worst loss since the series began. That year, FSU defeated only Wofford; the Stetson game ended in a tie.

The *Flambeau* ran several reports that indicated that coach Veller was unable to diagnose the team's difficulties. Veller, a longtime high-school and small college football coach, a former major in the Air Force, and a one-time player and assistant for Indiana University's team, had

3. Becoming the Chiefs (1947–1953) 63

been hired in 1948 with the hope of providing a solid foundation for FSU's future in football. It was helpful that Veller brought with him academic, as well as athletic, prowess.[71] But in an unexpected move, he resigned as head football coach in January 1953, although he would remain at FSU as an instructor in physical education.

Veller was succeeded in short order by Tom Nugent, who was fresh from a term of coaching at Virginia Military Institute (VMI). Nugent was universally regarded as an up-and-comer among young football coaches; he was one of the first in the nation to employ the "I" formation, a now common offensive football maneuver and one that would propel the Noles to more wins. And Nugent was no stranger to FSU fans; his VMI team had destroyed the Noles 28–7 in the third game of the season just past.

As if FSU's coaching changes were not enough, rumors were again flying in early 1953 about a long hoped-for match between the Noles and the Gators. Some were for it, some were against it. But regardless of one's stance on the matter, the prospect of a battle could only have excited—and perhaps even intimidated—members of both the Seminoles football team and the Marching Chiefs.

※ ※ ※

Recent changes to the football staff precipitated changes in the management of the band. As FSU began to contemplate its future in big-time football, university leaders must have known that a big-time marching band had to follow suit. In the spring of 1953, there were hints that Braunagel—a "loosey-goosey, fun loving guy" whose discipline was not exactly strict[72]—would not last in his current position. And indeed he did not, although he was not fired. The exact reasons for Braunagel's demotion were not discussed publicly—one Chief has surmised, "I think that Braunagel didn't want the responsibility of a new, improved band"[73]—but he proved a good sport about the matter. He remained the trumpet instructor at the School of Music, and would even serve as an assistant to the new Marching Chiefs director. Dean Kuersteiner could not have failed to recognize Braunagel's significant achievements at FSU; not only had he organized a band with aims higher than they had been previously, but he also established many of the traditions that last to this day.

In a few years, Braunagel would get another chance to lead the Marching Chiefs he helped in large measure to create. But not before a talented bandmaster from Ohio arrived at FSU determined to impose on the Marching Chiefs an original vision of discipline, creativity, and excellence. He brought with him to Tallahassee, besides his own enormous reputation, a gifted young arranger who would dedicate the rest of his life to the creation of a characteristic Marching Chiefs sound. Between them they would transform a regionally-appreciated marching band into a nationally-acclaimed powerhouse.

PART II.
MARCHING CHIEFS TWO TIMES!

◁ 4 ▷

Whit (1953–1962)

Manley R. Whitcomb

It is not at all clear that Braunagel's demotion was accomplished with tact. In April 1953, a speculative *Flambeau* headline read "Band Director from Ohio State May Replace Braunagel."[1] Although the banner suggests that no decision had yet been made with regard to Braunagel's fortunes, it seems likely that university leaders had already arrived at one. The remainder of the article gave a glowing report, as well as a fairly comprehensive biography, of the candidate, Manley R. Whitcomb.

"Whit" was a renowned bandmaster and a man steeped in the art of the college marching ensemble. In the marching band world that existed in the mid-twentieth century, Ohio State University's band—whose traditions date back to 1879, when several fifers and drummers gathered to play marching music for the school's ROTC cadets—was widely recognized as an ensemble *par excellence*. Whitcomb had enjoyed more than a decade-long association with the band that was by that time already a revered institution.

He had been a devoted musician since his youth. As a marching bandsman at his Milwaukee high school, he read books on the art of conducting and practiced what he learned to the accompaniment of sound recordings, while assisting his band director, who apparently was more at home teaching Latin.[2]

Following high school, Whitcomb attended and graduated from Northwestern University's storied music program. His principal instrument was cornet, but he minored in violin and dabbled at clarinet and piano. His real education came under the tutelage of Glenn C. Bainum, teacher of band techniques, arranging, and conducting at Northwestern, who "used a particularly sophisticated charting system for marching formations."[3] Upon graduation, he served for four seasons as an assistant band director at Ohio State University; he was appointed acting director in 1939 and named director in 1940. Like many men his age, he spent most of World War II in the military, during which time two assistants stood in for him at OSU. He resumed his duties in 1946 and remained in Columbus until 1953.[4]

Whitcomb's years at OSU were a clinic in creativity. He worked for, and then succeeded, Eugene Weigel, one of the early innovators in the art of the marching band. Weigel became the OSU marching band director in 1929 and soon implemented ideas that would change the national band landscape. He eliminated woodwinds in favor of an all-brass and percussion band in 1934, and initiated the 8-to-5 (twenty-two-and-a-half inch) step,[5] which would largely supersede the 6-to-5 (thirty-inch) step, although that replacement did not occur overnight.[6] In a move that was well ahead of its time, Weigel insisted that band members memorize their music, which would enable them to give greater attention to the details of field drill. He also introduced floating formations in 1924—this in an era "when most bands were 'block oriented,'" or formed simple letters.[7] Among other innovations: OSU's band was the first to wear spats; Weigel had the band sing from the field; and, in 1939, OSU's ensemble became "the only band to salute each opponent with a fanfare composed of the themes of the [opponents'] school songs. The fanfares are written by Mr. [Clare] Grundman and Prof. Whitcomb."[8] Most famously, Weigel introduced in 1936 OSU's now-exalted script OHIO.

Despite Weigel's groundbreaking tenure, Whitcomb's role with the Ohio State band—a thirteen-year span from 1939 to 1951[9]—should not be underestimated; officials at Ohio State "have credited Whitcomb with much of the development of that University's band program."[10] One of Whitcomb's greatest innovations was his use of the newly-invented copy machine, which enabled him to pass out drill charts to all band members. The spirit duplicator—also known as the "Ditto machine," so named because it was invented at the Ditto Corporation in 1923—is widely remembered today because of its light purple color and glue-y odor. Its essentiality to advances in the marching band has been insufficiently appreciated.

Not only did the copies of drill charts serve to streamline

rehearsals—in years prior, only Weigel had possession of the drill charts, and he was forced to explain the choreography to the band verbally—but it also enabled an advanced level of drill complexity. Marching band formations had previously been rudimentary for the main reason that the time taken to explain to band members where they were supposed to go was extraordinary, and teaching complex transitional drill was nearly impossible.

Whit sometimes came off as a little cocky. With tongue in cheek, he remarked that "the Ohio State Marching Band has made but five gross errors in the past sixteen years, and I'm not sure they were noticed."[11] But he nevertheless believed that the success of Ohio State's program was due to Weigel, and he took very little credit himself. In fact, Weigel's towering legend was one of the reasons Whitcomb made the move to FSU. Although the good weather and the promise of a less stressful position aided his decision, he recognized that here was a university on the rise and one that was desperately intent on forging a tradition of marching band excellence. Despite his trailblazing efforts—*Life* magazine had called Whit's group an "atomic-age band"[12]—there was little possibility in Ohio that Whitcomb would be able to blaze his own creative path in the mighty shadow of Eugene Weigel. As Whit himself said about his FSU adventure, "I knew that this would be my opportunity for an encore."[13]

Of course, those who hired him knew exactly what they were getting. By the time he arrived at FSU, he was a nationally-recognized bandmaster, "an authority on marching maneuvers and band drill."[14] George Corradino, who marched during Whit's first year in Tallahassee, remembers that "Whitcomb brought a reputation to the band"; hiring him sent a message nationwide that "they weren't horsing around down there at FSU when they got him out of Ohio."[15]

Whitcomb's appointment was not the only commitment the university made to its new marching band director. An enlightened administration knew that bringing in a respected leader was just one step toward securing FSU's band renown—another would be funding. In years past, the band's budget had been $500; the resources made available to Whit would top $10,000.[16] And with these fantastic resources, Whit "bought a tractor-trailer load of instruments—drums, cymbals, sousaphones" from a firm in Chicago. A student who was there at the time remembered, "He plain-and-simple bought the band and its sound."[17]

The "newly reorganized" Marching Chiefs led by band director Manley R. Whitcomb in 1953. Whitcomb was enticed to take the job in part on the promise of the acquisition of new military-style uniforms; these are black and include bright white spats. Notice that the women are back in skirts (courtesy of Heritage Protocol & University Archives, Florida State University Libraries).

In order to have a band, Whit needed musicians. One of the conditions he negotiated before accepting the job at FSU—besides his salary, his budget, and new uniforms to replace the old gold ones—was that rehearsals would be held Monday through Friday. The ambitious schedule and the promise of stricter discipline resulted in the loss of a good many students. Marching Chief Florence Ashby reports that of the ninety-six students in the block during Whit's first year, about seventy-five were freshmen. "The people who were not willing to go for that discipline just didn't go back out."[18] To bolster his numbers, Whit and his newly-assigned drum major sifted through all the applications to FSU in order to identify students who had participated in their high school bands. Once discovered, 147 students from Florida, Georgia, and Alabama received a personal invitation to join the Chiefs. Even the *Tallahassee Democrat* took notice of Whit's efforts, calling this recruiting blitz "his first official act."[19]

4. Whit (1953–1962) 69

Whitcomb arrived in Tallahassee in time to direct FSU's high school summer band camp. Not long after that, the Chiefs reported. "We came quite early in the fall," Ashby remembers, "since nobody marched 8-to-5." In order to master the technique, students were blindfolded and sent down the gridiron to ensure that they had learned it. Says Ashby, "He whipped us into shape pretty soon."[20]

"Music, Music, Music"

When it came to writing shows, Whit's imagination generally ran to several main ideas, which he outlined in a 1956 article for *The Instrumentalist* titled, "Your Band CAN Entertain."[21] Whit divided halftime entertainment into four broad categories: (1) Script Shows; (2) Formula Shows; (3) Musical Theme Shows; and (4) Idea Theme Shows. In Script Shows, "the center of cohesion and unity is the story. Without the announcements, the formations and the music would have little relationship." Whit used as an example the Chiefs' recent "Davy Crockett" show, a gridiron tale of the famous American frontiersman-politician who was currently enjoying a renaissance thanks to the popular ABC television series starring Fess Parker.

The Formula Show, in which "coherence or unity is maintained around the game itself," was another favorite. As Whit put it, "the usual formula show contains an effective entrance, a salute to the opponents, a salute to the home school, a special feature, usually unrelated to the rest of the show, and an effective exit." An entertaining presentation that required little ingenuity, Whit thought the Formula Show "a welcome relief from the pressure for new ideas."

Musical Theme Shows used music itself "as a central unifying force." Whit related that his effort to write a "Broadway Musical Comedy Show" required him to identify fifty to seventy-five Broadway selections, pare them down into a working list that would make for an engaging show, and enabled him to begin to develop ideas about accompanying choreography and drill.

Lastly, Whit's Idea Theme Show features a main idea "as its organizing force; music and formations are incidental without the idea to hold them together."

In practice, Whit was fascinated with campus life and activities related to the students. "Teen Age Capers" (November 1955), a typical

Here is a block-letter FSU formation at Homecoming 1955. As can be seen, the Marching Chiefs have long been able to keep the crowd enthralled during half-time (courtesy of Heritage Protocol & University Archives, Florida State University Libraries).

example of an Idea Theme Show, featured a variety of popular songs by Nat King Cole and others; formations included a hot rod with spinning wheels, a palm tree, and an ice cream cone. A salute to the "lowly freshman" (September 1957) included Gershwin's popular "I've Got Plenty of Nothing," played while in a cash register formation to indicate payments made at the end of registration; a brain—played to "Plink, Plank, Plunk," a Leroy Anderson tune "which accompanies a popular TV quiz program," titled "I've Got a Secret"—explodes following orientation week; and a teepee was formed during the playing of "Sorry No Vacancy," a reflection on the difficulty of obtaining a residence on campus while several dorms were under construction.[22] This show also featured a welcome serenade on the Rodgers and Hammerstein tune "Getting to Know You," rendered in honor of new university president, Robert M. Strozier.

In an October 1958 half-time show, the Chiefs prepared a show

4. Whit (1953–1962)

that was "dedicated to all." Whit thought the show was warranted, "Feeling that the grads of the Florida State College for Women will have a 'lost feeling' due to FSU's tremendous growth and development since becoming co-educational."[23] "Down by the Old Mill Stream" (1908), "In My Merry Oldsmobile" (1905), and other vintage tunes were played; the last-named featured a striking formation of a 1920-model touring car.

"Salute to the Trimester System" (September 1962) was one of Whit's stranger creations. Although the music selections were not unusual—"When You Wish Upon a Star" from Walt Disney's *Pinocchio* and Gershwin's *An American in Paris*—the formations were offbeat, if clever. Triangles represented the trimester itself; a splitting atom was intended to depict FSU's newly-constructed Molecular Biophysics building; a wristwatch stood for the girls' curfew; an automobile formation symbolized the ever-present problems of parking on campus. A similar show, "Salute to the Future of FSU" (November 1962) included the lullaby "Rock-a-Bye Baby" to a stork formation, and a steam shovel created to the tune, "Hi-Ho, Hi-Ho," from Disney's *Snow White and the Seven Dwarfs*. The theme song from the hit movie of the same name, "Three Coins in the Fountain" by Jules Styne and Sammy Cahn, conjured the university's iconic Westcott Fountain.

Whit, a Yankee to the core, was fascinated by the South. He produced "Dixieland Jubilee" (October 1957), which featured tunes associated with the South and formations that included an "old-fashioned riverboat complete with a smoking chimney and revolving paddle wheel."[24] Similarly, his "Salute to the Spirit of the Southland" (1959) show—performed at the game against regional rival University of Georgia—included the songs "Dixie," "The Yellow Rose of Texas," "Listen to the Mockingbird," and a *Suwannee River March*. The South was also highlighted in October 1961, when the Marching Chiefs commemorated the 100th anniversary of the start of the Civil War.[25] It was not a coincidence that the game opponent was the University of Richmond.

The state got a solid historical retrospective in "Florida, 400 Years Old" (October 1960). It included a variety of Spanish and English folk tunes, as well as an *Ave Maria* (probably Schubert's) and "Onward Christian Soldier." Formations included a wigwam, a cannon, and an outline map of Florida.

The topic of music itself often worked its way into the Chiefs repertoire. Weiss and Baum's popular 1949 song, "Music, Music,

Music," provided the idea for Whit's Musical Theme Show performed in September 1953. It featured a picture of a grand piano, twirlers performing a tuxedo-clad dance routine to a Rachmaninoff *Prelude*, and the Marching Maidens (as the majorettes were then called), who were "poured out of a teapot formation into a teacup formation" during a performance of another popular tune, "Tea for Two" (1925).[26] A show titled "Bands Through the Ages" (October 1957) presented Whit's take on early Roman bands, German polka bands, Dixieland bands, and modern concert bands. A special tribute was paid to the famous Sousa Band in rousing performances of his classic marches, *El Capitan* and *Stars and Stripes Forever*.

As mass entertainment became more common, Whit looked to television, the movies, and Broadway for inspiration. The music from these sources was not only fun for the Chiefs to learn and perform, but they were beguiling and accessible to the audience. Whit's November 1955 show, "The Movies," opened with the formation of a newsreel camera. Later, the band outlined the figures of the popular cartoon stars Sylvester the Cat and Tweetie Bird; and the theme from Disney's *Cinderella* provided the sonic backdrop to the formation of a giant pumpkin.

"Broadway Musicals on Parade" (October 1962) featured Cole Porter's "Another Opening, Another Show," and selections from *Kismet*, as well as a Rodgers and Hammerstein medley. It was reported that "Two hearts pierced with an arrow will be formed to [the song] 'I'm in Love with a Wonderful Guy' [from *South Pacific*]. The hearts will explode in [the letter formation] LOVE while the band plays 'If I Loved You' [from *Carousel*]."[27] Similar shows—*The Sound of Music* (November 1961), a Mickey Mouse-themed show (October 1956), and others—were successfully performed over the years.

Whit was enormously patriotic, and he routinely brought his love of country to the gridiron. His home-game debut, in fact, was a "Salute to Soldiers" (October 1953) rendered in honor of the Noles opponent, the Virginia Military Institute (VMI). "There's Something about a Soldier," a song made popular in 1934 by Betty Boop, was played to the floating formation of a soldier carrying his rifle; the Air Force was saluted by the formation of a floating bomber, while the Marine Corps "will be saluted with a tableau of the raising of the flag at Iwo Jima."[28] In a contest versus the Citadel, the Chiefs offered up "A Salute to the Armed Forces" (November 1961). The band, it was reported, "will march with a strictly military style and play traditional military music."[29] More politically, "The Sunshine State" (October 1962) was a retrospective of the state's accomplishments and "honors the Florida legislature."[30] Formations included a revolving sun, a sailboat, two maracas emerging during Ernesto Lecuona's "Malagueña," and a marching segment that was wryly dubbed "The Reapportionment Drill."

One 1959 show, titled "A Report on the Cold War," demonstrates Whit's keen sense of humor. Pitting American against Russian military aspirations, the band plays Irving Berlin's "Anything You Can Do, I Can Do Better" (1950). And offering hints of sarcasm, "The band forms a Coca-Cola bottle to demonstrate American superiority in the soft-drink field"; the Chiefs then salute Russian medical supremacy by forming a hypodermic needle to Cole Porter's "I've Got You Under My Skin" (1936). The navy hymn "Anchors Aweigh" salutes the USS Nautilus, the world's first atomic submarine, while Tchaikovsky's Piano Concerto pays tribute to pianist Van Cliburn, the first American to win the Russian Tchaikovsky Piano Competition. The show closes with the formation of a map of Florida and another sarcastic sentiment: "The Chiefs wish that Khrushchev could visit Tallahassee."[31] If we didn't know it beforehand, in this show we learn that Whit possessed a good deal of sass.

Whit was a savvy band director, and he had an astute understanding of the needs and wants of the typical football crowd. "It is well to remember," he insisted, "that most audiences have been conditioned to use both eyes and ears on the marching band; both the eye and the ear must be satisfied at all times." Careful attention to this maxim contributed in no small part to the success of the Marching Chiefs.[32]

Not long after Whit's arrival it was recognized that the Marching Chiefs—besides being imaginative and entertaining—were a valuable university asset. The organization's contribution to school spirit and the reputation of FSU was acknowledged in the 1955 yearbook, *Tally-Ho*. The volume was dedicated to the band, a direct result of the ensemble having served the university "so tirelessly, so endlessly." The yearbook did not neglect the band's incredible sound. The editor beamed that the Chiefs possessed "that certain wonderful faculty of getting the most original new sounds out of music we thought we were already familiar with, but upon listening to our band's version, [one] discovers that we have never, not ever, heard anything quite like it. They are unique; the best publicity bureau a university can have."[33]

"Hell-Raisers"

Whit established a number of traditions at FSU, ones that mostly had their origins at OSU. As we have seen, he introduced daily rehearsals—obviously the complex shows he envisioned could not be accomplished in just one or two rehearsals a week—and he also brought to Tallahassee the game-day "Skull Sessions," although, unlike today, they were not public run-throughs. A two-week long pre-season band camp would involve "squad leaders" (later "row leaders"), that is, student instructors who were responsible for teaching the new marching-movement system and show drill. Another tradition—one that has come and gone over the years—emerged; the playing the opponents' fight song was first recorded in 1954, when the Chiefs offered up the University of Georgia's in the opening home game of the season.[34]

One important technical innovation was the adoption of the now-standard 8-to-5 (22.5 inches) step, which Whitcomb borrowed from Weigel and introduced to the Marching Chiefs upon his arrival. Although now taken for granted, the 8-to-5 step—eight steps to five yards—was an oddity in the early days of the marching band, when there were no particular specifications for step size. Reports one Chief about marching before Whit arrived, "we just tried to stay in a straight line."[35] In the early era, keeping a uniform step size was beside the point, if only a straight line could be maintained. And if a standardized step was used at all, it was most often a 6-to-5 step (thirty inches), which was considered appropriate for the all-male band, although it was a bit cumbersome for women, many of whom were not able to take the larger strides. But the 8-to-5 had another advantage; it proved suitable for standard four- and eight-bar musical phrasing that occurs in most marches. As one marching band authority wrote in 1957, "Using the theory of four, the practical step becomes one-eighth of five yards in length.... Six steps to five yards has an advantage in faster downfield movement. This advantage is offset by the gain in musical phrasing of the eight-to-five and also the ability to use eight-to-five in forward and oblique movements."[36] Whit also introduced other marching-technical novelties: besides the 8-to-5, he taught the high-step (or "Chiefs step") and quick-step, a characteristic Marching Chiefs move accomplished by the now-famous Go Cadence.[37]

Naturally, the creation of the shows was of paramount importance. Contrary to today's more typical practice, arranger Charlie Carter

4. Whit (1953–1962)

explained that "the way we [Whit, Braunagel, and Carter] used to do the shows was to dream up a theme, make formations, and then find tunes that would fit the formations."[38] The theme or idea was the most important aspect of the show, and once decided, the formations were probably not too difficult to conjure. Previously, the transitional drills also did not present much of a problem, as scattering was still the norm. Carter explained that "each kid just got to his position the shortest way he could do it. So for a while it was total chaos, and suddenly it was a new formation."[39] Scatter drills did not occur merely because it was difficult and time consuming to teach and learn transitional drills. Scatter drills provide an interesting effect, one in which chaos instantly becomes order. More precise transitional drills were, however, slowly working their way into the Chiefs marching repertoire; before too long, they would dominate.

Whitcomb was later recognized as a pioneer in the effort to feature precision drill rather than routine scattering. In a 1963 article titled "Marching Band Trends in the Southeast" in the popular music education periodical *The Instrumentalist*, Richard Bowles enumerated several recent developments in the band director's world. Included were: highly precise and intricate drills; block formations that emphasized the music itself and the auxiliaries; pageantry that included smart uniforms and colorful regalia; and, most importantly, the sound of the band.[40] In his essay, Bowles singled out the Chiefs for recognition:

> The Marching Chiefs ... rank high in any listing of the nation's finest bands. Director Manley Whitcomb has abandoned the "picture" type of show; although the picture-type formations still result occasionally, they come about as a deliberate resolution of a beautifully unfolding drill, all performed to the accompaniment of gorgeous field sound buttressed by the fresh and original musical arrangements of Charles Carter.[41]

As Ellen Taafe Zwilich, Pulitzer Prize-winning composer and former Marching Chief, observed, Whit "was very exacting, and he knew what he wanted.... [He] was a team player like people in the theater had to be.... Very demanding, musically."[42]

※ ※ ※

"Big 8," FSU's celebrated drum line, has long been one of the most popular of the band's instrumental sections. The group was not always called Big 8. One drummer, who was a member of the section when the new director and arranger arrived in 1953, recalls that Charlie

Carter simply dubbed them the "Hell-Raisers."[43] How long it was named that—and how many besides Charlie actually called it that—is unclear.

How the group became Big 8 is also a matter of conjecture, as there are several competing theories. One involves speculations about the male physical apparatus; another revolves around membership in the Big Eight, an athletic conference formed in 1907, most of whose members later joined the Southwest Conference (now mostly the Big Twelve). Yet another says that just before a UF game it was noted that the Gators had merely one big drum—the giant novelty bass drum beaten throughout the football contests—whereas FSU could boast "eight big men."[44]

But the most plausible explanation—not unrelated to the "eight big men" theory—stipulates that the name was determined by the number of percussionists in the section. When Whit arrived, he established a drum section that featured four snare drummers, four tenor drummers, two bass drummers, and two cymbalists. Twelve percussionists in all. But because the tenor drummers were women—and were placed in the back half of the marching ensemble—they were not included in the total. Big 8, whose name consensus dates to 1955, was a males-only enterprise. The tenor drummers, whose style of playing included Scottish-style flourishes (that is, elaborate drumstick twirling), were called the "Coed Four."[45]

✣ ✣ ✣

The Marching Chiefs' "War Chant" is known to football fans throughout the nation; it is particularly vexing to those distraught opponents who hear it played constantly on gameday. Its origins have long remained mysterious to most of us. According to drummer John Clark, in 1953 the stands cheer, "Sittin' in a Wigwam," was a popular chant:

> Sittin' in a wigwam
> Beatin' on a tom-tom
> Who come?
> We come.
> Everybody will come.
> Scalp 'em [clap, clap]
> Scalp 'em [clap, clap]

In the same year, many School of Music students—those who were not already proficient at the keyboard—were enrolled in "class piano," a course during which a teacher instructs a mass of pupils in the art of piano playing. Students learned from John Thompson's widely used (and still popular) beginning method book for piano, *Teaching Little Fingers to Play* (1936). Thompson included a selection titled "From a Wigwam," a brief, minor-mode piece in 4/4 time. The tune itself is not too memorable, but the left-hand accompaniment—four quarter-notes (pounding out the open-fifth dyad C-G) with a natural accent on the first beat of each measure—paired marvelously with "Sittin' in a Wigwam." Before long the cheer and the beat, sounded by the drum section, were inseparable.

It is said that at one home game (after 1953), several events coincided to bring the "War Chant" into existence. As "Sittin' in a Wigwam" was being recited to the beat of the drums, the Noles on the gridiron were threatening to score. Fans fervently pointed to the endzone, as if to command the touchdown. All of a sudden—as outstretched arms with pointing fingers began to bend at the elbow to the rhythm of "Sittin' in a Wigwam"—the motion spontaneously became "chopping." The combined cheer and chop caught on quickly. Charlie noticed it, and invented a brief tune that would soon become synonymous with FSU gamedays. As Clark put it, "That thing just took off on it's own."[46] What we now call the "War Chant" was an instant classic, although for a time it seems to have faded.

In the mid–1980s, the band revived the "War Chant," and fans in Doak Campbell Stadium performed in unison a "Tomahawk Chop" arm gesture.[47] By 1990 two professional sports teams—baseball's Atlanta Braves and football's Kansas City Chiefs—had adopted both the tune and the chop, but they nevertheless remain most closely associated with FSU.

※ ※ ※

The drum cadence that takes the Marching Chiefs onto the field for pre-game shows is the first sound many hear from the band on gameday. Called "Come-On and Go," the "Go" portion is an adaptation of an original interlude written for Paul Yoder's *Haskell's Rascals* (1954), a composition for concert band and snare drum trio (although it seems commonly to have been performed with field drums). Yoder's piece, featured on the FSU Symphonic Band's spring tour in 1955, had been arranged for three drum-set players (to replace the trio of snare drums) and included a special thirty-two count double-time interjection composed by FSU graduate student and percussionist, Andy Odum. Odum himself was one of the drum-set players, along with percussionists Chris Welker and Jon Gilbert.

Between the Symphonic Band's spring tour and the start of the 1955 football season, Odum's addition to Yoder's *Haskell's Rascals* had been adapted for the Marching Chiefs by members of Big 8. The Go Cadence retains all of its original technique and spirit, and is one of the band's leading musical identifiers—when you hear it, you know the Chiefs are nearby. As for its creation, says Gilbert: "None of us can take credit for this; it was a group effort."[48]

It is worth noting that Chiefs leadership was not at first thrilled. "Whitcomb did not much like the new cadence when we played it for him," reports John Garrett, "and some of the Chiefs complained that they missed the steady beat of the military cadence. But most of the Chiefs liked it, and Whitcomb relented.[49]

※ ※ ※

Whit was nothing if not prepared. Undergraduate saxophonist Bentley Shellahamer remembers that "Rehearsals were always organized. Everything was always ready. They always started on time, and they never ran over-time. Everything was where it was supposed to be. [Whit's] rehearsal techniques were very efficient; things were very organized, businesslike, efficient, and we had fun."[50]

At OSU, Whit did not have to contend with the challenges that might accompany a co-ed band. In an attempt to vitiate any potential problems, he separated the boys from the girls on the field; that broke with FSU's recent precedent. Shellahamer relates that "When we would come out in company fronts and go down the field, the first two or three company fronts would be boys, then Big 8 in the middle, and then company fronts of girls."[51] When the band began forming pictures there was more integration, but they were still kept somewhat separate. "Whit didn't know how to work with females," says Shellahamer.[52] After a time, Whit seems to have adjusted to the idea of women in the marching band. They were not completely new to him; in 1942, women were admitted to his formerly all-male Ohio State symphonic band, not because of the shortage of men caused by war, but "merely [as] a concession to progress."[53] But at FSU, he had little choice but to use them given that there was a history of participation by women and the employment of woodwind instruments. Perhaps reflecting an older aesthetic and morality, Whit also made a significant change in the band's uniforms. As Corradino reports, "He put the girls in skirts."[54]

Early in his tenure, Whit asked the kids in the band to petition for the establishment of a chapter of the Greek band service organizations, Tau Beta Sigma and Kappa Kappa Psi (Gamma Nu chapter). Petitioners included President Doak Campbell, the mayor of Tallahassee, and other dignitaries, whose signatures gave enormous weight to the application. The first student installation occurred in May 1955. Whit was advisor to the fraternity; oboe instructor Nancy Fowler was TBS's faculty advisor, while Whit's wife, Lea Whitcomb, also advised.[55]

The organizations took part in many positive activities, including the sponsorship of at least one homecoming dance.[56] But one early and unfortunate episode bears recounting. Tau Beta Sigma and Kappa Kappa Psi were charged with establishing and managing an annual band banquet, a closing hurrah that celebrated achievement and friendship. To help inaugurate the first band banquet, Whit asked the students to invite Dr. William P. Foster, FAMU's distinguished director of bands. But as word of the invitation became known, A TBS sister recalls that, "Whit was told by an administrator that Foster," an African American, "would not be allowed to sit down with us."[57]

※ ※ ※

Band pageantry—the addition of excitement, color, and spirit to the football games—was important to Whit. During his first season as director, he invited two freshmen to join the band. They were Ed Franklin and Dick Puckett, also known as the "Flying Seminoles." The duo had been a twirling sensation at Miami Jackson High School, where they were called the "Flying Twirlers." The Jackson High School band was a fine one—it won a 1949 competition in New York, and the twirlers received many, perhaps even most, of the accolades. In addition, Franklin and Puckett twirled at the Dominican Republic's presidential palace and at an All-Star major league baseball game in Chicago.[58]

Drum major Richard (Dick) Mayo, who attended high school with the twirling duo, encouraged Whit to recruit them to FSU. An audition on Landis Green was scheduled; Whit was in attendance, as was President Campbell. As Puckett remembers it, following their try-out, Whit said to Campbell: "I want them." Campbell then looked at the duo and said, "Well boys, what will it take to get you." Puckett quickly responded: "Everything." The twirlers had been offered scholarships at several other colleges and universities, but Campbell's acquiescence to their requirements—tuition, books, food, laundry service, and spending money—aided their decision. On his speedy retort to the university president, Puckett has judged that "I would never have said that if I wasn't eighteen."[59] Franklin and Puckett were joined on FSU's field by another feature twirler, Paula Parsons.[60]

In 1956—the final year seniors Franklin and Puckett appeared with the Chiefs—two new Flying Seminoles were added; they were Wesley B. Carroll (known as "B") from Statesboro, Georgia, and Ted Daniel from Clearwater. "We did a number with all four of us," Puckett recalls, "and it was rather hectic."[61] Carroll and Daniel twirled on their own for just the 1957 season.

As we have seen, Whit was no stranger to the benefits of publicity; the Marching Chiefs enjoyed the services of publicity director Irvin Lipscomb for at least the 1960 season.[62] He recognized that a couple of good feature twirlers in tribal outfits—a *Flambeau* reporter was quick to note that Daniel and Carroll dressed in "skimpy Seminole regalia,"[63] as had Franklin and Puckett—could garner attention and substantially add to the audience's excitement. Whit valued the entire twirling corps (the Marching Maidens), and in a likely calculation to keep them coming to FSU, the School of Music inaugurated its Summer Twirling Camp in 1957 with 234 young twirlers.

Once the era of the Flying Seminoles was over, the tradition of feature twirling was carried on by Janice Freeman and Beverly Calvert, known as the "Garnet and Gold Girls"; they had twirled with the Chiefs since 1959.[64] Unlike Franklin and Puckett, Freeman and Calvert had not twirled together before matriculating to FSU. "When they first began twirling with the Chiefs," Lipscomb tells us, "their styles and methods of execution were completely different."[65] However, following a good many practice sessions, Calvert could report that "we unconsciously integrated our methods until we had developed an identical technique."[66]

FSU's twirlers were among the first heralds of the Marching Chiefs'—and indeed the university's—embrace of Indian motifs, although FSU's 1950 *Tally-Ho* yearbook brimmed such references. In the late-1950s, Carter started arranging Indian-style pieces for the majorettes; the Garnet and Gold Girls wore Indian headdresses; and the band rocked the stadium with a campus favorite, "Seminole Spirit."

Not everyone appreciated the stylistic gesture however. In 1958, one writer, baffled by the band's inauthenticity, asked, "Have you ever noticed our Marching Chiefs represent the Seminoles spirit by playing music associated with the western Plains Indians? Or that, during some football halfs, the majorettes get out on the field and perform a Plains Indian Rain Dance?"[67] The writer could not have been heartened when, a month later, the cartoonish "Sammy Seminole" mascot made his debut at Homecoming.[68]

If the majorettes and feature twirlers employed Indian affectations, Whit insisted that the winds and percussion maintain a more traditional look. The new uniforms—which had purportedly been selected with community input—were black with gold trim and designed in a recognizably military style.[69] Whit's vision of pageantry was also manifest in the band's drum major, although he had no intention of dressing his on-field leader in Indian garb. Perhaps in an embrace of his past OSU experiences, Whit unsuccessfully tried to talk one drum major into wearing an Ohio State-style outfit, complete with high boots and riding pants.[70]

The drum major position, of course, has three main purposes: starting and conducting the music; assisting with the instruction of drill and maneuvers in rehearsal; and, importantly, establishing the tone of school spirit via costume and choreography. The relative weights of these jobs has fluctuated over the years, but they have nevertheless remained staples of the drum major's duties. From the outset, Whit knew the drum major had to grab attention. He selected Mayo, a talented young musician from Miami who had already become an important part of Whit's planning team, to fill the post. As Corradino, one of Mayo's close friends, relates, Whit "immediately trained Mayo to be a drum major and taught him to strut, and all that stuff." The strut—a maneuver in which the drum major high steps downfield with a treacherous backward lean—could be a thrill to watch, and Mayo, FSU's first strutter, may also have been one of its best strutters. "When Mayo strutted, man, his drum major's hat almost touched the ground," says Corradino. "He did it well, but he had a good teacher."[71]

※ ※ ※

Although Braunagel had taken the Chiefs on the road, it was during Whit's era that football's cultural influence on campus began to surge; as that happened, the desire to stoke spirit and provide

Marching Chiefs drum major Richard (Dick) Mayo leads the band down the field, circa 1954. Whit's drum majors adopted a Big Ten lean-back strutting style that was complemented by a traditional uniform (courtesy of Heritage Protocol & University Archives, Florida State University Libraries).

half-time entertainment at the games—even at away games—was deemed essential. Like today, excursions to in-state rivalry games, high school exhibition games, and a variety of community outreach parades were common. In something of an anomaly, the Chiefs even marched in Tampa's Gasparilla Parade in February 1955. One milestone accompanied the band's Orange Bowl appearance—and Whit's very first FSU show—in Miami on September 25, 1953. It was noteworthy because it marked the production of the Marching Chiefs' first pre-game show, "a new tradition at FSU."[72]

Several big away games garnered attention for the Chiefs. The Noles played Villanova in Philadelphia on October 27, 1956. While in the northeast, band members raised money to travel to New York City where they appeared on Dave Garroway's NBC "Today Show" on Monday, October 29. The broadcast featured, in addition to some of the Chiefs and the Flying Seminoles, a number of FSU circus acts. The band was represented only partially—mostly by the majorettes, unsurprisingly.[73] The Chiefs were so big that "we couldn't get into the studio."[74] In honor of the show and its host, Charlie Carter wrote "The Dave Garroway March," but he later changed its title to "The Capitol Hill March" (pub. 1964) following the inability of the Chiefs to serenade Garroway in person. Efforts had been made to land a Chiefs appearance on the popular "Ed Sullivan Show," but those plans never materialized.[75]

The Chiefs did not make it to every important away game, however. Following the successful trip to Philadelphia and New York City a year before, it was hoped by some that the Chiefs would attend the 1957 FSU versus Boston College game in Chestnut Hill. Funds were not allocated, though; that development moved one writer to conclude that "the university is losing an opportunity to gain a lot of positive publicity."[76]

As the football program continued its gradual ascent, bowl appearances became anticipated events. FSU's second bowl trip took the Chiefs to El Paso's Sun Bowl in a match against Texas Western University (now University of Texas at El Paso or UTEP) on New Year's Day 1955.[77] The half-time show, "A Salute to Texas," is one of that era's most beloved. Besides the traditional "Mexican Hat Dance," the brand new and hugely popular Perry Como hit "Papa Loves Mambo," and several other tunes, its Spanish/Mexican theme also included Puckett and Franklin choreographed in a bullfighting scene—as matador and bull, respectively—to the dramatic strains of "Malagueña." It was reported that "The band's colorful panorama at intermission," which included forming a bull's head, "kept the fans happy."[78] But band member Paul Ort gives much credit to the Flying Seminoles: "Half of our standing ovation belonged to them."[79]

Mayo was sharp that day. He had been a respected drum major for a couple of years by now, but at the Sun Bowl he was by all accounts at his finest. And Texas Western's drum major apparently knew it. One Chief recalls that "he tried to imitate Mayo, and ended up on his butt."[80] Another Chief sensed more than a mere imitation attempt: "Their drum major was trying to out-do Dick Mayo."[81] Mayo had strutted masterfully, but it didn't go quite so well with the home team bandleader, whose effort to match Mayo proved disastrous: "Whoever that drum major was hit himself on the chin with his baton, knocked himself out, and had to be carried off on a stretcher."[82] The Sun Bowl offered the

Chiefs a few other bright memories, including a quick excursion to Juárez, Mexico, and a brief stop in New Orleans during the return trip.

The 170-member Chiefs also marched at the nationally-televised Senior Bowl, an all-star game, in Mobile, Alabama, in January 1962. The pre-game and half-time entertainment featured shows by both the Chiefs and the Mississippi Southern College band. In keeping with the locale, Whit offered up "The Sound of Music along the Gulf Coast," which highlighted selections from *The Sound of Music* and a variety of sea-related numbers.[83]

Small Scandals

College-related nonsense was not a new phenomenon at FSU, or anywhere else. But what had been harmless hijinks in the 1940s erupted into more contemptible actions in the fall of 1955, albeit now the antics occurred in the stands and not on the field. "While we have long been proud of the Marching Chiefs' spirit in cheering the team at football games," wrote a *Flambeau* editor, "we were appalled at their actions last Saturday night." Under the headline "Band Spoils Record," the observer went on to chide the Chiefs for "diverting the spectators' attention to imaginary fights in the stands and invisible flying saucers in the clouds."[84]

But the Marching Chiefs were not accountable for the entire mess, at least according to Jim Ed Glass, who had been sitting near the band and who responded to the *Flambeau* in a letter of his own. Glass observed the consumption of alcohol behind the band, where he saw quantities of "whiskey bottles, drink mix, and paper cups."[85] Besides that, when the Chiefs left the stands to line up for the halftime show, a spectator picked up and played an instrument that had been left behind. This prompted a scuffle when the band returned; one Marching Chiefs drummer was shoved by a fan and "knocked unconscious." Glass finally admitted the points made by the *Flambeau* were correct; the band had jokingly pointed to UFOs in the clouds and drew attention to imaginary fights in the stands. These injudicious escapades by the Chiefs could more easily have been overlooked had they not coincided with another, bigger problem, one related to university funding.[86]

FSU's Artist Series was a widely respected but costly endeavor. It had long comprised premiere events not only on campus, but throughout the entirety of north central Florida. For years the series had been an artistic and cultural staple in the region and had introduced students and the general public to innumerable celebrities, artists, and ensembles. In 1955, however, the series was noticeably abridged from its former halcyon days. "Wiljohn," a *Flambeau* columnist and member of the music fraternity Phi Mu Alpha, groused that during a recent round of budget cuts, the Artist Series suffered defunding, but the Chiefs line was increased. "The rumor, well substantiated," wrote Wiljohn, "has it that the reason we only have three guests appearing on this year's Artist Series is because the rest of the money was given to the Marching Chiefs."[87]

Wiljohn's column sparked the ire of many—probably mostly Marching Chiefs—for within days he could report, in a column titled "Have the Chiefs Declared War?," that "anyone who mentions them without praise or Hosannahs on their lips" risks attack.[88] Wiljohn went out of his way to walk back any charges he had levied and noted that the Chiefs are the "foremost leaders of this school's spirit and downright the best single representative of FSU." While he also acknowledged that the Chiefs were too quick to dismiss criticism, he was happy that those feelings did not permeate the band's administration. "Mr. Whitcomb has shown a very fair attitude toward the whole procedure," Wiljohn admitted. "Had I been him, I should have strung me up first thing, and then advised the *Flambeau* to get a new columnist."[89]

By month's end, the grumbles had mostly subsided. Karl Edwards, a senator in the student government, introduced a resolution in support of the Chiefs and the budget increase. Edwards reasoned, "due to the fact that the Marching Chiefs have received so much adverse criticism from certain quarters of late, I feel that the Senate should recognize the powerful contribution of this organization to the welfare of Florida State University."[90] Edwards's resolution passed unanimously.

Damned Gators

Since plunging into the icy waters of big-time college football, an ongoing goal of FSU students and supporters had been the scheduling of a game against the University of Florida. Of course, in this pursuit the Noles had absolutely nothing to lose. But the Gainesville team was in no hurry to establish a new rivalry against an upstart college and a team which had until very recently been a school for females. The entire scenario, many Gators likely thought, was completely beneath them. By the early 1950s, however, several influential parties were turning up the heat, and there seemed little possibility that an intra-state gridiron match would not occur. It might even happen rather soon.

Part of the difficulty of arranging a game stemmed from an agreement reached when the two schools became co-educational. To allay fears of a new rivalry, in 1947 the Board of Control and the university presidents determined that "for the time being, collegiate athletics between the two schools was out of the question"—which is to say, as far as Gators were concerned, it was out of the question.[91] By 1950, however, President Campbell was ready to revisit that decision. He was aided by coaches and physical education instructors from both universities who hoped to establish a tradition of play among all in-state teams. For the time being FSU was willing to stipulate that sports *other than football* could be scheduled, "the reason being that the Florida people heavily subsidize football, and FSU does not subsidize any sport."[92] Later that year, the FSU track team became the first squad to make the journey to Gainesville for intercollegiate play.

Naturally, that move only bolstered those who were clamoring for a gridiron match. But the idea was again squelched. An article on the whole matter was penned by Don Bacon for UF's *The Alligator*; it was reprinted in the *Flambeau* under the title, "Florida State Is Still Whimpering." Bacon chided Noles supporters:

> Now the Seminoles are crying because they couldn't force Florida to meet their team on the gridiron.... They tried pressure in the state legislature, pressure on the Florida [governor's] administration, and called for sympathy from the state citizens. If the powers to be [sic] over at Florida State had used up some of that time, energy, and money in showing the scholastic and social advantages of attending FSU, they would have accomplished more.[93]

One of the chief opponents of a football contest between FSU and Florida was UF athletic director Bob Woodruff. Following a December 1954 meeting with FSU's athletic director, Howard Danford, it was reported that Woodruff agreed to continue to schedule golf, tennis, track, and swim meets, but only if FSU refused to seek competition not only in football, but also in basketball and baseball.[94] The stakes since the 1950 negotiations seemed to have changed rather dramatically. Campbell later provided a sober assessment of the matter, writing,

4. Whit (1953–1962) 87

> In order to understand the nature of the problem one must bear in mind the fact that for 50 years the University of Florida had enjoyed the unique distinction of representing the State in big-time intercollegiate sports. It is easy to understand that the alumni and loyal fans would find it difficult to recognize a newcomer in the field, to say nothing of considering the new institution on anything like equal terms.[95]

Not wanting to claim all the credit for the efforts himself, Campbell added, "It should be noted that the then football coach at F. S. U. [Tom Nugent] did his full share of 'needling' the Coach and Director of Athletics at the University of Florida."[96]

UF's shenanigans forced State Senator James E. Connor—himself a Gator—to barge into the matter. He presented a bill to the Miscellaneous Legislation Committee that directed the two schools to play football. "Woodruff is shifting and shinning because FSU will give [the Gators] a close game," Connor complained. "My idea is to put the heat on and see that this game is arranged."[97] And indeed it would be. On February 21, 1955, the Board of Control mandated the playing of a football game. But the bill injudiciously left the details to the universities, one of which was in no hurry to see it through. Florida finally relented, and in 1956—working two full years ahead of schedule—planners finally scheduled the first game. It would occur on Saturday, November 22, 1958.

It was expected that legions of students from Tallahassee would make the trip to Gainesville; early estimates predicted that 5,000 would attend, but as game day neared it was feared that the Noles turnout would be double that number. Virtually every state highway patrolman in northern and central Florida was called to duty for what promised to be a tidal wave of traffic and its accompanying mayhem.

The Marching Chiefs attended the game, of course. A combined pre-game show with the Fighting Gator Band was followed by a half-time show and raucous support in the stadium's north end zone, dubbed the "poor relations" section by the *Flambeau*. The first meeting inevitably forced comparisons between the bands, and from the outset the Chiefs were full of pride knowing that they would be the better unit. Whit urged humility. "Listen," he said, "of course you're better than they are. But remember: you work harder, you're more dedicated, and you're better musicians to start with. So don't try to rub it in too much."[98]

Once on UF's campus the band was treated to at least one unwanted obscenity. Perhaps in a show of might, Whit had the Chiefs march across the Gainesville campus to get to UF's band room for a pre-game warm-up. Majorette Penny MacArthur Janowski remembers that at one point in the journey, "there was a huge sheet coming out of a dorm window." The sheet "had a great big screw on it—painted on it; it was a huge sheet, full bed, like a queen size sheet—and it had this screw painted on it in black, and under it, 'You, FSU.'" The sentiment—Screw You FSU—was pretty lewd by the standards of the day. Janowski was mortified: "I thought it was the dirtiest thing I had ever seen in my life."[99]

On that first highly anticipated and magnificent FSU versus UF game day, the damned Gators prevailed, 21–7. But the Chiefs had the last laugh. Tradition stipulated that the Gators should ring a large church bell following each home victory, and this they did after FSU's defeat. Somehow, though, the bell ended up in Tallahassee. As reported by one reliable source, "It came back in the belly of one of the [Chiefs] buses."[100]

※ ※ ※

If the loss to the Gators was disappointing, there was at least the consolation of a bowl bid. The Noles were invited to the first annual Bluegrass Bowl (December 13, 1958) in Louisville, Kentucky. It was the team's third bowl invitation and its first in a cold climate; temperatures that did not exceed the thirties led some to call it the "Br-r-r-grass Bowl."[101]

At first it was not clear that the Marching Chiefs would have a role at the Bluegrass Bowl. Funds had not been set aside for travel to Louisville, and none seemed forthcoming from either the School of Music or the university. One day before the game—and the same day the Chiefs were to leave for Thomasville, Georgia, to catch the train that had been chartered for their travel—it was announced that two state agencies would subsidize the trip. Florida's State Development Commission and the State Department contributed $5,000 and $1,500, respectively. The expenditure, said one official, "is in line with the ideas and purpose of the commission in promoting the state."[102] The Marching Chiefs would "show Florida's importance industrially, culturally, and as a vacation land."

Whit had already created a show and formations that would pique the curiosity of the audience—potential Florida tourists all—including a rocket (to represent Cape Canaveral), Bok Tower, palm trees, and a state map outline. It turned out to be a perfect counterpoint to the actual weather in Kentucky that day. Drum major Bennett Shelfer remembers that "The field was completely frozen, and the wind was so cold; your lips would stick to the mouthpiece."[103]

Whit Retires

Following the 1963 spring term, Whit retired from his position as director of the Marching Chiefs. After a career spent in marching band leadership and decades of dealing with the "grind of the football schedule,"[104] he now wished to pursue other musical avenues. The decision was also precipitated in part by a couple of personal reasons: he had a child relatively late in life, and leaving the Chiefs would enable him to devote more time to him. Charles E. Beutel tells us that Whit "doted on his son."[105] Besides that, at least once Whit suffered a major heart attack while on the rehearsal tower.[106] It would not be his last; other heart attacks of varying intensity would occur over the next few years.

With the Chiefs in the rearview mirror, Whit's time now would be devoted to graduate music education and especially to his beloved symphonic band. Despite his consequential achievements on the gridiron, Shellahamer has pointed out that "Whit was always more of a concert band

Drum major Bennett Shelfer shines his shoes just before going onto the field, circa 1960 (courtesy of Bennett Shelfer).

guy."[107] This may have perhaps been indicated as early as 1955, when Whit organized a sit-down Christmas concert that featured both the Chiefs and the symphonic band; "This is the first time the Chiefs have played in a concert," the band leader said, "but we've had so many requests that we decided to try it."[108] Off campus, Whit took on leadership roles with the College Band Directors National Association (CBDNA), where he cemented his already solid national reputation. And although Whit had been an icon at FSU since he arrived, public recognition came to him only recently when the Manley R. Whitcomb Band Complex was dedicated in 2013.

Notwithstanding his retirement, Whit's creative interests seem not to have strayed far from the possibilities inherent in the marching band. In 1967, Whit wrote an article titled "The Future of the College Band." In it he chronicled trends, described what he thought would be the coming fashions in artistry and performance, and provided personal insights about what the marching band *ought* to be.[109] He imagined a time when the auxiliaries would "carry the visual part of the show," while "the band concentrates on playing." He also anticipated the growing use of "composed shows," ones wherein movement and original music—not arrangements, but serious pieces composed expressly for the medium—are "treated as a unity." Finally, Whit expected that marching bands would soon realize enormous improvements in musical performances; these could be best effected in part by better, more thoughtful selections of music and by more imaginative arrangements of them.[110] He concluded with a hopeful prediction:

> It is my personal belief that future college bands will achieve standards of musical excellence and possess a rich musical repertoire that exceeds our fondest hopes. The gridiron shows will become increasingly better and achieve at times high standards of musical and artistic creativity.[111]

Whit had already ensured that a number of these trends were already occurring with his own Marching Chiefs. Artistry and entertainment had long been top priorities. Despite a few lapses here and there, in Tallahassee the future of the marching band was already in progress. And the band director who impelled the Chiefs to new heights could rest assured that his able successor would carry on the vision that they shared.

5

The Art of the Marching Band (1963–1970)

Charlie Carter

Whitcomb wrote "The Future of College Band" four years after he had retired from directing the Marching Chiefs. In it he laid out many of his hopes for the future of the national band movement, especially those related to the improvement of musical performance, although he had already instituted many of his ideas during his tenure with the Chiefs. Whit began to tackle his main musical goals—better performances of better music that is skillfully arranged—the moment he arrived in Tallahassee.

Of course, he could not have done it alone. Whit brought with him from Ohio a twenty-six-year-old named Charles Carter (known affectionately to all as Charlie), a trusted musical partner, whose kindness, wit, and eccentricity was surpassed only by his genius. Carter would remain the principal arranger for the Chiefs for the next five decades. During that time, he not only created the Marching Chiefs signature sound, but he also demonstrated to millions of listeners that music arranged for the marching band could transcend the mere gridiron tunefulness to which they were accustomed. Indeed, music for the marching band could be art.

⁎ ⁎ ⁎

Charlie was born in Oklahoma in 1926. By the time he was five years old, the dire economy that resulted from the Great Depression forced the Carters to move to the outskirts of Columbus, Ohio, where they resided with family.[1] Charlie exhibited an early knack for the visual arts—especially cartooning—and for music. While most of his family had only scant musical interests, one brother-in-law was a music teacher; he gave Charlie lessons in music theory and arranging. Charlie took up the trombone, and by the time he was in high school he was performing in a variety of big bands and combos, for which he composed original works and arranged popular tunes. Among the latter is an arrangement of bandleader Kay Kyser's popular foxtrot, "The Wise Old Owl" (1941). That marked Charlie's first effort; according to the arranger, it was "a disaster."[2]

Arranger Charlie Carter is at work at his desk in this undated photo. Charlie's magnificent arrangements, crafted especially for the Chiefs over five decades, made him a legendary figure at FSU (courtesy of Heritage Protocol & University Archives, Florida State University Libraries).

Charlie graduated from high school in 1944 and headed to nearby Columbus, where he enrolled at The Ohio State University and joined its band. The director was William McBride, who served as interim director while Whit completed his hitch in the Army. Very few could avoid military service in those days, and Charlie was no different. He had barely begun classes at OSU when, in February 1945, he was drafted into the Army. At first assigned to a standard service unit at Fort Riley, Kansas, he subsequently learned that the base had a band, and he transferred to it as soon as he could. He played trombone and arranged dance-band music.[3] Following his September 1946 discharge, he made his way back to Columbus and OSU.

Although enrolled at OSU as a music education major, Charlie did not have a particular passion for that field. But he was proving himself an exemplary theory and composition student, and by the end of his junior year he decided to change his major; this occurred just as Charlie's interest in composing original works for band was growing.

Charlie sought a graduate education outside Columbus, and, then as today, the Eastman School of Music in Rochester, New York, had a strong attraction to eager young musicians. He enrolled in its master's program in the fall of 1951. Although originally recommended for admittance into the theory department, Charlie pressed chairman Wayne Barlow for entrance into the composition program. Barlow accepted him based on the merits of one of his early symphonic band pieces. Charlie studied orchestration with Bernard Rogers, a prolific composer whose students included the likes of Clifton Williams, Dominick Argento, and other now-famous composers.

Having completed his degree program at Eastman, Carter returned to Columbus, where he labored at a menial job and arranged music on the side. In short order, Whitcomb contacted him to commission a piece for an upcoming convention. That renewed acquaintance moved Whit, just prior to the start of the 1952 football season, to offer Carter a job as OSU's full-time marching band arranger.

✦ ✦ ✦

When Whit and Charlie moved to Tallahassee in 1953, they had not been working together very long, although they had already developed a professional and personal relationship. If Whit had been excited about his "encore," Charlie was somewhat more muted in his enthusiasm about the move from Ohio. "Even though I was in a good situation arranging for the Ohio State University Marching Band," he told one researcher, "I wanted to work with Whitcomb. Everyone idolized him. I really respected him and was flattered that he even asked me to go to the Florida State University. We also had a miserable winter in Columbus—lots of snow and cold weather. So the idea of heading south sounded encouraging."[4]

Charlie's first months in Tallahassee did not get off to a promising start, as there was a misunderstanding about his role at the university. While Charlie thought he had been offered a job as Whit's assistant director—a faculty post, he reasonably assumed—he later learned that Whit expected him to be an assistant of another type—a doctoral graduate assistant.

Charlie resigned himself to this end, and he seems to have applied himself to most of his classwork only half-heartedly. His composition classes, however, were another matter; they excited him enough to inspire some of his best music, including several works that have retained their place in the symphonic band repertoire. Despite these successes, Charlie dropped out of the doctoral program in 1956, but he kept his position as the Marching Chiefs arranger, albeit at a meager salary. Financial matters would be an ongoing concern for Charlie, and he considered opportunities elsewhere. Even a move to Gainesville was rumored. But his love of Tallahassee and his many friends in the capital city compelled him to stay. And with the pressures of pursuing an advanced degree behind him, Charlie could now devote his full attention to his own creative work.

⁕ ⁕ ⁕

Charlie shared with Whit the management and oversight of a relatively new musical pursuit in Tallahassee, the Flying High Circus Band. The Circus Band accompanied the unique student club that had been founded in 1947 by Jack Haskins.[5] Haskins appreciated the Circus Band, as we know from an early letter he penned to a band member. "The band, as a unit, did an excellent job—nothing short of professionalism," Haskins wrote to Marjorie Nell Fogarty. "We thought it was good last year, but there was no comparison with this season's organization.... Believe me when I say—the band made the show."[6] Charlie helped to run the Circus Band from 1954 until its dissolution in 1963, when the Flying High Circus leadership discovered that it could save money, and probably lend more consistency to performances, by using recorded music.

Charlie continued his regimen of composing weighty works for symphonic band, but of course another enduring artistic monument is the vast body of music he composed and arranged for the Marching Chiefs. He brought a distinctive style to his arrangements; anyone becoming familiar with Charlie's music will soon detect telltale characteristics of instrumentation and harmony that are his alone. Professor Clifford K. Madsen, FSU's Robert O. Lawton Distinguished Professor of Music and former assistant director of the Marching Chiefs, credited Charlie with "two things, technically, that are marvelous. He writes the best tenor lines of anybody in the business, and he has on-the-beat dissonances that resolve.... Those are his characteristics, and those are techniques that anybody can use, but he seems to use them with more skill than anybody else."[7]

5. The Art of the Marching Band (1963–1970)   95

Robert (Bob) S. Thurston, Charlie's biographer and devoted protégé, has thoughtfully assessed Charlie's musical style; it is worth quoting here at length:

> Charlie had scoring down to a science, which made him efficient and prolific—but he never lost touch with the art, which made his music uniquely and unmistakably his. A big part of that was his very nature: cheerful, happy, humble. He was likeable, and he liked to be liked. His music had a strong commercial bent, and he indulged it without guilt. He had no desire to write "great music," as he put it, using air quotes, referring to pieces that might go over big in academic circles but nowhere else. He chose, early on, to keep his work accessible to player and listener alike, and to reach as many people as he could.
>
> He treated every arrangement he wrote for the Marching Chiefs the same as he would have treated a concert scoring of the same arrangement. The Chiefs just had a smaller instrumental palette. His scoring for the Chiefs rarely deviated from his preferred doublings (flutes and clarinets doubling trumpets; alto saxes doubling horns; tenor saxes doubling baritones), nor from a list of instrumental settings he relied on (i.e., who played the melody, who played the countermelody, etc.). Charlie had eleven different scoring templates he found to be the most effective for getting the biggest, fullest sound from a marching band while varying the color as much as possible from one phrase or section to the next.
>
> Probably his most distinctive trademark was his gift for countermelodies, which he gave most often to the trombones (his own instrument) and baritones, colored with tenor saxes. He wrote out the melody first, almost always in the soprano voice. Then he gave it a robust bass line, defaulting to roots and fifths but always on the lookout for an interesting third or other color tone. Then he wrote a counterline that worked harmonically by supplying the missing chord tones, and rhythmically by moving where the melody sustained, and sustaining where the melody moved. When needed, he let the alto voices cover what was left; often they simply doubled the melody an octave lower.
>
> The formula was simple on paper but Charlie took it beyond "just" craft, in a way that was hard to explain yet easy to recognize.[8]

Tallahassee Democrat reporter George Allen summed up Charlie's achievements eloquently. Listening to the Marching Chiefs, he wrote, "is a musical treat akin to a concert in a fine hall."[9]

Despite the praise that had been heaped on him for decades, Charlie himself was mostly matter-of-fact about his work. He noted in 1986 that, "We pretty much used the same scoring that the Ohio State University band had for their arrangements. With the addition of woodwinds in the Marching Chiefs [OSU was an all-brass band], we wrote two separate clarinet parts and a flute part an octave above the melody. By the second year, we split the trombone parts and added a baritone part. The result was an eight-part arrangement, which is still the standard today."[10] But there is another key to Charlie's musical magic. As Marching Chief Johnny E. Clark, a drummer in 1953, astutely notes, "Charlie wrote for the strong sections."[11] His own humility aside, Charlie has been credited with "musical innovations and arrangements [that] keep Seminole fans at their seats throughout the halftime intermission."[12]

During the early 1960s and early 1970s, Charlie's daily work schedule varied little. Given his aversion to traffic and congestion—and to the parking irritations that have vexed FSU in every decade—he preferred to work at home. Upon waking, he would shower and brush his hair a specific number of times. His daily attire was simple and unchanging: khaki pants, a pocketed white t-shirt, and the ever-important white handkerchief, which he neatly lodged in his shirt pocket. Following breakfast, he worked until lunch time, after which he would spend a few more hours at his writing desk. In his later years, when his energy was more easily sapped, he skipped an hour or two of work to enjoy an afternoon nap. Evenings were spent in the company of friends and colleagues—Charlie was a very sociable man—and he often enjoyed a glass of bourbon. "After dinner," wife Sara Pankaskie remembered, "he would quite often listen to music … he loved swing music, and band composers…. He'd listen to music, and he'd absorb it. You'd never hear it come out directly [in his own arrangements and compositions], but you could hear the influences weeks, months, and years later."[13]

Charlie had his share of personal peculiarities. As former Chiefs director Robert Sheldon explained, Charlie "was child-like in a lot of ways," a quality that was sensed by many others.[14] "He was a very sweet man, and had a lot of quirky behaviors." For one thing, he was prone to bouts of nervousness over rather trivial matters. "He would get upset very easily," according to Sheldon. "If the pencils were not lined up on his desk exactly the way they were supposed to be he would have a panic attack."[15] Sara Pankaskie relates that "Charlie had a bit of OCD [obsessive-compulsive disorder]."[16] In addition, he had suffered from very poor eyesight from his childhood, and the result was that he often spoke to others from an uncomfortably close range.[17] Charlie also received plenty of perhaps unwanted attention for "Charlie stops" (also known as "Charlie breaks"), the frequent restroom bus delays that he required during away game trips.

Charlie loved his FSU students, and he worked and fraternized with them often. Activities invariably began at Charlie's home, where

5. The Art of the Marching Band (1963–1970)   97

he and the kids would listen to music, develop show ideas, and select tunes. Remembers one Chief, "Charlie had by far the best record collection and the best stereo of anybody we could know."[18] One committee of students was elected to select the tunes that would be featured on a Blood, Sweat and Tears show. "We would spend time over at Charlie's house," Flush section leader Chuck Beutel remembers, "listening to recordings, and picking out the things that we thought would work."[19] Once the songs were decided, everyone knew that they would sound impressive on the field: "It was really easy to sound good when you were playing Charlie Carter arrangements."[20] Once Charlie had arranged a score for the Chiefs, band members wrote out the individual parts, and when they were ready, he organized reading rehearsals to proof them and make revisions as needed.[21]

One may reasonably conclude that in some ways Charlie's professional career never lived up to his own expectations. For reasons defying common sense, the School of Music never elected to place him on a career path that might one day confer tenure. His paychecks were always pitiably small, and at least once he was not even paid on time.[22] Toward the end of his career, and after years of dedicated toil, Charlie struck a deal that gave him the title Arranger in Residence and ensured long-term employment, which he sought mostly for the health insurance policy, the use of which was becoming increasingly necessary. It is true that a portion of the blame for his employment woes rested with Charlie himself, but his treatment by the university is a rare stain on an otherwise creditable history.

Neither Charlie's personal quirks nor his professional troubles obscured the magic of his music, of course. He was a brilliant arranger, whose contributions to the Marching Chiefs are unmatched. Ellen Taafe Zwilich recalls that "he was a wonderful arranger. In those days [Whit's era], the Marching Chiefs was a relatively small group, and we could play big band stuff. Charlie was amazing."[23] Charlie's fame grew over time; Sheldon recognized the arranger's achievements even before he directed the Chiefs: "He was a legend, as far as I was concerned."[24]

"Brownie"

Robert Braunagel, the one-time director of the Chiefs who had then become Whit's assistant, did not seem like the natural pick to re-assume the post of director. In fact, he was not Whit's first choice. Cliff Madsen recollects that Whit approached him to run the Chiefs. Madsen was no stranger to the marching band. A native of Utah, he had only recently been the director of Brigham Young University's Cougar Marching Band. But despite Madsen's experience and qualifications, Dean Kuersteiner believed that Braunagel, having spent a decade as Whit's loyal deputy, should get first crack at the job.[25] Once hired, Braunagel convinced Madsen, who had become a close friend, to serve as his associate director. Madsen has reflected that, "Charlie Carter, Braunagel, and I were like the Three Musketeers.... Everything that happened with the marching band for those [first] two or three years, we were all actively involved in."[26]

That Braunagel was selected to succeed Whit speaks volumes about his easy-going temperament, his earlier willingness to be a part of Whit's team, and his devotion to FSU. The promotion of Braunagel—

Brownie reviews his Marching Chiefs on the practice field in 1970. He was nearing the end of two decades of close association with the band that, in many ways, he created (from *Florida Flambeau*, 1970. Courtesy of Heritage Protocol & University Archives, Florida State University Libraries).

a beloved figure who was affectionately known as "Brownie"—was announced on May 7, 1963. The *Flambeau*'s page-one notice, titled "Marching Seminoles Get New Chief," reported that Brownie had been Whit's assistant, but made no mention that he had once been the marching band's director, although that fact was generally known by the band members.[27] By now it probably mattered little; his strengths were undoubtedly bolstered, and any deficiencies he might have had in his early years as director were certainly corrected during his ten years as Whit's assistant.

Brownie had the opportunity to learn a great deal from Whit, who was not only a serious teacher and thinker on matters related to marching band, but someone who could also articulate an original vision of the marching band's potential as an art form. But if Brownie took Whit's many lessons to heart, he nevertheless spared little time in attempting to put his own stamp on the Marching Chiefs. "Experimentation," he told the *Flambeau* in 1963, "will be the password for the Chiefs this season." Many of the innovations were related to the band's sound. New arrangements were "designed to give the Chiefs a richer, fuller sound through the use of high sustained trumpet parts." Percussion placement was also a new feature, because "in the modern pre-game shows, drums will be placed in the center of the football field, and four bass drums will be featured in place of the usual two. This is expected to add further depth and color to drum cadences."[28]

Of course, there was also the matter of drill; Brownie had a keen sense of what the audience in the stands was seeing, and he brought to bear special talents with respect to perspective. This was especially useful as Doak Campbell Stadium grew. As one Chief said, "He was an absolute genius at his visual-spatial abilities ... just amazing."[29] Madsen relates that, in a time when many bands used scatter drills to move from formation to formation, Brownie, like Whit before him, used transitions as an opportunity to entertain the audience. "Braunagel took great care in the transitions being very, very pretty and nice on the field."[30]

Brownie worked the band pretty hard. Skull Sessions of the day were held onstage in Opperman Music Hall; they were recorded so that, on the following Monday, Brownie could match the recorded sound with the black-and-white film that had been taken at the game. His media thus aligned, he would point out the band's errors, and not always diplomatically.[31] But it wasn't in Brownie to be overly-harsh;

one Chief observed that Brownie "had sort of an odd leadership style, because there was never a lot of demanding until things were so wrong that he didn't have any other choice. It was always more encouraging and cajoling and teasing about what was wrong and what needed to be fixed, and everybody appreciated that."[32] The Chiefs had an abiding affection for Brownie "and loved to find ways to make him smile."[33]

Brownie sought to increase audience interest and participation in the football games by the introduction in 1963 of a new "musical cheer" during which "the words 'Go Seminoles,' 'Fight, Team, Fight,' and 'Scalp 'Em' will be shouted by FSU supporters during pauses in the music."[34] In addition, "top secret" majorette uniforms were planned, as was an entirely new pre-game entrance. There was general excitement about Brownie's many changes, and students were eager to show them off. One Chief looked forward to the upcoming trip to Gainesville, "when they will show the music-starved Gators what a marching band looks like."[35]

Another musical favorite was invented in this era. It was occasioned by the first win over the Gators on November 21, 1964. An historic contest in Doak Campbell Stadium, the game marked the Gainesville team's first appearance in Tallahassee. So momentous was FSU's victory that it prompted the "largest celebration since the end of World War II. They had to close off the streets."[36] The win inspired Tommie Wright to compose his "FSU Victory March," which he then submitted to Brownie for review. Wright undoubtedly expected that Brownie would have it arranged for the Chiefs, but instead it sparked something of a competition. Wright's "March" was thought by some to be plodding, tedious, and uncharacteristic of similar songs. In an effort to produce a better result, Carter and Madsen joined forces to compose an alternative simply titled "Victory Song."[37] Madsen remembers "that was a real joint endeavor."[38]

Brownie had already selected his winner, but in full appreciation of School of Music politics, he determined to let others decide which victory tune was most effective. He assembled a band to play both selections in competition in the Westcott Building auditorium (now Ruby Diamond Concert Hall). A faculty panel was convened, and invitations were issued to the entire student body, including all fraternities and sororities. Brownie conducted; he is reported to have taken the Wright selection so slowly as to make it "insufferably long."[39] On the

5. The Art of the Marching Band (1963–1970)

other hand, the Carter/Madsen tune was played up-tempo. It was bright. Brisk. Tuneful. Nevertheless—and even though Brownie had a thumb on the scale in favor of the Carter/Madsen march—the faculty judges declared Wright's "FSU Victory March" triumphant.

Brownie undoubtedly gave the panel's selection is just respect. But the audience—band members, sorority sisters, and frat boys—chose the "Victory Song." It remains a traditional favorite at FSU.

"Never lost a halftime show"

Brownie's halftime shows were, like Whit's, wide-ranging and eclectic, and he drew inspiration from a variety of sources. History was a common theme. In "The World's Fair, Past and Present" (October 1964), formations reflected iconic fair structures, such as the Crystal Palace

The Marching Chiefs in rehearsal in 1969. Sporting the band's name on the drums was an excellent branding strategy. And if the tubas at this time were perhaps not the most virtuosic section in the band, at least they had a cool name—"The Royal Flush" (*Florida Flambeau*, 1969. Courtesy of Heritage Protocol & University Archives, Florida State University Libraries).

(London), the Eiffel Tower (Paris), and George Ferris's remarkable Wheel (Chicago). Recognizable music was also deployed to signify important events. Glenn Miller's "Pennsylvania 6–5000," for example, celebrated the introduction of the telephone at Philadelphia's 1876 Centennial Exhibition. And two selections from FSU composer Carlisle Floyd's renowned opera, *Susannah*—which had been mounted at the 1958 Brussels World's Fair—were played by the Chiefs, a gesture that was entirely appropriate, as Floyd had just been recognized as a University Distinguished Professor.[40]

Pop culture was also on Brownie's menu. During his tenure, television was gaining influence in America. Color television, still something of a rarity in the 1950s, was more widely available by the next decade. As more Americans looked to television for news and entertainment, Brownie took advantage of its popularity. The "Wonderful World of Television" (October 1963) featured themes from the beloved cartoon show *Huckleberry Hound*, as well as the westerns *Rawhide* and *Gunsmoke*. Brownie resurrected the TV-themed show idea again in 1965, this time using tunes from *The Munsters, Perry Mason, Gomer Pyle, Candid Camera, My Mother the Car, Petticoat Junction*, and other favorites. Drill included "a company front…. Herman Munster, a train, a car, and the scales of justice."[41]

Given their residence in the state capitol, the Chiefs could scarcely avoid politics. A "Political Spectacular" (October 1964) gave both presidential candidates some free advertising: "The AUH2O formation and 'Go with Goldwater' will salute Republican candidate Barry Goldwater. The Democratic nominee will be represented by an LBJ formation played to 'Hello Lyndon.'"[42]

Campus culture was reflected in "FSU in Review" (October 1964), which included "formations depicting campus life": a pennant, a typewriter, a triangle ("representing the trimester"), and a dollar sign.[43] And in a nod to campus romance, "A girl's figure will be the formation as the band plays 'I Can't Give You Anything but Love.'"[44]

The 1966 season featured a pronounced turn to popular culture with shows based on the music of Henry Mancini, whose animated *Pink Panther* television series was beloved; a salute to Disney; and music from the kitschy *Batman* series. But more serious music was not neglected. Works by Paul Yoder, an enormously influential composer of school band music, were also included on the season roster. Appearing for Band Day, Yoder himself conducted some of his own

5. The Art of the Marching Band (1963–1970)   103

compositions, "Down the Gridiron" and "Firehouse Special" among them.[45]

By 1970, Brownie's vision of what was possible on the gridiron extended not to merely an individual show, but to an entire season. "In a new approach to half-time entertainment," a *Flambeau* writer enthused, "the Marching Chiefs will present a coordinated musical theme throughout the 1970 football season."[46] Each show comprised four segments, each with a self-contained motive. The segments were: "Those Were the Days," the "Bent Arrow Award," "Happiness is...," and "The Spirit of Our Times."

One show, performed at the October 1970 Miami game, provides an example of how Brownie's scheme worked. The "Those Were the Days" portion—intended to reflect on simpler, happier times of yore—featured marches by Sousa and Fillmore. The "Bent Arrow Award" segment—a light musical take on human foibles—was dedicated to "the loser at the pari-mutuel window"; the formation was a silver dollar, and the band played two tunes, Bobby Sherman's hit, "Easy Come, Easy

The Marching Chiefs perform at Doak Campbell Stadium, circa 1970 (photograph by J. Barry Mittan. Courtesy of Heritage Protocol & University Archives, Florida State University Libraries).

Go" and Gershwin's "I've Got Plenty of Nuthin.'"[47] "Happiness Is..." celebrated those activities that add joy to life. In a tribute to the City of Miami, the Chiefs formed a surfboard and a boat to the theme from the television program, *Hawaii Five-O*. Finally, "The Spirit of Our Times" gave way to hit songs of the day, including Tony Orlando and Dawn's "Candida" (1970) and Richard Harris's "The Yard Went on Forever" (1968).

※ ※ ※

The Chiefs continued to enjoy their reputation for a "tradition of fun-loving antics."[48] One particularly memorable escapade occurred during the 1963 Miami game. According to the *Flambeau*'s Bob Mitchell, "At the height of the Marching Chiefs [half-time] program," UM's mascot took to the field in an effort to derail the show. The mascot, an Ibis—that is, an ornithological specimen "dressed up to look like a seagull, but looks more like a deranged canary"—failed, but band members were determined to get even. Plans were laid for a "sportswriter" to invite the foul fowl to an interview and photo session at Miami's iconic Fontainebleau Hotel.

The bird bought it, and, upon its arrival, "90 to 100 Marching Chiefs lurked in the shadows" waiting to pounce. "The poor bird, having no place to go, stepped backwards, into the fountain." The Ibis's companion quickly ran to the hotel to call the cops. At this point, Mitchell reported, "The Chiefs ... made an orderly exodus."[49] The ruse perpetrated on Miami's Ibis remains one of the greatest capers in Chiefs history.

But the Miami misadventures did not end there. As the Chiefs headed out of town, one of the buses broke down in front of the Boulevard Drive-In Theatre. With time on their hands and a movie marquee within reach, several band members determined to change the lettering on the marquee to read "FSU All Time" and "UM O [zero] ha." (The gridiron Noles had drubbed the Canes, 24–0.)[50] The owner of the theater arrived and demanded the restoration of the original lettering; when he didn't get it, he alerted the police, who "were greeted by wild cheers and were soon surrounded by 120 band members who were chanting 'Freedom' and singing 'We Shall Overcome.'" The police were inclined to let the whole thing go as a prank, but the theater owner insisted on a written complaint. The prospect of the Chiefs being part of an official police record raised some concern. As remembered by

5. The Art of the Marching Band (1963–1970)   105

Gene Crowe, Brownie got on the bus and said, "You know, we may have gone too far there. I'm a little bit worried because there is a police report."[51] At about that time, someone handed Brownie the police report, which had mysteriously come into the possession of an enterprising Chief. Thus ended what has become widely known as the "Run-in at the Drive-in."

✦ ✦ ✦

Over the years, "Flushing the Field" has been one of the most hallowed of Marching Chiefs traditions. That it developed as a result of embarrassment to the not-always-respected sousaphone section has been largely forgotten. In 1966, the various instrument sections were rated from best to worst based on musical ability and overall contributions to the band. The five-member tuba section, as declared by a staff vote, was rated dead last. "It was just awful," says Chuck Beutel, tuba section row leader at the time. "I was just crushed." Tuba section morale plummeted, and solutions were desperately sought: "What can we do, what can we do?," was the question. The answer: "Well, maybe we can come up with a gimmick."[52]

The tubas were forced to re-imagine themselves as "The Flush." As originally conceived, the name "was indicative of the way we sounded," Beutel says. That is, toilet-like. "We weren't great players." Beutel himself was an accomplished bassoonist, who played the tuba because he wanted to be part of the Chiefs. But something had to change. "We were looking for a gimmick that would instill some pride in the section." It was immediately recognized that a toilet comparison surely would not do that.

Instead of "The Flush," another section member came up with the idea of being the "Royal Flush"; that dispensed with the toilet association and related the tuba section to the game of poker, a somewhat more positive connotation. "We each selected a card [with which] to associate ourselves," and in short order Poker hands were painted on each instrument and case. The five members of the Royal Flush were an ace (for the row leader), a king, a jack, a ten, and a joker. Because there were no women in the section, there was no queen.

But the Royal Flush, having invented a cool name, required another ploy to fully restore their due respect and increase their coolness. By the time the Miami game rolled around, a scheme to "Flush the Field" had been invented. "When the Chiefs made their exit to the far sideline," Beutel explains, "instead of the sousaphones going directly to the far sideline, we went—on the fast cadence—to the center and ran around the circle." It was not, of course, an entirely spontaneous event, as it had been choreographed in advance. Brownie and Big 8 also knew what was happening; according to Beutel, "The drums kept the cadence going; I had set it up with the drums."[53]

※ ※ ※

Given that the Marching Chiefs were well established, well appreciated, and hugely popular with FSU audiences, several former Chiefs wondered why there was no alumni band. The topic first bubbled up in 1969, when Mike and Judy Pate and Curtis and Jo Ellen Falany began to dig into the matter more seriously. After several bottles of bottom-shelf champagne, "We had a long conversation and decided that what FSU needed is an alumni band. What we really wanted to do was to get back together with our friends."[54] While Pate is clearly proud of the many good things that the Alumni Band has done to date—scholarships and other financial assistance to the band program—he insists that the program started out as something considerably less ambitious. The notion of an alumni band, "was not some altruistic, long-term vision that we could ultimately become a fundraising and support arm for the Chiefs. It was really about getting back together and re-connecting with old friends."[55]

The first appearance of the Alumni Band occurred on November 14, 1970. Despite the fact that the *Flambeau* reported that sixty alums had signed up to perform, only twenty-seven appeared.[56] Pate recalls that "On the night before the game we would all gather at Charlie's house, where he put old [Marching Chiefs] tape recordings on" for the participants, who spent much of their time affixing garnet and gold bands to the hats that had been donated by the local Budweiser distributor.[57]

The first Alumni Band was featured during pre-game. The small ensemble marched out in a company front ("that was all we could form," says Pate) and played the "Fight Song." Their efforts were by no means unappreciated. "The stands went nuts. They thought it was the greatest thing they had ever seen."[58] The group then joined the Chiefs, which had formed a tomahawk. In that year's pre-game show, the handle of the tomahawk served to guide the entering football team from the end zone to the sideline. Alumni leaders pleaded for Brownie to include

5. The Art of the Marching Band (1963–1970)   107

them in that climactic moment; he agreed, and added to his formation an Alumni Band feather, which rested atop the Marching Chiefs tomahawk.

The first performance by the Alumni Band occurred on the twentieth anniversary of the naming of the band as the Marching Chiefs and the premiere of the "Fight Song," but it seems that no one actually realized it. Says Pate, "It was just a happy coincidence."[59]

As of this writing, the Alumni Band typically hovers near 300.

※ ※ ※

Another tradition appeared in 1969: the "Hairy Buffalo" party. Although post-game parties were nothing new on campus, the Hairy Buffalo—an alcoholic beverage made from a variety of white liquors combined in a garbage can and mixed with punch, Kool-Aid or some similar fruity addition—tended to make such events more memorable (or less memorable) than ever before.

As recounted by W. Alan Smith, a handful of Marching Chiefs Kappa Kappa Psi brothers journeyed to Oklahoma State University (Stillwater, Oklahoma) to attend the fraternity's 1969 national convention. There they met brothers from the University of Connecticut "who introduced us to a concoction they called the 'Hairy Buffalo.' We brought the idea back with us and introduced it on the first Chiefs' road trip that Fall—to Miami. We adapted what we borrowed from UConn to FSU tastes, and a tradition was born."[60]

※ ※ ※

It is an article of faith that the Marching Chiefs "never lost a half-time show." It is said; it is believed. The phrase, dear to all who ever wore the uniform, has been repeated since the '50s, but it gained popular currency in 1960, when it appeared on the cover of a university magazine. A variation of the phrase was picked up by the *Tally-Ho* yearbook in 1963, which, in the most optimistic terms stipulated that, "Regardless of the football game, we always win the half-time show."[61] A *Flambeau* writer gleefully reiterated the sentiment, and it has been proclaimed many times since.[62]

The notion of half-time show supremacy was a subjective one until 1970, when the ABC television network aired the "Chevrolet All-American College TV Band Contest." The competition purported "to determine the best NCAA [National Collegiate Athletic Association]

The Marching Chiefs form a diamond at Doak Campbell Stadium in this 1964 photograph. Two things to notice: the centerfield Seminole head has yet to appear; and the stands remain full for another entertaining show (courtesy of State Archives of Florida/Florida Memory. Image no. TD015741).

band in the country," by presenting a round of "semi-finals" between various bands that were a part of ABC's "Game of the Week." This was perhaps not the fairest system of determining the nation's best band; after all, if a university's football team was not selected for broadcast on ABC, it's marching band was entirely out of luck.

Nevertheless, the Chiefs who took the band motto as gospel also knew the risks that the contest posed. "The rallying cry for the Marching Chiefs was ... if we don't win this one, we can't say that any more," remembers W. Alan Smith. "We took that challenge very seriously. That was our goal that year—to prove that our slogan was the case."[63]

Those few bands fortunate enough to be in the competition were judged on playing, uniformity, and marching, "as well as the general effect the band had on the audience."[64] FSU had recently defeated the University of Houston Cougar Band with its "Fancy Colors" show at the old Tampa Stadium (later known as "The Big Sombrero") to move to the final round; the victory landed the Chiefs a front-page photo in the *Tallahassee Democrat*.[65] The win was no small accomplishment,

5. The Art of the Marching Band (1963–1970)   109

given that the "Spirit of Houston" band was led by Bill Moffit, a respected marching band arranger and innovator whose fame would grow enormously over the next several decades. FSU's triumph—declared by judges including big-band phenom Les Brown, Jack Lee, and the already-legendary Florida A & M marching band director William P. Foster—was unanimous.

Other semi-finals pitted Stanford University against University of Arkansas. The great trumpeter Doc Severinsen was one of the onsite judges for that contest; Arkansas won. The University of North Texas took on the University of Tulsa. Louisiana State University conquered the University of Alabama.

Within a month following the semi-finals, the judges convened in Denver to watch film, compare and discuss the regional performances, and declare a national winner. The panel crowned William F. Swor's LSU "Golden Band from Tigerland." The prize was a coveted expenses-paid trip to the East-West Shrine Game in Oakland, California, a wonderful excursion for a band that hails from the Bayou.

Although ABC's new emphasis on the marching band did not go unappreciated, Braunagel took the whole thing with a grain of salt: "The contest is mainly a gimmick to get more people to watch the half-time show," he said. Nevertheless, "it did give the band a real lift."[66] The Chiefs placed second in the final rankings.

At least this once, the Chiefs did lose a halftime show.

Forging an Art Form

One of the most potent manifestations of Brownie's pledge of experimentation was the November 1963 production of *Ballet for Band* by Dr. John Boda. As Brownie told one reporter, "this is the first time that any band has ever done this type of thing."[67]

Boda's *Ballet* is a specially composed piece for marching band, one that takes into account the ensemble's unique instrumentation, the placement of instruments on the field, the nature of sound produced outdoors, and the possibilities and limitations inherent when the musicians are in motion. Brownie, of course, had a significant role in ensuring that the overlay of drill was complementary to Boda's score. An FSU professor of music whose renown rested on numerous compositions, his service as assistant conductor under George Szell and the magnificent Cleveland Orchestra, and his own brilliance, Boda was a mild-mannered, unassuming man whose neo-classical style compositions reflected a spirit of adventure tempered by a respect for tradition.[68]

Boda's *Ballet* was linked by FSU's publicity department to other works composed specifically for outdoor performances by the likes of Handel (*Water Music*) and Berlioz (*Grande symphonie funèbre et triomphale*). In addition, "The significance of this program," a press release announced, "is contained in the fact that it represents an effort to find a medium in which the American Composer can establish a direct line of communication to the mass audience of America."[69] The same release expressed a good deal of confidence in the fans at Doak Campbell Stadium. Boda's score was not "the usual 'music to eat hot dogs by,'" the writer admitted; nevertheless, the local football crowd "[has] shown a sufficient appreciation and interest in the Chiefs to entitle the FSU fans to the honor of being the first collegiate football audience to witness this signal effort."[70]

Boda's *Ballet for Band* is in a three-part form. Former Marching Chief, composer, and Boda protégé Paul Basler has said that his mentor "mentioned that when he was asked to write the work he decided not to alter his compositional style to 'fit' what was considered the [norm] for marching band music.... The piece is very typical of his compositional style—filled with high energy, rhythmic syncopation, a use of many major seconds and explosive percussion punctuation."[71]

As described by the *Flambeau*:

> The opening section is strongly rhythmical and features the brass and percussion groups. While playing the band forms constantly changing patterns which gives the impression of looking through a kaleidoscope. The second section is a waltz. Music and formations in this section "gives the impression of a Martian Carousel," said Braunagel. The finale comes on unexpectedly and features the same groups as in the opening sections.[72]

Boda's *Ballet* was an unexpected hit. The *Tallahassee Democrat*, in an editorial titled "More, Please," lamented that, having corralled thousands of people in a Doak Campbell stadium on a Saturday, the university did not take the opportunity to "show off some of the more cultural and educational aspects of its programs."[73] But here football fans were treated to something wonderful and unique:

> Some 24,000 people listened and watched as the band accompanied its symphonic music with a series of formations representing different styles of

5. The Art of the Marching Band (1963–1970) 111

crosses. You might say it was a captive audience, since it had no place to go, but it was obviously captivated by the performance. We can recall no greater applause for the band in Campbell stadium. Thus, a fine piece of music work was presented to an audience perhaps 20 times as great as it might have been able to attract on its own. It was a splendid show by a superb musical group....[74]

So successful was it that the *Democrat* hoped that other FSU cultural assets might appear at the games: choruses and soloists could sing school songs, theater ensembles could perform "snatches of drama," painters and sculptors could exhibit beneath the stands. In an effort to display the many wonders of the university, it was suggested that "even chemists and physicists might offer demonstrations of the modern magic."[75]

But that day was about Boda's *Ballet*, which Madsen has called "a monumental achievement and innovation."[76]

✧ ✧ ✧

Brownie's idea of providing audiences with original marching band shows founded on the bedrock of new compositions did not end with the *Ballet for Band*. The following year, Charlie Carter was invited to write original music that would premiere at the 1964 FSU versus UF game.[77] The crowd was expected to number 42,500 fans, several thousand more than the stadium could comfortably accommodate.[78]

Carter's *Marching Chiefs Fantasia* was similar to Boda's show in that the drill, written by Brownie, was largely abstract.[79] But other features demonstrate Charlie's sure knowledge of the marching band as a genre and his own devotion to audience-accessible musical styles. Opening with a flourish, the *Fantasia* is in four parts; the script from the show provides an idea of its structure:

> Fanfare ("Company Front Entrance: Opening with a brilliant fanfare, the band moves downfield to the driving rhythms of the quick-step march"); I. March and II. Drill (transition march, waltz, and march; "Triangular and Kaleidoscopic Patterns: Forming in three trinagle [sic] patterns, the sequence starts in ¾ time and changes to march tempo"); III. Dance Tempo ("Stage: The music takes an abrupt change of style into a modern jazz idiom as the band forms a stage and presents the majorettes and feature twirlers"); IV. Grand Finale ("Drill sequence: The music changes to a grandiose mood as the Chiefs present a constantly changing drill sequence ending in a company front finale.")[80]

Although this was an original show, Charlie was astute enough to utilize conventions of football entertainment that would resonate with audiences. His work employs strains of big band-style swing (Charlie's favored genre), as well as hints of beloved school songs. The drill included the recognizable fast-paced Chiefs step, the band's excellent feature twirler Cookie Winchester, and the most recent iteration of an FSU twirling duo, Bookie Reynolds and Jerry Williams, better known as the "Seminole Twins."

Carter's show was perhaps a little too routine to linger in the memory. It got scant notice compared to Boda's earlier effort, and, as of this writing, the *Fantasia* has not received an encore. One Chief, who performed the show at its premiere, recalls that "I mentioned [the *Fantasia*] to Charlie," a few years later while taking an arranging class, "and his reaction was, 'Oh, somebody actually remembers that show!'"[81]

※ ※ ※

Boda wrote a second original composition for the Marching Chiefs. His *Ballet for Band No. 2*, was premiered on October 25, 1969. Braunagel proudly noted in a *Flambeau* article that this was a third production of "a serious type half-time show" given by the Chiefs. In this newest effort, Boda's scheme was not drastically different from his first *Ballet for Band*:

> The three-part show, in ABA form (fast, slow, fast) opens with a march tune in which four designs are executed by the band. The second part is built around tone clusters and features the brass sections, with the band moving in a series of expanding kaleidoscopic circles. The music then returns to the march section, and the band performs three more abstract designs to complete the show.[82]

Tone clusters and abstract designs were not typical marching band fare, and to accomplish them required much practice. One Chief remembers that "The rehearsals were really, really intense and tough," and that the audience reaction was mixed.[83] Unlike Boda's earlier effort, the second one was not roundly appreciated. "The crowd was really kind of taken aback that there were no breaks," said W. Alan Smith, and "the music itself was so strange and unfamiliar." It was "one of the most creative things we did while I was there. We rehearsed that show virtually the entire season before we finally put it on."[84]

Although wholly original shows would crop up from time to time on the Marching Chiefs roster of performances, they never regained the momentum that they achieved during Brownie's second term as director. If his vision of originality in the marching band medium was perhaps fleeting, it was nevertheless an important milestone in the history of the genre. It was one thing to play popular songs and to create familiar formations for vast crowds at the football stadium; it was quite another to perform new works by esteemed, serious composers and to set them to abstract, modernistic drill. The football gridiron, once a place for high-quality entertainments, was now a canvas for art.

"Ghosts of FSCW"

The Homecoming Pow Wow of October 1964 was not unlike those that had been produced in the previous decade-and-a-half. There were parades, banquets, and student-created and performed skits, a vestigial Odd-Even tradition that through the decades came and went. Their more recent resurrection may have been an attempt to mirror aspects of UF's "Gator Growl," which incorporated skits to provide homecoming with—besides school spirit and pageantry—a sometimes irreverent comedic edge. On Friday evening October 9, a number of FSU sororities and fraternities offered up skits in front of students and faculty. The audience also included plenty of alumni and townsfolk, and as the Pow Wow had long been a family affair, locals were warmly welcomed. Often there were even children in attendance. But what was intended as an evening of wholesome fun erupted into another small scandal that impacted the Marching Chiefs.

Despite having been refereed and approved by a faculty committee, some of the skits were considered obscene; besides that, many of the most prominent organizations on campus were mercilessly attacked—or "parodied," as defenders of the presentations termed it. Angry letters from alumni and townspeople poured into the office of FSU President John E. Champion. Many also registered their disapproval with the *Tallahassee Democrat*, which in turn led to coverage in a variety of newspapers, including the *St. Petersburg Times*, the *Miami Herald*, and the *Atlanta Constitution*.

As one of the largest and most visible organizations on campus, the Marching Chiefs were naturally among the groups most targeted for criticism, although we do not know the exact nature of the affronts. Within days of the Pow Wow a group of unnamed Chiefs penned their own letter to the *Flambeau*. "The exhibition by certain sororities this weekend," the Chiefs claimed, "was one of the most disgusting and vulgar things witnessed by the Marching Chiefs and thousands of others. We get embarrassed to think that anyone could stoop that low to get a few laughs. It was all in very poor taste and was not appreciated by anyone."[85]

Others agreed and even found the affair an insult to the whole of FSU. One student, who was unaffiliated with the Chiefs, wrote, "To think that some people would do such a thing to the school we all love and cherish!"[86] Another declared that the "badly produced, badly acted, mistaken farce ... could hardly be labeled as in good taste regardless of the time or place."[87]

Many others defended the skits, claiming them perfectly appropriate on several counts. First, skits at other universities—like the one just down the road—were as bad or worse. Why the uproar over an activity that was routine elsewhere? Second—in an enormous slight to both alumni and Tallahasseeans—the event was supposed to be by students for students, and if alums and townies felt as though they should stay away, they were probably correct.

In many ways, FSU's 1964 Pow Wow marked the arrival of the volcanic sixties. Issues of race (FSU had been integrated just two years before), women's liberation, the Vietnam War—the 1969 Homecoming theme was "Peace is Relevant"—and others occupied the thoughts of many Americans. FSU students and the Marching Chiefs were no different; as one band member observed, "The Chiefs were a microcosm of everything that was going on."[88] Curtis Falany, in a reflection that neatly encapsulates the magnitude of the changes that were occurring at the time, remembers that upon his arrival at FSU in 1965 the women's dorms were carefully monitored. Undergraduate girls were required to be in their dorm rooms by 11:00 p.m. on weeknights; on weekends they could be out until 12:30 a.m. Once inside, they were expected to remain there until 6:00 a.m.[89] "By the time I left," Falany says, "they had co-ed dorms."[90] The dress code for women was similarly stifling. Marching Chief Steven L. Sparkman reflected that "When I started [in 1965], the girls had to wear trench coats to practice and from practice, because they couldn't walk on campus in shorts."[91] Shorts were tolerated on Chiefs Field during rehearsals, but not otherwise.

Sometimes the Chiefs were at the center of social concerns. In 1968, for example, President Champion received a list of demands from the Afro-American Student Union, one of which requested that

5. The Art of the Marching Band (1963–1970)   115

he prohibit musical groups from playing the old Confederate anthem, "Dixie," which had long been a campus favorite. Said one Chief, FSU students would "rather hear that than hear the 'Fight Song,' almost."[92] Champion said that he could not forbid it, but he also noted that the Marching Chiefs had not played it so far that year, "and it is doubtful that they intend to do so."[93] But "Dixie" was not dead. FSU President Stanley Marshall recalled that the song also caused consternation in his administration; the *Flambeau* printed letters advocating for and against its playing. The song "was quietly dropped during the football season of 1969," Marshall wrote. "To my great relief the 'Dixie' proponents made no protests."[94] In this Chiefs were well ahead of a good many other Southern bands. UF and Georgia did not scrap "Dixie" until the mid–1970s. Alabama's Crimson Tide Band was legally obligated to play it owing to legislation passed by defiant lawmakers in 1967; the same legislation required the presence at football games of the Confederate flag.[95] Ole Miss nixed its use of "Dixie" only in 2016.

Sensitivity to representations of the Seminole Tribe also began during this era. The football mascot Sammy Seminole was tolerated for the time being, but the basketball mascot proved too controversial to maintain. In an effort to be more accommodating to the concerns of Native American students, the basketball spirit mascot, Chief Fullabull, considered a variety of other names and changed his to Chief Wampum-Stompum.[96] Naturally, that one was deemed equally unacceptable. The issue was resolved when the mascot reviewed a list of names submitted by actual Seminole Indians, and finally selected Chief Yahola (a purported variation of Osceola), a Seminole word meaning "victorious."[97]

As far as concerns the Pow Wow skits, what in another time might simply have been passed over as silliness and immaturity had now morphed into issues of freedom of speech and the rights of students to air grievances. One letter to the editor of the *Flambeau* acknowledged that "the band practices long, hard hours. And the majority of the student body appreciates their effort. However, this does not take away the right of any student to make critical remarks or poke fun at the band or any organization or person on this campus."[98] And when the University meted out punishment to most of the fraternities and sororities involved, another student asked, "Isn't the democratic system based partially on the freedom of dissent?" Referring to some of the complaints vented in the skits, the same person asked another question:

"What better place than the Pow Wow to express the objections of the student body?"

From today's vantage point, one might question whether in fact the Pow Wow was the most appropriate venue for such venting. That aside, one anonymous correspondent to the *Flambeau* laid blame for the controversy squarely at the feet of the University and its history of over-protectiveness, a characteristic that was a remnant of its FSCW days. "In actuality, the student body of FSU has been subjected for years to pressures restricting [the] free flow of ideas as well as [the] free flow of actions," the writer complained,

> And the result of this suppression was demonstrated in the first uninhibiting opportunity borne on campus for college students to portray themselves as college students not masquerading sophists.... So, hark, all potential college material, FSU offers a liberal education ... but, beware, the ivy covered spirals deceive—through the hallowed halls the ghosts of FSCW loom. If you're not afraid of hoblins and goblins, then have no fear—FSU is like a Mother, dear![99]

The Chiefs Go Bowling

FSU played Oklahoma in Jacksonville's Gator Bowl on January 2, 1965. In its first post-season trip since the 1958 Bluegrass Bowl in Kentucky, FSU logged an impressive win over the Sooners, 36 to 19. That game marked a streak of appearances at four bowls within a five-year span, although the next three would result in two losses and a tie. The Chiefs, of course, had little trouble getting to the bowl games held in the South, but one trip required assistance from some extraordinary sources.

The 1966 Sun Bowl, held on Christmas Eve in El Paso, Texas, featured FSU in a contest against the University of Wyoming Cowboys. The team-name narrative alone—Wyoming's Cowboys versus FSU's Indians—would ensure a fascinated and sizable national audience. But the trip was a long one, and the costs of taking the team alone would approach $54,000, an extraordinary amount considering that the Bowl Committee guaranteed FSU just a measly $60,000 payout.[100] Taking the Chiefs to El Paso would be an expensive frill, university leaders concluded, and it was never seriously considered.

Word that the Chiefs were not attending the game got around quickly, and that notion caused a tumult on campus. In short order, the *Flambeau* became a crucial supporter of the effort to send the band

5. The Art of the Marching Band (1963–1970)   117

to Texas. The newspaper's December 2 issue included a front-page article, a letter to the editor, a "Frankly Speaking" column that recorded the opinions of students, and a "special editorial," which was in fact a feature-length commentary.[101] The *Flambeau* was suddenly demonstrating zealous support for the Chiefs in a way band members had not seen before.

FSU student body president Larry Gonzalez spoke up on the matter. He said, "With the exception of the Florida-FSU game, the controversy over sending the Marching Chiefs to El Paso has rallied perhaps the greatest concern from members of the student body in years."[102]

Gonzalez and his followers organized a fundraising campaign. FSU students were collectively asked to contribute $6,000, to which another $28,000 would be cobbled together from a variety of sources. This included funding from the athletic department, which, it was believed, could be pressured, maybe even embarrassed, into contributing to the Chiefs.

This cartoon aptly reflects the Chiefs' frustration at their inability to secure funding for travel to El Paso's 1966 Sun Bowl. After a good deal of hullabaloo, the money was found (*Florida Flambeau*, 1966. Courtesy of Heritage Protocol & University Archives, Florida State University Libraries).

Besides these steps, Gonzalez and other university personnel went to the state capitol to mine for additional governmental funds. Florida's

Citrus Commission was one target. Although neither football nor the Marching Chiefs were directly related to that panel's mission, the commissioners convinced themselves that FSU's presence at a nationally-televised football game could bolster fruit juice sales. It was later reported that "The SSB [Student Seminole Boosters] told Gov. Burns that the Citrus Commission wanted to aid the Chiefs and that if he would give them the word, they might come through with the funds." The Governor later called a band student leader and told him to "notify the Chiefs to pack."[103]

The journey to El Paso was arduous, but a twelve-hour flight delay, the result of dense fog in Tallahassee, did not sap the Chiefs' spirits. As the fog began to break, the band lined up and went through the show on a runway.[104] According to Mike Pate, "We used (as best we could) cracks in the runway as not-very-well-established yard line markers."[105] And while the game itself, televised by NBC, resulted in a disappointing 28–20 Noles loss, the halftime show was broadcast in its entirety.

FSU's next two years of bowls were thankfully more local. The Gator Bowl in Jacksonville (December 20, 1967) pitted the Noles against Penn State; it ended in a 17–17 tie. A year later, FSU took a 31–27 loss versus LSU at the inaugural Peach Bowl (December 30, 1968). The Chiefs got scant local media attention for their efforts at either the Gator Bowl or the Peach Bowl, although at the former a *Flambeau* writer proffered that "The majorettes will be twirling their best routines of the season."[106]

※ ※ ※

In retrospect, Brownie's ascent to the post of director of the Marching Chiefs following Whit's resignation seems like a perfect metaphor for the times. Whit, while not an unfriendly man, was focused and intensely disciplined; his style had been honed by a number of years spent with OSU's all-male, military-style marching band and a hitch in the armed forces. But his was a style that, by the 1960s, was falling out of favor. Authority at all levels of the university was being questioned; students protested myriad real and perceived problems and issues; and—following decades of financial distress, multiple hot wars abroad, and now the Cold War—students were yearning for a less formal, less restrictive atmosphere.

As far as the band was concerned, the atmosphere became

5. The Art of the Marching Band (1963–1970)   119

noticeably more relaxed. One former Chief admitted that "Brownie ... was totally your best buddy."[107] These are words that could never have been uttered about Whit, but which aptly reflect the mutual affection between Brownie and his students. Brownie was both friend and leader. He thought the new leniency was an improvement over the old ways. According to a *Flambeau* reporter, "Under informal supervision, the band has 'no discipline,' according to Braunagel, who feels that most bands are run autocratically. The relaxed working atmosphere, plus the long hours of practice, contributes largely to the group spirit, an important part of the organization."[108]

Brownie's era was perhaps marked by a reduction in top-down discipline, but there is no evidence that it was accompanied by diminished quality. In fact, the Marching Chiefs of that era almost unanimously recall that even if rehearsals started late and ended late—something unimaginable under Whit—everything that needed to be accomplished was accomplished. "I do remember the sense that

In this 1960s photograph, the Chiefs are marching to the double-time Go Cadence. This is a rare glimpse at the back of the old black uniforms (courtesy of Heritage Protocol & University Archives, Florida State University Libraries).

every Friday," Marching Chief Chris Haughee said, "as we started rehearsal, we would look at each other and say 'There's no way we're gonna be ready by Saturday.' ... But Brownie was able to work magic and get it done."[109]

If his half-time shows sometimes took a bit longer to perfect, Brownie's vision of originality on the gridiron—which was greatly enhanced, as always, by Charlie's imaginative arrangements—took the marching band genre to unprecedented artistic heights. It also conferred additional prestige upon the already nationally renowned Marching Chiefs.

⬧ 6 ⬧

World Renowned
(1971–1976)

"With an ever present flair"

In 1970 the brilliant American musician Leonard Bernstein was at last a free man. Having resigned his conducting post at the New York Philharmonic just a year before, he embarked on a number of musical projects at home and abroad that sated his incredible appetite for creation. He started composing again; this was a beloved aspect of his career that he had mostly put on hold since he started with the Philharmonic in 1957. And, besides continuing to guest conduct notable orchestras worldwide, Bernstein also initiated several music-educational projects for American and British television. He was an energetic and innovative artist, and his legions of fans admired his immense talent and his obvious dedication to "the show."

One of those Bernstein fans was Richard (Dick) Mayo. Mayo holds the distinction of having been the first Marching Chiefs director who was himself a Marching Chief. He played bells (glockenspiel) when he joined the band and did some dancing on the field when Braunagel was director[1]; he was recruited to be the drum major in 1953, Whit's first year in Tallahassee. Mayo recounted that "Whitcomb came into the music library and asked if I would like to be the drum major." There may be more to the story than that, for, as one Chief—who heard it from Mayo himself—says, "that sounds very casual for Manley Whitcomb."[2] Nevertheless, Whit gave his new, inexperienced drum major lessons in conducting, twirling the mace, and strutting in hopes he would be ready for the coming football season.[3]

Mayo was also a talented oboist and pianist. He was awarded his Bachelor of Music Education degree in 1955, and then went on to pursue a Master of Arts degree from Columbia University in New York City. It was probably during his New York years that he came under the influence of Leonard Bernstein.[4]

Mayo was brought back to FSU in 1970 by Whitcomb to serve as assistant marching band director under Brownie. Mayo had always been a Whitcomb favorite; this hire not only helped Brownie as he entered the twilight of his career, but it also cemented Mayo's status as heir apparent. At FSU Mayo's duties included—besides the Marching Chiefs—the teaching of a variety of music education courses and the running of the jazz/rock ensemble (known then as the "lab" band because of its preference for "experimental" music), which had been founded by Brownie in 1956, "to acquaint members with the best forms of modern and popular music."[5]

Marching Chiefs director Richard (Dick) Mayo had been Whit's first drum major and later served as Brownie's assistant. Here he rehearses the band from Chiefs tower with the assistance of Harry E. Price and Susan Allen (courtesy of John F. Ervin).

6. World Renowned (1971–1976) 123

Mayo was named the new director of the Chiefs in April 1971.[6] His rise to that position was reported with little fanfare in the *Flambeau*. The first article to mention it simply noted that he was the new director; the biggest portion of the article stressed recruiting, a Mayo priority, even though the band that year numbered a healthy 184.[7]

⁕ ⁕ ⁕

As with most conservatories and music schools, FSU's School of Music was founded on a fairly conservative classical aesthetic. Three noteworthy early nods to popular culture were Sykora's swing band, the marching band, and the circus band. Mayo added to those in important ways: he introduced several new courses to FSU students, including jazz and rock history, and organized a new class titled "Jazz and Rock Lab Performing Ensembles in the Middle, Junior and Senior High Schools," which was intended to aid music teachers as they were forced to grapple with the needs of the "Now Generation."[8] Mayo was committed to the presentation of a variety of popular American music styles, even during a time when such music in higher education was still viewed with suspicion. He oversaw the school's two large jazz/rock bands and two combos, and was an organizer of "Bach, Rock, and All That Jazz," a "new approach to musical tours" that took a number of FSU ensembles on the road for publicity and recruiting. "A teacher has to be informed," Mayo insisted. "He can't tune out his students and their interest in, and involvement with, contemporary music."[9] That sentiment could very well have been sounded by Bernstein himself.

⁕ ⁕ ⁕

Mayo's first Marching Chiefs show was "Innovations in Sound," a title that reflects not only the ongoing emphasis on the quality of the musical performance itself but also Mayo's own creative aesthetic. Combining the classical with the popular, the show featured music by Richard Wagner and John Philip Sousa, as well as jazz favorites by Louis Armstrong, Buddy Rich, and Tallahassee's own Cannonball Adderley. "Innovations in Sound" was performed at FSU's first home football game of the season versus the University of Kansas. The Jayhawks band did not make the trip; in its stead, Mayo invited Dr. William P. Foster's FAMU marching band to perform at halftime.

Continuing the spirit of innovation, Mayo made numerous

FSU's majorettes, seen here in 1973, have long been considered among the finest in the South. They are renowned not only for their excellent twirling, but also for the pageantry and vivacity they bring to the shows (courtesy of Heritage Protocol & University Archives, Florida State University Libraries).

6. World Renowned (1971–1976)

changes in his first year, ones that were designed to excite the crowds and to enhance his recruiting efforts. They also contributed to Mayo's own fervent love of "the show"; as one Mayo confidante has reported, "He loved to attract attention."[10]

One new element of "the show" was the scatter drill, a technique that Mayo resurrected.[11] During the scatter drill, band members wander around the football field in a seemingly random fashion until, at a particular point in the music or in a drum cadence, they pop into place in a new formation. The suddenness of the arrival of the formation creates a powerful effect—chaos instantly gives way to order and provides a visual thrill that is often accompanied by an assertive downbeat. As Sara Pankaskie recalls, some band members reacted with surprise: "'What? That's not military!' And Mayo was like 'Well, yeah, that's the point. We're not a military group, we're a performing group!'"[12] Scatter drills had not been featured regularly since before Whit's time.

The pursuit of a contemporary sound had been inaugurated by Brownie in his November 1969 half-time show, titled "The Now Music for the Now Generation." It was based on the music of the popular jazz/rock band Blood, Sweat & Tears, which had released four chart-topping albums between 1968 and 1971. The show featured three Blood, Sweat & Tears arrangements and included the on-field use of three drum sets and three amplified bass guitars.[13] Another highlight of the early Blood, Sweat & Tears charts was that band's trumpet player Lew Soloff, who often screamed in his instrument's upper register. Brownie, himself an impressive trumpet player, noted the brass talent in the Chiefs; says one member of the band, "We had a killer trumpet section."[14] Mayo seized upon the talent of the Marching Chiefs trumpet section—which during Brownie's later years became known as the "Screech Squad" because of their ability to play high notes—to perform an arrangement of "Get It On" (1971), a fiery tune that had been made famous by the jazz/rock trumpet virtuoso Bill Chase.

Other pop artists influenced the Marching Chiefs and their sound innovations. Santana's 1970 album titled *Abraxas* greatly affected Big 8. By 1971 Mayo added percussion; in addition to the twenty-two drummers who played the traditional battery of snares, bass drums, and cymbals, several new instruments were added: bongo-conga clusters (the congas were jettisoned the next year); timbales; various sizes of tri-toms; and marching timpani.[15] These, it was thought, would make for "a more contemporary sound," and Latin percussion was becoming increasingly popular.[16] One Chief has reflected that "It was really the Santana album that led to all of that."[17]

The Latin percussion instruments that were increasingly popular among members of Big 8 had an unanticipated effect on the pre-game show. Heavier instruments, and drummers who were now bogged down with all manner of harnesses, straps, and multi-drum sets, were now having difficulties participating in the Go Cadence. According to George Rosete, "There was no way we were going to be able to 'double-time' it out on the field to the Go Cadence. The drums were too heavy and cumbersome."[18] Rosete, who drum-majored for one year before deciding to return to his beloved Big 8, took matters into his own hands: "I approached Mr. Mayo with the idea that we could … position ourselves with a cadence that led into the Go Cadence and [then] segue into it so that the rest of the Chiefs could then come on as always (double-time). He left it up to me to come up with something. That's why I wrote the Come-On Cadence." Says Rosete, "I am honored as well as surprised that the Chiefs continue to use my cadence to enter the field even now, 40+ years later."[19]

Besides jazz/rock, Mayo was attracted to other contemporary musical styles. He made regular treks to New York City to hear Broadway's newest hits—popular shows that included *Hair* (1967) and *Godspell* (1971), among others—and to assess their appropriateness for his purposes.[20] And a 1973 Marching Chiefs show, titled "Jazz: America's Music," included not only more traditional jazz selections, but also another round of "special adaptations" of music by Blood, Sweat & Tears.[21] Mayo's innovations paid off in other ways. The Chiefs now numbered 225, plus sixteen majorettes and twenty-two members of a "department in charge of props used during the half-time shows."[22]

Charlie Carter was also charged with making the sound more contemporary; as one *Flambeau* writer noted, the music "is voiced higher and is much brighter this year."[23] The acquisition of better instruments was no small contributor to the Chiefs' new sound. Mayo was especially happy with the improvement in the tuba section. "We got rid of the plastic, fiberglass 'toilet bowls' that we had for tubas—the white ones—," he said, "and we went out and got good King brass sousaphones. That made a great difference in the volume."[24]

Although they generally got along, Charlie's working relationship with Mayo was sometimes quarrelsome. Sara Pankaskie remembers that "Brownie had pretty much let Charlie do what he wanted to do….

6. World Renowned (1971–1976)

Mayo had other ideas. He wanted more contemporary music, he wanted big endings on every tune. So, he and Charlie clashed sometimes on the musical aspects."[25] Another Chief recalls that "Charlie liked swing tunes, and he liked [jazz and pop] standards, and he liked show tunes. He did not like rock 'n' roll."[26] Charlie appreciated sophisticated writing, and the simplicity of the music he was now being asked to arrange was nothing less than enormously irritating. "I remember one tune ... one of the rock tunes," says Pankaskie. "Charlie said, 'It's only got three goddamned chords in it!'"[27]

※ ※ ※

Mayo's vision of the marching band included the incorporation of entertainment elements besides music and maneuvering. In the early seventies he established the Arts & Props Committee. Its purpose was twofold: first, it enabled Mayo to keep enthusiastic students in the band orbit even though, for a variety of reasons, they did not make the final band block; second, Mayo fully intended to use the gridiron as a stage on which he would mount massive and elaborate productions. To accomplish this he needed a corps to handle the props that would bring his shows to life. Marching Chief John Carmichael acted as chairman of the Arts & Props Committee; although he was still marching in the band block, he was proud to be part of the group: "We were the people who put things together."[28]

A patriotic show offered an early opportunity for the committee's involvement. Mayo asked the group to create an American flag that would cover much of the football field; he also wanted it to have a noticeable texture, which was provided by the application of crêpe paper; when affixed to the flag, the thin tissue would supply the effect Mayo envisioned.

The flag was a massive project—a number of students worked through the night to make sure it would be ready for the rehearsals and the show. The undertaking also required lots of Elmer's Glue, which was used to ensure that the crêpe paper adhered to the flag. Having gone through massive amounts of the stuff, the Arts & Props Committee had decided by the next morning their name should be the "Glue Crew."

Although everyone appreciated the Glue Crew and its importance to band pageantry, some thought that there were sometimes elements of overkill. The group itself was sometimes enormous; one Chief

The Marching Chiefs on parade in this early 1970s. The military-style black uniforms have now given way to garnet uniforms with wide gold trim (courtesy of Heritage Protocol & University Archives, Florida State University Libraries).

recollects that, "the Glue Crew expanded in size during [Mayo's] tenure, because ... you were always making stuff, and doing stuff; and it wouldn't be unusual for Glue Crew to be forty to sixty kids."[29]

Mayo's broad entertainment and production vision was not universally appreciated. W. Alan Smith remembers that Mayo brought "a lot of apparatus on the field." At times, he thought, "It made the field look cluttered, and took away from the marching itself."[30] One widely remembered half-time show—performed in Mayo's single year as Brownie's assistant—is "Fancy Colors," based on the band Chicago's 1970 album (now known as *Chicago II*). The production in Doak Campbell Stadium required six or seven intricate props, but as Smith puts it, "There was all sorts of junk on the field."[31] Another observer recalls that, "They made more props than you can imagine."[32]

✣ ✣ ✣

In keeping with Mayo's renewed emphasis on sound, the ideas for a Marching Chiefs half-time show now began with the music. This contrasted with the method used by Whit and Brownie, whose conceptions for the most part began with the formations; the search for appropriate accompanying music then followed.[33] For example, a November 1972 show titled "Movies" played on the famous pop tunes "What's New Pussycat?" and "Baby Elephant Walk." Only after Charlie had made the arrangements did Mayo devise the respective cat and elephant formations.

Mayo is directly responsible for one of the Chief's most cherished sonic traditions, the "Before Game Fanfare, pt. 2," the grandiose selection that now introduces the band at pre-game. He heard the tune on an album produced by the well-known pop/rock band The Osmonds. Mayo had discovered "Are You Up There?" on the group's eleventh studio album, *The Plan*, which was produced in 1973. Generally speaking, *The Plan* is one of the Osmond family's most ambitious albums, one that explores the family's Mormonism, while also presenting musical ideas that are more sophisticated than one generally expects from a 1970s-era teen pop band. The tune's comparative complexity is undoubtedly what inspired Mayo to take the album to Charlie to have it arranged.

Going hand in hand with sound innovations was team spirit among the sections. Mayo encouraged the sections that did not already have a name to adopt one. Of course, Big 8 has been Big 8 since the 1950s, and the Royal Flush and Screech Squad were named in the 1960s. Most of the rest of the section names originate from Mayo's years.[34] With the exception of the original three, section names have changed over the years. Current section names are: Chiefs Flutes; Pieces (clarinets); Section X (saxophones); Hornz (French horns/mellophones); Roamin' Bones (trombones); and T.O.N.E.S. (baritones).

As instrumental sections were acquiring their own identities, new sections of a different type were being added. Mayo—in his ongoing quest to improve "the show"—introduced a flag corps, rifles, and a color guard in the fall of 1975.[35] It was not a universally approved expansion. Given the emphasis on sound and drill, it might have seemed reasonable to question why these additions were necessary. According to Bill Haggard, "All of us on the student staff were like 'what the hell are you doing'"[36] But by then the students closest to Mayo knew that argument was pointless. "He was always looking for the new creative thing."[37]

Big 8 member Tim Wise recalls Mayo's nearly spontaneous creation of "The Focus." An elaborate variation on the scatter drill, The Focus was a completely new entrance that Mayo presented to the band at a Saturday morning run-through just before a noon Georgia Tech game. As Wise describes it, "it looked like an out-of-focus camera lens. From way up in the stands [it looked as though] everybody's running, and then it just looks like a blob on the field. And in eight seconds, suddenly an image clarifies."[38] That particular show featured music by Elton John, but according to Wise it was the drill, in combination with Charlie's arrangements, that astounded: "People just jumped out of their seats. They couldn't believe it; they'd never seen anything like it." The Focus was never performed again. A tour-de-force maneuver envisioned by a confident director who had faith in his band to execute it on the spur of the moment, perhaps Mayo thought that repeating it would simply be gratuitous. Or perhaps Mayo was off to his next imaginative feat. Whatever the case, The Focus "was a one-time event."[39]

The Marching Chiefs are used to taglines. In the early Mayo era, the band announcer proclaimed at the end of every show, "With an ever present flair for the dramatic, ladies and gentlemen, the pride of the State of Florida, the Florida State University Marching Chiefs."[40] Mayo's creative genius and flair for the dramatic were obvious to everyone.

"Anti-Football Views"

The Marching Chiefs were greatly affected when, in September 1972, the *Flambeau* became an independent newspaper. What had been a wholly-owned property of FSU was now a not-for-profit entity. Although free of the shackles of university oversight, the newspaper was now in need of funds from non-university sources. As it sought to increase revenues by expanding the amount of space it dedicated to advertising, the *Flambeau* substantially altered its news coverage. More common now than previously were stories about the university administration, its use of power and money, and its internal political machinations; the workings of student government; the tribulations of national government; and other causes of the day, including the women's lib movement, the Vietnam war, and civil rights.

The increase in political news—university, local, state, and national—naturally led to a diminished space for other concerns. Gone

6. World Renowned (1971–1976)

was the detailed and mostly positive coverage of aspects of campus life that had been typical a few years before—Greek life, clubs, activities, shenanigans. Gone, too, was the regular coverage of the Marching Chiefs. To paraphrase a line from Bob Dylan's 1964 hit album, the times at FSU were definitely a-changing.

※ ※ ※

FSU increasingly faced a lack of confidence in authority and a growing resistance to bureaucratic decision-making. This issue became prominent when, in the same month the *Flambeau* went private, it reported that new Marching Chiefs uniforms were going cost $18,000, an amount that would be skimmed from the Student Government Association (SGA) budget allocation from the university. Most galling to SGA leaders was the fact that the university simply kept the funds and paid for the uniforms directly, without the benefit of a fund transfer that would give the SGA a chance to ruminate over the matter. This effectively exempted the SGA from any say in the expenditure of its own resources.

Former SGA senator Tom Sullivan was apoplectic. He claimed that FSU president J. Stanley Marshall had committed a "fiscal atrocity." Further, Sullivan complained, Marshall held a "dictatorial control over students' monies," and "as long as this power exists we will have extravagant football expenditures on the one hand and a newspaper stripped of all funding on the other."[41]

The funds expended on Marching Chiefs uniforms were, it was thought by some, symptomatic of negative issues related to FSU's ascendant football ambitions. As always, *Flambeau* readers were quick to chime in. Letters to the editor decried the costs of sports and its detriment to the university. One of them, headlined "Sports Financing Undermines Library," railed against "sports and sports financing" which continued to be the "number one attention-getter" on campus.[42] Another writer, in an article titled "Anti-Football Views Clarified," believed that "the academic quality of FSU could probably be improved," but for the administration's insistence on funding athletics.[43]

The fielding of a losing football team did not help the situation. Not only were students complaining, but gameday attendance was dwindling. By October 1974 the Athletic Department and Mass Communications were working overtime "to create renewed excitement about its sagging football program."⁴⁴ Among the season's game-time activities were parachutists, prize giveaways, fireworks, and "the blonde in the garnet and gold bikini who gave the referee the game ball ... and a kiss after descending to Earth in a helicopter."⁴⁵ Naturally, these ploys invited parody; one writer suggested that the crowd could be increased and energized if organizers would "trot out some of the more hated administrators," who could be yelled at by the fans. Other attractions might include the random igniting of cherry bombs throughout the stands; having assistant coaches jump from the top of the press box (without the benefit of parachutes); and "Sado-Masochism Night," at which "everyone who shows up at the game wearing leather trusses and carrying whips could be admitted free."⁴⁶

The fortunes of marching bands are often linked to those of the football program, and as "anti-football views" surged during this period, so did criticism of the Chiefs. One alumna complained that the alma mater and "Fight Song" were no longer being played at the football games; that the shows were dull; and that they were being repeated. There was more: "Our Marching Chiefs seem to have forgotten how to march. They march on to the field, form one or possibly two formations, but never the FSU initials, and march off the field. Where has the dazzle gone?"⁴⁷ Such criticism could only have cut Mayo deeply.

The Marching Chiefs have never responded well to public criticism, and many students were downright thin-skinned over this slight. One Chief replied that the letter "has created an uproar in the ranks of the number one band in the nation."⁴⁸ Another Chief, responding to the same letter, wondered "Why is it [that] alumni are always so eager to find fault with their old alma mater."⁴⁹ As the battle of words continued, another correspondent, one critical of the Chiefs, reckoned that "there are many marching bands that are far superior to FSU's." He named Grambling, LSU, USC, and Texas Southern (Houston), before declaring the band from Southern University (Baton Rouge) "the finest marching band in the opinion of experts."⁵⁰ The writer did not identify the experts.

During the dismal 1974 football season some band members again felt violated, or at least underappreciated, and one Marching Chief had had enough of FSU's football fans. "So while you're sitting in the stands half drunk and yelling rude obscenities at the band," the writer scolded, "try to think of a game without the Marching Chiefs. Then, maybe you

6. World Renowned (1971–1976)   133

can apply that magnificent yelling ability towards cheering the FSU team."[51] The public sensed the band's irritation and followed up with letters that were happy to extol the Chiefs' many virtues.

※ ※ ※

If in the early- and mid–1960s Tallahassee was forced to confront issues of integration, coed dorms, the playing of "Dixie," and other matters, the 1970s ushered in vitriol; the times were perhaps even becoming a bit anarchic. One instance occurred in May 1968, when editors of a student literary magazine made known their intention to publish "The Pig Knife," a story that contained vulgar language that some deemed shocking. When the university's Board of Student Publications approved its publication only to be told that the administration—that is, President John Champion himself, who enjoyed the final word on such matters—rejected it, students were incensed. Vigils lambasted the censorship over the course of an entire week; they prompted the founding of a new organization, the Student Grassroots Movement. Before long, faculty members piled on. In the end, Champion resigned over the matter.[52]

New President J. Stanley Marshall's tenure began with similar turbulence. When, in early 1969, a radical activist organization called Students for a Democratic Society (SDS) was denied official sanction by the university, the group's leadership seethed. The SDS initiated a demonstration in the student union, but given their failure to win the university's approval to meet on campus, Marshall sought and received a court injunction to have fifty-eight students forcibly removed from campus by the police. At one point, officers aimed their rifles toward the students, prompting the standoff to be called "The Night of Bayonets." The protest was not without serious repercussions, but violence was thankfully avoided.[53]

Although certainly less consequential, there nevertheless was a good deal of angst on campus—at least in some quarters—related to the downward trajectory of FSU's football program following the resignation of the beloved head coach Bill Peterson, who fielded his first Seminole team in 1960. Peterson was largely responsible for the respect FSU garnered throughout the 1960s. He was replaced by Larry Jones, who had been a competent assistant, most recently at Tennessee, but whose first two years in Tallahassee were less than creditable. 1971's respectable 8–4 season was followed by a disappointing showing in

1972, when the team's 7–4 record included a 42–13 crushing by the Gators. But the worst was yet to come.

In the 1973 season, the Noles went 0–11, a devastating record that prompted one reporter to issue a football program "autopsy." Drum major Tom Drick recalls that during this period "[The team was] so bad, we played the 'Fight Song' for first downs."[54] And even if the millions of dollars required to bring the team to national prominence could be acquired, "it may be too little, too late"; in the writer's estimation, the best FSU could hope for in the foreseeable future "is to gain the stature of a Mississippi State, a TCU or a Clemson, i.e., to play .400-.500 ball."[55] Other areas of the football program were equally dismaying. Thanks to an investigation begun by the *Flambeau* and finished by the *St. Petersburg Times*, Jones had been charged by the NCAA with running a "brutal and dehumanizing" training program. The accusations were concerning, to say the least, but following a thorough review by a panel headed by former Governor Leroy Collins, Jones and FSU were cleared of all wrongdoing. But the damage to Jones's and the university's reputation was done. Even President Marshall's impassioned threats of a lawsuit against the *Times* could not repair it.[56]

This would not be the last time that either the team, under its new head coach Darrell Mudra,

Drum major Tom Drick wears traditional Big Ten-style apparel—tall headgear, a high collar, and epaulets—as he conducts the Marching Chiefs with a baton in 1971 (photograph by J. Barry Mittan. Courtesy of Heritage Protocol & University Archives, Florida State University Libraries).

or the Marching Chiefs were faced with criticism over this issue or that. But for the time being there was a respite; things got remarkably smoother for everyone once the Noles snapped a twenty-game losing streak with a 21–14 victory over the Miami Hurricanes in November 1974.

Syria and Jordan (1974)

Fifteen days in the Middle East in August 1974 gave the Marching Chiefs an appellation that has been cherished ever since: "World Renowned."[57] The occasion was an event hosted by the Syrian government in the ancient city of Damascus. The fair was in part the result of thawing relationships with a number of nations since the Six-Days War of 1967. As President Marshall put it in his memoir, *The Tumultuous Sixties*, the U.S. "had severed relations" with various Arab countries in the wake of the War, "and now, seven years later, the new ties were to be celebrated by having one of America's great college bands perform at an international trade fair in Damascus, Syria."[58]

The U.S. did not enjoy diplomatic relations with Syria, but it sought an entrée via cultural exchange. At the time, School of Music Dean Wiley Housewright served on a "Cultural Programs Abroad" panel sponsored by the Cultural Division of the federal State Department.[59] This fortuitous relationship resulted in the Chiefs' invitation to the fair. It was reportedly "the first time in seven years a cultural group from the U.S. has been a guest of the Syrian government."[60] FSU's band would represent the U.S., one of thirty-three nations planning to participate.[61]

The band's Syria trip was preceded by another FSU music-related international excursion that summer. Mayo had just spent two weeks leading jazz band performances in Poland, Czechoslovakia, and Romania. The schedule was grueling, and, between planning two international tours, preparing the shows and the music (as graduate assistant Harry E. Price said, "While we were touring Poland, we were writing drill"[62]), the director was frazzled. Said Bill Hinkle, a former assistant director with the Chiefs, during this period, "Mayo was a basket case."[63] Just two weeks intervened between the trips.

The Marching Chiefs was not the only FSU musical group to attend the world trade fair; also in tow were the Wind Ensemble—

supplemented by a few School of Music faculty members—and the Jazz Lab Band, 155 musicians in all. They would perform on a specially-designated "America Day," which was set aside to highlight aspects of American culture. The Jazz Band and the Wind Ensemble, which played on alternate days, concertized at the Syrian palace, while the Chiefs performed at the city's soccer stadium. The yard lines were a particular nuisance; although the dimensions and line markings of an American football field had been sent to the host site in advance, they had been laid out inaccurately. Cloth strips—not paint—marked the field, and the lines had to be adjusted upon the Chiefs arrival. Drum major Bob Duke remembered that "The first part of the first rehearsal was spent re-lining the field."[64] As for the shows themselves, one routine resulted in the formation of a camel; others included the spelling of Arabic words. Band member John Carmichael recalls that "we were hoping we spelled it right and didn't say anything offensive."[65] That was in part because machine-gun-armed soldiers were posted at intervals of about twenty feet around the entirety of the stadium.

During the fair Syrian military forces were on constant alert. "There were soldiers walking around with guns," band member Karen Burton observed, "and we saw Russian MIGs flying over the city, but we were not confined, except that we couldn't take pictures of military installations outside of town."[66] At various times during the trip, gunfire could be heard from the nearby hills.

Cultural exchange was an essential component of the trip, and the Marching Chiefs had opportunities to engage in conversations with those locals who could speak English, as well as with students from the city university. But Mayo cautioned students to "Remember that we are guests of Syria and the rules of good sense apply in conversations with Syrian people. Please, no comments on Israeli and Syrian conflicts. You may exercise your right of free speech concerning cultural and domestic (US) problems."[67] As far as commerce was concerned, Marshall wrote that "The trade fair was about what you'd expect—open-air exhibits of products of many kinds, to be examined and bargained for by merchants who appeared to come from many countries, some well beyond the Middle East."[68]

If the daily calls to prayer took some of the Chiefs by surprise, a more unwelcome visitor was dysentery, which affected a number of the band members. Said Burton, "It's hard to march when you don't feel so well."[69] As far as the food was concerned, Carmichael recalls

6. World Renowned (1971–1976)   137

that "sometimes it wasn't too bad, but other times it was just awful"; now and then, some Chiefs could be seen getting sick on the marching field.[70]

On August 22 the Chiefs took a three-day side trip to Amman, Jordan, where they "played before large crowds of Jordanians," including King Hussein, Ethiopian Chief Haile Selassie, and their wives.[71] The Jordanian Army Band, which hosted the Chiefs at Jordan's Royal Stadium, reciprocated with a performance of its own. Duke remembers that the entire scene was spectacular; locals could even be spied clambering over the walls to watch.

Following the trip, FSU's publicity office issued a press release recounting the band's exploits. In it, two diplomats—Denton Keith, of the Office of Public Affairs at the U.S. Embassy in Damascus, and Thomas Scotes, a Chargé d'affaires with the State Department—claimed that "It would have taken five years to make the friends [the Marching Chiefs] made for us in two weeks."[72]

The Marching Chiefs' international travels of 1974 continued to resonate the following spring, when King Hussein traveled to FSU to accept an honorary doctorate.

❧ ❧ ❧

Mayo engaged in a massive and ongoing effort to educate the public about what it took to be in the Chiefs. In *Flambeau* article after article, he makes a point of informing readers about the time students spend in rehearsal and on the field. "Most people," Mayo explained, "don't realize the amount of time that is put into each seventeen-minute performance." He calculated that for every minute of performance the Chiefs put in ten hours of rehearsal; for every hour of rehearsal, Mayo and his staff prepare for five hours.[73] Mayo also explained the concept of providing drill charts to students and discussed methods for dealing with the treacherous traffic patterns that often resulted from transitioning from one formation to the next.

A 1974 *Flambeau* feature, "Marching Chiefs Excel in Skill, Precision," is one of the lengthiest articles in Chiefs history. In it Mayo declares that "My concept of this organization is that of an educational laboratory of learning which helps people work and live together while showing growth and maturity." The writer reveals a number of facts about the Chiefs—about ninety students per year are admitted, 60 percent are music majors, 40 percent graduate each year, and others. And

Here Mayo is shown rehearsing drill and wearing his ever-present necktie (from *Florida Flambeau*, 1971. Courtesy of Heritage Protocol & University Archives, Florida State University Libraries).

it was perhaps a sign of the times—as well as an indication of Mayo's friendly and permissive personality—that, under his leadership, "students are highly self-reliant and self-disciplinary."[74]

Sound was sometimes emphasized in the press. In 1975 *Flambeau* writer Vanessa Williams interviewed staff assistant Bill Haggard, who echoed many of Mayo's themes, but focused on the Chiefs' sonic virtues. "Our top priority is sound," Haggard said. "We want to look good, but the music is most important."[75] Another bragging point was the Chiefs' enrollment: that year the band hit a record 260 members.

Dis-Spirited '76

The 1975 football season had not been kind to FSU. That year the team went 3–8, and, although it was an improvement over the 1974

6. World Renowned (1971–1976)

mark of 1–10, it was not enough to save the coach. Darrell Mudra never really seemed to fit in at FSU—his insistence on coaching from the press box did not help his image—and the *Flambeau* had fueled speculation four months before that Mudra's job was in jeopardy.[76] During these lean years of football, many Marching Chiefs "determined that the fans were coming to see us instead of coming to see the football [game]. It made the band come together, since we kinda felt that football wasn't getting it done."[77] Following the last game of the season, funds were quietly raised to buy out Mudra's contract, and he was fired on January 4, 1976, halfway through his four-year contract.

When it was learned that President Marshall had been behind the clandestine fundraising effort that led to Mudra's ouster, there was real trouble.[78] Marshall denied it, of course, but there had already been plenty of angst for Marshall, whose often tumultuous seven-year tenure bore the brunt of a number of converging difficulties. Even the president's 1969 appointment had been clouded by anti–Marshall resolutions from various student and academic groups. Now the administration not only had to contend with the current social and political issues of the day, but more immediate student concerns: tuition increases, library closings, an increasingly bloated university bureaucracy. It was also thought that Marshall was aloof from faculty and students. One letter to the editor of the *Flambeau* accused Marshall of being "The Richard M. Nixon of Florida State University."[79] When, in the early months of 1976, state public officials began venting their opinions that Marshall's time was nearly at its end, the president took the hint. He resigned in March.[80]

To the losses of Marshall and Mudra, one can add Mayo's resignation, which was announced in April.[81] Mayo thought he had done about as much as he could as a band director at FSU, and he was frankly exhausted.[82] But it is also clear that he was unhappy with his budgetary situation. Mayo made known his displeasure with "the lack of public and legislative support" that the university was receiving. He might have been dismayed with salaries in the School of Music, as well. He was the fourth faculty member to resign that spring; another was the eminent composer Carlisle Floyd, who left to accept a more lucrative financial deal at the University of Houston.

Mayo was also bogged down by School of Music politics, as were a number of his colleagues. It seemed not to be a secret that "Mayo had to fight for every nickel and dime,"[83] and charges of administrative cronyism had long been simmering; they would boil over in an investigative article in the *Tallahassee Democrat* just a couple of years later.[84] In addition, his attempts to give the "popular performing idiom" a larger presence at FSU met with strenuous resistance. Bill Hinkle remembers that despite the advances Mayo had achieved at that time, "You couldn't mention jazz. [It was] a four-letter word."[85] Further, Mayo was devastated by Marshall's resignation, as "we had gotten enormous support from him, which was very critical to the band program."[86] Given these issues, along with his own "burnout factor," Mayo felt that it "just seemed like a good thing for everybody—me and the program as well—to move on to something else."[87] Mayo's assessment was not wrong, for even students had noticed that he "had kinda checked out."[88]

But along with Mayo's genius came no small amount of pride, and perhaps a tinge of arrogance. His own gloss on his departure from FSU does not completely comport with the memories of others. Madsen recalls that, "Every once in a while if he didn't get what he wanted, he'd go to the president of the university and threaten to resign." President Marshall oftentimes acceded to Mayo's demands. But another leader would have none of it: "He tried that one time with [Dean Wiley Housewright]," and, according to Madsen, the Dean "got up and said 'well, it's been nice having you here.'"[89] Harry E. Price also noted Mayo's bad habit: "He resigned one time too many."[90]

Mayo was well respected and beloved, but he was not without a few eccentricities. One Chief has observed that "Mayo was always dressed in a three-piece suit. Always."[91] His choice of on-field apparel might have emanated from his respect for the always nattily dressed Leonard Bernstein and a desire to command a Bernsteinian sort of respect himself. Whatever his motivation, Mayo usually radiated a degree of formality. Besides that, Mayo didn't have a driver's license; of course, he had not needed one in New York. In Tallahassee several of his protégés regularly drove him around town. Grocery stores. Drycleaners. Liquor stores.[92]

It is not too much to say that Mayo was one of the most creative people ever to direct the Marching Chiefs. Madsen has even gone so far as to say that "He was one of the most talented guys we've ever had around here [i.e., the School of Music]. He could do it all. And did it all." And not only was he a superb musician, he was a good man. Says Madsen, the Marching Chiefs "thought he was wonderful, and he was."[93] Following his departure from Tallahassee, Mayo took a position with the Friendship Ambassadors Foundation, an organization that promotes cultural exchange and youth leadership; it was the same company that had been responsible for the jazz band's invitation to Europe in 1974. Mayo also maintained ties to the music education profession as a clinician. In later life his health began to falter, and, as George Corradino put it, "He became an invalid."[94]

Several anecdotes will illustrate Mayo's ingenuity. As recounted by Bill Haggard, at one Chiefs practice, "He didn't speak during the entire rehearsal. He just looked at us [and] used hand signals. It was really interesting, but he really had our attention."[95] Many Marching Chiefs also recall that Mayo was unafraid to make changes on gameday. If a better show could be effected by changing points in the music or in the drill, Mayo did it; it bothered him not at all that it was Saturday morning. Haggard again: "When he was at his best, he was really phenomenal."[96]

Mayo thought in terms of innovation and entertainment, and he had a huge canvas—the football gridiron—on which to paint his masterpieces. During his five years as director, the Chiefs inaugurated several of their most important traditions—the "Before-Game Fanfare, pt. 2," the use of contemporary pop music, the Glue Crew, and a number of section names among them.[97] Importantly, he also maintained the historic emphasis on student leadership and perhaps even expanded the roles taken on by students. Mayo believed in teamwork and gave his charges important responsibilities. Not only did the student leadership teach others music and drill, but students were often charged with the writing of drill for the halftime shows.[98] As a former Marching Chief and student leader himself, Mayo recognized the value of student leadership. And given his workload, he was compelled to give his students some responsibilities; it is worth noting that when Mayo left FSU he was replaced by three people.[99]

Although Mayo had learned the band director's trade in the carefully planned and tightly controlled atmosphere favored by Whit, his own temperament was less disciplinarian and much more like Brownie's. Yet he possessed a flamboyance—an eagerness to put on "the show"—that none of his predecessors could boast. It seems entirely unsurprising that, on Mayo's watch, the Marching Chiefs became "World Renowned."

※ ※ ※

Mayo was succeeded by William Raxsdale, who had been a nationally-recognized band director at Acadiana High School in Lafayette, Louisiana. Raxsdale had received both a bachelor's and a master's degree in music education at the University of Southwestern Louisiana and was currently serving on a committee of the College Band Directors National Association. According to one report, Raxsdale "spends most of his summers instructing [at] clinics and preparing competition shows for championship bands."[100] Like Mayo, Raxsdale was hired to lead the Marching Chiefs and to do minimal work with the jazz department.

Raxsdale's term as director of the Chiefs occurred just as the drum corps movement in America was ascending; it was a style he wholeheartedly embraced. Drum corps organizations, which had existed for decades, had a direct relationship to military organizations from World War I onward. But unlike their collegiate counterparts—which had been formed in order to magnify school spirit and to provide a social outlet—the drum corps, all-male in their earliest days, were often competitive, and participating organizations sometimes even received compensation for tournament wins. What began as a loose association of drum corps units became highly organized when a governing body, Drum Corps International (DCI), was founded in 1972. It established rules for member organizations and guidelines for competitions that were managed under its aegis.

Drum corps was a different animal from the traditional collegiate band, including the Chiefs. All-brass instrumentation was typical of corps style, and instruments were usually single-valve, bell-front, bugle-type horns (although this restriction has been relaxed over the last twenty years or so). Drill design was routinely intricate and often abstract. An expanded percussion section was placed on the pressbox sideline—also known as "the pit"—where it was not encumbered by the challenges of marching while playing. Drum corps also focused attention on a show's visual impact by use of an elaborate admixture of auxiliaries and props. Corps style dispensed with the traditional marching band "high-step" in favor of the "glide step," a movement that smoothly thrusts the foot forward, as opposed to the raised knee that characterizes the Chief step. In short, drum corps style was wholly incompatible with that developed over several decades by the Marching Chiefs.

Upon his arrival, Raxsdale made wholesale changes to Marching

6. World Renowned (1971–1976)

The pre-season band camp ritual, during which new students—freshmen, gunkies, or rookies, depending on the era—learn what it takes to be a Chief, can be grueling. This '70s-era photograph shows the steely determination of one particular flute row (courtesy of John F. Ervin).

Chiefs tradition in favor of drum corps style. "We made a lot of changes as far as the amount of marching done," he said in a later interview. "Where basically the band would do maybe five pictures, ... when I came here we'd do anywhere from 30 to 40 pages of drill, actual marching. [Prior to that], they would do what they call a whirlwind [i.e., a scatter drill]—the whistle would blow, or the drums would kick it off, and they'd just literally run from one position to another.... It was a big change of philosophy."[101]

This "change in philosophy" created a firestorm. Among Raxsdale's sins: he introduced the glide step and almost completely eradicated the beloved Chief step. No Chief step meant no arm swing, which was another hallmark of Marching Chiefs tradition. More radical than those changes was Raxsdale's decision not to present a new show at each home game.[102] This is a typical scenario in the drum corps world, in which the idea is to work on a single show with the goal of bringing it to perfection. As Clifford K. Madsen has noted, Raxsdale "could not produce a new show every [Saturday] night, and the Chiefs were just not used to that.... The 'corps style' was anathema as far as anybody at Florida State was concerned. Raxsdale was not sensitive to this, nor to the leadership that had been carefully developed all the way back to Whitcomb; [that is,] the student leadership. There has always been some strong student leadership, and he was just not sensitive to it."[103]

Raxsdale had additional shortcomings. Generally regarded as a somewhat insecure man, he rarely connected with the students on a personal level, and he seemed unable to grasp the importance of Chiefs tradition. In fact, many traditions he thought were simply stupid, and he was almost completely unable to build trust with the band members. In addition, many questioned not only his judgment but his musicianship.[104] And his relationship with Charlie Carter, always a concern, was "strictly business."[105]

After a short time Marching Chiefs student leadership made it known to School of Music administration that they were not happy; many of the unhappiest Chiefs simply quit. Nancy Haughee estimates that at least sixty members dropped out. In fact, she said, "We had to re-chart every show to factor in how many people had quit.... We had gaps and holes, because some of the departures would be last minute, some would be during rehearsal, some would be after."[106] Raxsdale seemed oblivious to it all. Chris Dickinson, Raxsdale's drum major, says, "He was pretty insensitive to what was happening.... He just didn't seem to be aware of the discontent that was in the majority of the band members."[107] The 1976 Senior Show, a tradition in which the seniors performed on-field for the last time, was memorable. In full recognition of the grim marching season just passed, the small cohort of remaining senior Chiefs played Marvin Hamlisch's anguished tune "The Way We Were."

The problems were perceived by the fans of the Marching Chiefs, as well. One *Flambeau* letter-writer admitted that "I, like many others I know, had often found the Marching Chiefs to be the only highlight of the game.... The sound alone could bring an audience to its feet." But now, in the opinion of the writer and many of his friends, they were "having difficulty hearing the band while it was on the field." Further, "the band seems to be forming nothing but circles and squares instead of the pictures and intricate designs for which they have gained fame."[108]

Raxsdale was the director for just a single season, but his reputation outside of Tallahassee seems not to have suffered too much from

6. World Renowned (1971–1976)

his association with the Marching Chiefs. He went on to write several books about marching band technique, including *Contemporary Color Guard Manual* (1980), *Contemporary Show Design Manual* (1981) and *The Marching Band Director: A Master Planning Guide* (1985). Each of these continued to advocate for a marching band style that had met with dismal approval at FSU.

※ ※ ※

Mayo's era provided many points of pride that remain dear to the Marching Chiefs. Those years saw additions of traditions and increases in enrollment. Perhaps more importantly, Mayo's outstanding showmanship turned the ensemble into a half-time entertainment leader, and his insistence on musical perfection resulted in a group whose sound was unmatched.

It is undeniable that the mid–1970s were dark years at FSU. In light of a football coach firing, a presidential resignation, and the departure of a hugely talented band director—not to mention the coming and going of another band director whose gridiron aesthetics proved entirely incompatible with the ideals of FSU—to some the situation might have seemed hopeless.

But the future was about to get rosier. Three men—an already-hired football coach, a newly-inaugurated president, and a soon-to-be hired bandmaster—would not only right the ship, but they would guide their respective areas of responsibility—the team, the university, and the Marching Chiefs—to new heights of excellence.

Part III.
Marching Chiefs Three Times!

⏵ 7 ⏴

Football Rising
Bowden, Bernie, and Bentley
(1976–1990)

Tradition Returns

If FSU had dreamed in the early 1950s of becoming a national football powerhouse—and had even shown flashes of promise during several seasons—the last ten years had been a disaster. To rectify the matter, Bobby Bowden was named FSU's new head football coach by President Marshall in January 1976. It was not Bowden's first venture to Tallahassee, as he had been an assistant coach at FSU from 1963 to 1965 under head coach Bill Peterson. But Bowden's hiring, like Mudra's termination, was controversial. Although he had been a successful head coach at the University of West Virginia and was thought to be a man who could take the Noles football program to prominence, Bowden was hired after just an eight-day search; university policy clearly stipulated a minimum job listing period of three weeks.

Once he arrived in Tallahassee, FSU fans wondered how involved Coach Bowden would actually be in the day-to-day football operations. Mudra's style had been untenable at FSU; he was considered by some to be too informal and undisciplined, and many believed he delegated too much of the decision-making to his assistants. Bowden reassured the attendees at his first press conference that he would be strict and that he would be in charge. And unlike Mudra, Bowden himself would decide on a weekly basis who would play and who would ride the bench.[1] He wasted no time in stressing his authority. "Discipline is his

7. Football Rising (1976–1990)

byword," one reporter stated, "and although open to suggestions, he asserts that he and he alone has the final decision on any and every matter."[2]

Bowden's 1976 squad won just five games, but among them were the last three contests of the season, which to many fans portended good things to come. As the team progressed, stars began to emerge. Two 1977 standouts were Leon High School's own quarterback duo, Wally Woodham and Jimmy Jordan. But they were not the only ones, and Bowden's commitment to recruiting beyond the region would lead to spectacular results in relatively short order. *Flambeau* sportswriter Godwin Kelly tried to tamp down hopes that the team would get to a bowl that season. "The Seminoles are going to break the elusive .500 mark this year, but just barely." Despite that grim projection, he closed hopefully: "Don't worry, though, because the team is just starting to roll."[3]

Kelly got it wrong. The 1977 squad ended up with a 10–2 winning record, a Tangerine Bowl victory—FSU's first post-season win since 1964—over Texas Tech, and an eleventh-place finish in the national UPI poll. Against a variety of odds, football at FSU was definitely rising; in fact, it was beginning to overshadow other aspects of the university. By 1980 one student wag could remark, "Now that everyone knows where Campbell Stadium is, we might ought to post directions to the rest of the campus."[4]

※ ※ ※

Following Marshall's resignation in March 1976—amid a flurry of accusations and ill will—Dr. Bernard (Bernie) Sliger was named interim president while the Board of Regents conducted a national search for Marshall's replacement. Sliger was the logical choice to serve as interim-president; he had been the university's Executive Vice President under Marshall, and he was well acquainted with FSU's current opportunities and challenges.

According to the board's by-laws, Sliger was not actually eligible to become president. The difficulty lay in a rule that prohibited an interim-president from being considered for the presidency. Sliger, however, had more than a few supporters on the board, and they passed a resolution in a 9–0 vote that allowed for his consideration. Said one board member flatly, "We never abided by the policy."[5]

Sliger became FSU's president in February 1977. His promotion was aided by a gentle and conciliatory temperament; while still interim-president, and in the midst of severe financial difficulties, he held the first president's ice cream social, an event intended to thaw relations with students. But once selected as president, there were several pressing matters with which to contend, including a miserly legislature, the strengthening of programs for minority students, and the weighty matter of faculty retention. The latter was particularly vexing, for teaching talent was leaving in droves. Sliger tried to shift focus away from the university; using the recent departure to the University of Houston of music professor and internationally distinguished composer Carlisle Floyd as an example, Sliger said that faculty didn't leave FSU solely for monetary reasons: "Houston is a better place to write operas and to have your operas performed than Tallahassee."[6]

As the football craze at FSU began to intensify, Sliger was forced to give it due attention, as well. Not that it was an onerous task for him. When asked if he supported the university's athletic ambitions, Sliger, a former high school basketball and track coach, said simply, "I'm an enthusiast."[7]

※ ※ ※

If Bowden and Sliger were heralds of better fortunes at FSU, the same may be said of the new director of the Marching Chiefs. In the summer of 1977, following Raxsdale's departure, Bentley Shellahamer was directing an ensemble at FSU's summer band camp. No stranger to FSU's music school, Shellahamer had spent a number of years in Tallahassee, first as a student, then as a music teacher. During the band camp Brownie encouraged him to apply for the vacant Marching Chiefs director position. Shellahamer, of course, was also no stranger to the Chiefs.

Shellahamer was born in Baltimore, where he started to learn saxophone. When the family moved to Miami, he continued to play in junior high school and at North Miami High School, where he eventually served as the band's drum major. He had already determined to be a band director when, during his junior year, he first saw the Marching Chiefs perform at Miami's Orange Bowl in a game versus the Hurricanes (November 4, 1960). The Chiefs performed Whit's "Three Coins in the Fountain" show, which convinced him that FSU would be his college destination. Months later, when Shellahamer heard FSU's touring symphonic band perform, the decision was clinched: "That's where I want to go to school."[8]

Shellahamer was a Chief for three seasons: '62, '64, and '65.

7. Football Rising (1976–1990)

Following graduation in 1966 Shellahamer taught at Tallahassee's Rickards High School for three years; he had been interning there when the band director left to seek a graduate degree, and Shellahamer was offered the job. He received his master's degree from FSU in 1970, having participated in a one-year program for which he received a tuition award from the National Defense Educational Act (NDEA). The program trained music educators to become music supervisors. Following another year at Rickards, Shellahamer took a job at the new Piper High School in Sunrise, Florida. Although not without some significant obstacles, it did not take long for Shellahamer to turn Piper's music program into one of the most respected in the state.

Following a difficult 1976 season, Bentley Shellahamer returned the Marching Chiefs to their former glory (*FSView/Florida Flambeau* Collection, MSS 2006–012. Courtesy of Heritage Protocol & University Archives, Florida State University Libraries).

As the end of the 1977 summer music camps neared, Shellahamer decided to apply for the Chiefs job. It was already July, and, given the proximity to the new football season, the hiring committee had to act fast. He was appointed director that month.

Of course, there was more to it than just managing the Chiefs. Teaching, conducting various ensembles, and student advising were sizable parts of the job. He would also be responsible for the activities of the "All-American Showtimers," a summertime performing group founded by Mayo in association with Callaway Gardens, and one that included the jazz band, singers, and even the circus. By the time he arrived in Tallahassee, however, the "Showtimers" had thankfully folded.

Besides his own enormous workload, Shellahamer had to grapple with the psychological state of the Chiefs on the heels of their recent experiences. "Morale was low ... very low," he remembers. "A lot of Chiefs had quit; the ones that hung on were doing it out of loyalty to the band and to the university."[9] Like most observers, he tied the morale deficit to the evaporation of cherished traditions. Surely the hiring committee knew that he would be able to step into the breach in a way that no stranger to the program could have. And indeed, as the Chiefs learned about him and his methods, and as they regained their trust in the organization, Shellahamer got his due rewards. "My first year was like heaven," he reflected, "Because I put all of those [traditions] back."[10]

⸙ ⸙ ⸙

Shellahamer's early shows brought back some of the thematicism that had been typical prior to Raxsdale; he also reintroduced the idea of a new show at each home game. But he elected to keep some elements of drum corps style. The Chiefs step, with its crisp arm swing, became the norm, but he also preserved the glide step, which is a perfect physical reflection of slower, more *legato* strains of music. Traditional pictures were returned to the visual repertoire, but abstract maneuvers and formations also retained a place in selected shows. Finally, where Raxsdale introduced detailed transitional charts from formation to formation, and Mayo sometimes used scatter drills in place of transitional drills, Shellahamer took the middle path and used both. "When I took over," he explains, "we blended traditional and corps style."[11]

Shellahamer's first halftime show was based on Sylvester Stallone's hit movie *Rocky*. It marked a slight change in work habits from earlier times, as he requested music from Charlie Carter before he would write the drill. As Shellahamer recounts, he would say to Charlie, "I need a minute and a half of Rocky," and once the music was in hand, the drill was created. This differed significantly from Whit's style of working; having already written the drill, Whit would say to Carter "I need 64 counts of music." Not that Shellahamer received the music very quickly: "I would give Charlie the music to write, and he wasn't fast, so I

7. Football Rising (1976–1990)

wouldn't get the music until three or four days before I had to put it out for the Chiefs, so I'd be up all night for a week writing drill."[12] Shellahamer's shows were typically begun two or three weeks before they were needed.

In the Braunagel era new pre-game shows were introduced every season incorporating the variety of fanfares that over a decade had accumulated in the band library.[13] While writing one of his early pre-game shows, Shellahamer discovered the "Before Game Fanfare, Part 2," the powerful opener borrowed from the Osmond family, which had been birthed in the Mayo years. Charlie had arranged the tune in the original key, per Mayo's instructions ("Charlie hated—absolutely hated—being told to copy something off a [phonograph] record," Shellahamer recalled. "Mayo requested that often."[14]). In 1978 Shellahamer asked Charlie put it in a more comfortable key. The Chiefs played the "Fanfare," and it proved to be a hit with the band and the football crowd. Shellahamer kept it in the repertoire, and by the 1980

Drum major Jim Bruce leads the Chiefs in a parade circa 1978. Bruce, Shellahamer's first drum major, would be the last to sport the Big Ten look (courtesy of Heritage Protocol & University Archives, Florida State University Libraries).

season the "Fanfare" was the traditional pre-game opener. It remains so to this day.

※ ※ ※

One of Shellahamer's most memorable shows occurred at a home game versus the University of East Carolina (September 20, 1980). A patriotic show, it was performed in the midst of the Iranian hostage crisis, which had kept a large cohort of Americans in captivity for nearly a year. The show garnered notice in the *Tallahassee Democrat* in an editorial titled "Thanks, Marching Chiefs":

> In the cynical world of 1980, genuine moments of patriotism are rare. Especially because our national pride has been bruised during the past 10 months as American citizens have been held hostage in Iran, it is easy to overlook the uniqueness of this country and its many strengths.
>
> So it was heart-poundingly appropriate Saturday night for the Florida State University Marching Chiefs to remind more than 50,000 football fans that 53 of their countrymen were finishing their 322nd day of imprisonment half way round the world.
>
> The band pulled all the traditionally American levers. The crowd was asked to sing. "America the Beautiful." Colored balloons filled the air. And, at just the right moment, a flurry of fireworks burst into the night sky over the Pensacola Street overpass.
>
> The crowd stood and sang and cheered lustily. They were asked to remember the hostages with a moment of silence.
>
> And after it was over, the band won a long, well deserved standing ovation.
>
> These days more than ever, Americans need to remember that they live in freedom. And the Marching Chiefs provided that reminder with a most impressive show.
>
> Thanks, Marching Chiefs. Your hard work was worth it.[15]

Shellahamer later learned that "all across Tallahassee the next morning preachers and churches were talking about that show."[16]

"Where our traditions come from": *FSU at Ohio State, October 3, 1981*

When the 1981 football schedule was unveiled, Shellahamer immediately got the idea to take the Chiefs to the October 3 game at Ohio State University. "When we found out we were playing Ohio State," he later recalled, "I was very aware of the connection to FSU."[17] Not only had Whit and Charlie immigrated to Tallahassee from Columbus, but several other School of Music faculty luminaries also enjoyed a strong

7. Football Rising (1976–1990)

association with OSU. Among them were oboist Nancy Fowler, clarinetist Harry Schmidt, and trombonist William Cramer.

At the time, the Chiefs received enough money from the athletic department to take two big trips a year. Shellahamer enjoyed free rein to select which games to attend, and he decided that OSU would be one of them. He immediately telephoned OSU band director Paul Droste, who was delighted at the idea. Shellahamer found that Droste and his entire staff "were very welcoming."[18]

Plans were laid to take the now 300-member Chiefs to OSU. The trip included a practice break in Knoxville at the University of Tennessee's Neyland Stadium. Travel then continued to the small town of Orrville, Ohio, located about a hundred miles northeast of Columbus. Arrangements had been made for the Chiefs to stay in the private homes of the citizens of Orrville, home to the J. M. Smucker Company, known everywhere for its jams and jellies. A final Chiefs run-through before Saturday's contest occurred at Orrville High School's Friday night football game. Fred Blosser, principal of the high school, sent accolades to the Chiefs via the *Flambeau*: "They completely won the hearts of the people of Orrville.... Thank you for allowing your students to turn a cold October evening in Ohio into a very enjoyable experience."[19]

A highlight of the FSU–OSU band reunion was a ceremony held before the game. Charlie was in attendance, of course, but Whit was the main honoree. Not only was he recognized for his contributions to the band profession, but he conducted the National Anthem at pregame. Shellahamer remembers an inspiring vignette: "At one point, Brownie was sitting on one side of me and Whitcomb was sitting on the other side of me, and they both had been my college band directors, and here we were at Ohio State. That's pretty cool."[20]

The band also received high marks for its performance at OSU. When asked to describe the crowd reaction to the Chiefs—the fervid emotions poured forth by more than 87,000 spectators—Shellahamer recalls that "They were sort of blown away. They thought we were this nice little band from the South come up to visit.... We did the Skull Session in St. John's Arena, and when we opened with the 'Fanfare,' they went 'Oh, My God!'"[21] And if that was not enough, the Chiefs half-time show—which featured John Williams's energetic "Raiders March" from Steven Spielberg's just released movie *Raiders of the Lost Ark* and the hit song "Don't Cry for Me Argentina" from the Andrew Lloyd

Webber-Tim Rice musical, *Evita*—simply killed. The impression left by the Chiefs was reinforced by the team, which shellacked the Buckeyes that day, 36 to 27.

The OSU trip had another singular outcome. Not long afterward, Shellahamer determined to enroll at OSU to pursue a doctoral degree in music education. There he would spend two full academic years learning in the place that, in many ways, had sired the Marching Chiefs. But beyond the opening that trip provided for Shellahamer to pursue a wonderful personal opportunity, the band's Ohio excursion reconnected the Chiefs to their ancestral home, one that had been left behind more than a quarter-century earlier, when Whit and Charlie packed up a car and headed south. The reunion was a monumental event. "Just taking the band up there was an emotional experience," said Shellahamer, "because that's where our traditions come from."[22]

✳ ✳ ✳

Andre Arrouet led the Marching Chiefs in 1982 and 1983. Naturally, Shellahamer had a hand in selecting the interim director. With a bachelor's degree from Appalachian State University and a Master of

Following the lead of the majorettes, drum major Ken Williams adopted a Native American look in 1980. Since then, such apparel has been the rule for drum majors (photograph by J. Barry Mittan. Courtesy of Heritage Protocol & University Archives, Florida State University Libraries).

7. Football Rising (1976–1990)

Arts degree in music education from the University of South Florida, Arrouet's closest tie to FSU was by marriage. But he was widely respected by his colleagues for his work at Melbourne High School, and he was known to be affable and trustworthy. While in Tallahassee, it was expected that Arrouet "will seek his own doctorate in music ... between football seasons."[23]

The transition from Shellahamer to Arrouet was not pain-free, but one observer noted that any stress the Chiefs might have had regarding Shellahamer's departure was mitigated by the latter's friendship with Arrouet and the knowledge that he intended to return. Announcer David Westberry has said that Arrouet "wanted everyone to enjoy themselves and to understand what a wonderful experience and opportunity they had before them to be in this organization."[24] The new director was himself a bit giddy about his new gig; as Westberry concluded, "It's like somebody gives you the keys to the Porsche for a couple of years."[25]

During Arrouet's tenure, a truly wonderful new tradition evolved from an old one. Borrowed from Ohio State, the Skull Sessions had begun at FSU under Whit in an attempt to drill the performance into the heads (skulls) of the Chiefs. They also served as an opportunity for Whit to record the music and evaluate the band's performance. Originally held in Opperman Music Hall, the Skull Sessions were later moved to the band room of the new music building.

Following the Chiefs' trip to Ohio State, Shellahamer got the idea to present FSU's Skull Sessions after the manner of the OSU band; that is, he determined to give the pre-game music run-throughs outdoors and invite the public to attend. The advantages were two-fold. Students would still work through the show mentally, but now band fans could listen in, creating a public relations coup—OSU's audiences were huge, and it was thought that fans of the Marching Chiefs would also line up to be part of the performance. In addition, the outdoor performances solved a practical problem. As Arrouet was quick to note, "We got too big" for indoor Skull Sessions.[26]

If Shellahamer developed the outdoor Skull Session idea, it was ushered in by Arrouet. The first public Skull Session was held at FSU's new baseball field, Dick Howser Stadium. Arrouet recounts that "we actually tried to do [the Skull Sessions] in sit-down style"; that is, folding chairs were placed around the infield and spanned from first base to third base. Although it worked well for rehearsal and performance purposes—the baseball stadium concerts were an immediate success—it was rather hard on the infield of what is now known as Mike Martin Field. "After that first year," Arrouet remembers, "[Baseball coach] Mike Martin said 'Hey fellas, you can use the baseball stadium, but no more chairs in the infield.'"[27] From now on, the band would stand.

During a portion of the 1981 football season, the Marching Chiefs were photographed by Heinz Kluetmeier for a feature spread in *Sports Illustrated*. The article, which appeared a year later in December 1982, was titled "All Horns Up!!!" The attention was particularly noteworthy because it was the first time the magazine had directed its spotlight at a college marching band. Although the write-up is short on text and long on photos (it did manage to fit in "Florida State may occasionally lose a football game, but never a half-time show"), it nevertheless gave the Chiefs national acclaim in a way that other marching bands could only have envied.[28]

✧ ✧ ✧

The "Flush," as FSU's tuba section is affectionately called, performs for the crowd, circa 1984 (courtesy of Bob O'Lary/Olary.com).

7. Football Rising (1976–1990)

For the first time in a long time, the Chiefs were facing jabs from the audience about the on-field sound. As Arrouet recalls, during his first year "we were getting criticism for not being heard."[29] He had solutions; he talked to Charlie about scoring matters and even changed the key of the "Fight Song" to make it more piercing. Additionally, Arrouet "was into big endings," and Charlie started to create more thrilling climaxes rather reminiscent of the Mayo era.

Arrouet relied on plenty of help to make his two years with the Chiefs successful. Graduate assistants were numerous and always on-hand, and former drum major Jim Bruce, who was now acting as Field Coordinator, wrote much of the drill. The music, still mostly arranged by Charlie, was complemented by contributions from others in the Marching Chiefs orbit, including Bob Thurston. Half-time shows were often nostalgic and popular, with selections from *West Side Story*, a Beatles show, and a lush arrangement of John Williams's main theme from the hit movie *E. T.: The Extra-Terrestrial* (1982) among the highlights.

Band Day is an enduring tradition at FSU. This 1984 photograph shows high school students on the field performing with the Marching Chiefs. The drum major is Bill Faucett, the author of this book (photograph by Deborah Thomas. Courtesy of the State Archives of Florida/Florida Memory. Image no. FFL2360).

As we have seen, the grueling football season schedule has never been kind to FSU's marching band directors. Arrouet mentions that "often I didn't get to bed until two or three in the morning." But, for the short-term at least, he found it a rewarding job, especially on game day. "Getting to Saturday was really tough," he said. "But I loved Saturday."[30]

❉ ❉ ❉

In early 1983 Gerald D. Poe, director of the University of Florida "Pride of the Sunshine State" marching band was contacted by representatives from CBS.[31] For Super Bowl XVIII, a match that would pit the Oakland Raiders against the Washington Redskins in Tampa, the broadcast network administrators hoped the Gator band would consent to perform at pre-game. Upon learning about CBS's offer, NFL commissioner Pete Rozelle suggested a production that would include, in addition to the Gator Band, the Marching Chiefs.

Poe contacted Arrouet to talk it over; the decision was not an easy one, for, as Arrouet has said, "When we hang up the uniforms [following the final FSU game], it's pretty much done."[32] The Super Bowl, of course, would require gathering and rehearsing in January, well after the end of the college football season.

Although playing at a Super Bowl was not entirely without appeal, Arrouet and Poe had a muted enthusiasm for the project, at least at first. They fully expected that the demands they intended to unleash on the Super Bowl honchos would result in the withdrawal of the offer. Among the requirements: all expenses would be paid, including hotel rooms, buses, per diems for students, and honoraria for the directors and their assistants. In addition, the directors required a $10,000 gift to each university that would establish a band scholarship. So far, so good; NFL administrators hadn't flinched yet. But they soon would.

Arrouet and Poe insisted that each student be allotted a ticket to the game. "That's impossible," the organizers cried. "Do you know how much these tickets cost?"[33] The NFL had already begun preparations to treat the bands to a game-watching party in a hangar at a nearby airport, but the directors would not relent. Unsure of what to do, Arrouet reminded them that Tampa's "Big Sombrero," as the old Tampa Stadium was known, had a wide pedestrian walkway around the bowl's entire circumference at about the vertical mid-point. The 600 or so necessary folding chairs, Arrouet insisted, could be placed on the walkway. Against all odds, NFL leaders agreed to the seating plan; or, as Poe wryly said in his published report of the event, "special seats were made available."[34]

Rehearsals occurred in Tallahassee and Gainesville; each band would perform three minutes of their own music and drill followed by a combined fifteen-minute performance. Charlie Carter wrote a new march titled "Super Chiefs," while Gator Band arranger Gary Langford produced a new version of Florida's state song, "Old Folks at Home" (better known as "Way Down upon the Swanee River"). The sight of a combined FSU-UF band might have taken some observers by surprise, but in fact it was not unique: the Chiefs and the Gator Band had appeared on the field together several times since the first gridiron meeting between the teams in 1958.[35]

The Voice

There is no member of the Marching Chiefs organization better known to Doak Campbell Stadium's football enthusiasts than its announcer. It is difficult to construct a complete lineage of Chiefs announcers, as they tended not to get mentioned in the various press releases, program booklets, and news features that otherwise name the principals in the band—directors, drum majors, etc.—although early on their names sometimes appeared on record labels and their voices were even heard on the band's recordings.

Nonetheless, a few names are known to us. Don Westbrook was a student-announcer in the mid- to late-1950s, as was Frank Knight. J. Dayton Smith, best known for having composed the "Hymn to the Garnet and Gold," also announced during Whit's years. Three announcers during the Braunagel era were Fred Vorce, trumpet player Steve Sparkman, and Doug Minear. Tommy Barfield informed audiences during the Mayo era. And Big 8 member Tim Wise announced in 1979 and 1980.

All of these could boast special qualities of vocal timbre, dramatic interpretation, or humorous sincerity, but none could match the longevity of one special announcer who continues to serve the Chiefs. David Westberry began announcing in 1981; it has been a term that, over the span of four decades, has provided more than a little organizational stability.

Westberry marched with the Chiefs for three seasons, 1978 through 1980, but his band experience dates back much farther. "Marching bands are something I've been around all my life," he said. "From the time my brother and I were born, that's all we knew."[36] His early exposure to the sometimes esoteric band world occurred courtesy of his father, Leonard L. Westberry, a 1952 FSU graduate in music education. Besides participating is his Dad's St. Augustine High School band, Westberry played in several ensembles at Florida Junior College in Jacksonville. Although a career in music education might have been predicted for Westberry, he ultimately chose another path. He graduated from FSU's College of Business in 1981 and immediately accepted a position with the Auditor General's office of the State of Florida in Tallahassee.

Westberry's decision to accept a government job proved providential when auditions for a new Marching Chiefs announcer were advertised following the resignation of Tim Wise. "I was very reluctant to try out," Westberry reports, but he was encouraged to do so by a number of friends, several of whom were still marching. The auditions, held on Chiefs Field, were open to all comers; members of the Chiefs were invited. Westberry ultimately prevailed in the competition. "I knew and loved the Chiefs," he said, describing the transition from player to announcer. "It was an easy and natural fit for me." The terms of his engagement were not entirely clear, but as of this writing—some thirty-five years after he delivered his first half-time script—"There was never a mention of re-auditioning."[37]

Once "hired," Westberry quickly forged a routine that he would by and large maintain. He attended rehearsals at mid-week in order to get a feel for the show; Friday afternoon and Saturday morning continuity rehearsals were crucial for nailing down details of the script—which is usually drafted by the director and tweaked by the announcer—and for perfecting the timings.

Westberry was forced to adapt to the many changes that occurred as a result of football's increasing popularity and an accompanying rise in technology. In the 1980s, "When television got more involved," he relates, "it was always an issue of timing." Precise schedules were followed to facilitate television coverage of the National Anthem, selected portions of pre-game and half-time entertainments, and, of course, advertisements. It was incumbent upon the band director and the announcer to ensure that the band could meet increasingly rigorous

7. Football Rising (1976–1990)

The brass section, fronted by majorettes, performs at half-time in Doak Campbell Stadium, circa 1986 (courtesy of Bob O'Lary/Olary.com).

timetables, while at the same time ensuring positive university exposure.

As technology advanced, the announcer's job got slightly easier. "They [television producers] were more intense over timings" early on, but as tape recordings evolved toward digitization, "it became less of an issue because they would come on to our broadcasts after the pregame ... a lot of times they may be taping some of it and cut and splice it as though it was live."[38] These editing sleights-of-hand eliminated an enormous number of game-day marching band pressures.

Through the years Westberry's affection for the Chiefs has only grown; his dedication is all the more impressive given that the announcer's post is uncompensated.

Shellahamer Returns

Shellahamer returned to his position at FSU in time for the 1984 football season. Because of Arrouet's fine stewardship, the band was in remarkably good shape, and the transition back to a Shellahamer routine was smooth.

Shellahamer's later shows were characterized by the same fun, variety, and creativity to which audiences were accustomed. A Caribbean-themed show featured a medley of beloved tunes and gave special attention to the island crooner Harry Belafonte. Film composer John Williams was saluted with performances of his main titles from the movies *1941* and *The Cowboys*, and others. And British music got some well-deserved attention with a performance that included a classic for wind band, Gustav Holst's First Suite in E-flat (1909).

Shellahamer's 1988 *A Seminole Saga*, a musical depiction of a day in the life of a Seminole Indian village, was considered by the director "my best show ever."[39] Although it was introduced in the script as "an entirely new concept for marching band presentations," Shellahamer was in fact resurrecting a conception that had been utilized by Braunagel in the 1960s. Here was a creative and completely novel idea set to new drill and music.[40] The music was by Charlie Carter, his second original show following the *Marching Chiefs Fantasia* of 1964.

The Chiefs beautifully execute a field formation, circa 1985 (courtesy of Bob O'Lary/Olary.com).

7. Football Rising (1976–1990)   163

A Seminole Saga, a "four-act multi-media drama," opened with Tallahassee city commissioner Steve Meisburg, guitar in hand, singing his locally popular song, "Seminole" (1981), while standing at midfield. As the ballad continued, the Chiefs quietly took to the field in a concert formation and began the first scene, "Awakening," which depicted "A new day" as it "breaks over the Seminole Village."[41]

The second act, "The Hunt," was a crowd-pleasing defeat of an alligator, a principal Seminole nemesis. Here the Chiefs form an alligator at one end of the field while a bow and arrow are formed at the opposite end. The bow is drawn, and an arrow—its brilliant silver tip created by the gleam of the Flush—soars across the field and plunges into the despised gator, which does not survive. The reference to UF, though not explicit, was not lost on the spectators; saxophonist Carter Vaverek recalls that "the crowd went pretty wild."[42]

"The Battle" was the *Saga*'s third segment. The music was a variation and expansion of the "War Chant," although it was more angular, brassier, and carries more rhythmic punch than its standard version. As "enemy forces gather[ed]," two opposing blocks met at midfield and "tragedy, death, and sorrow" ensued. "Their blood," the announcer lamented, "is on our hands."

The *Saga* closed with a "Victory Dance," a tightly-choreographed color guard feature complete with props (in this instance, a Seminole dwelling) and fire batons. The music, played from a concert formation, was powerful and triumphant.

Although there were moments of precision drill, especially in the second and fourth tableaux, the formations included lots of block and concert sets that highlighted Charlie's rich, symphonic harmonies and lent sonic muscle to what, after all, was a forceful and captivating tale of struggle and triumph. In this original conception for marching band, the Chiefs steadfastly maintained their traditional emphasis on sound.

The final half-time show of the Shellahamer era was "A Night at the Opera." It is perhaps not surprising that Shellahamer, an excellent and knowledgeable musician, would create as the culmination of his career a show based entirely on a musical genre. But perhaps more telling are its selections. "A Night at the Opera" was framed by the music of Andrew Lloyd Webber's blockbuster musical, *The Phantom of the Opera*; its main theme opened and closed the show. There were intervening operatic bonbons by Wagner and Bizet, but *Phantom*'s forceful strains, along with inventive chandelier formations, made it the driving force of the entire spectacle.

Shellahamer's last season as Marching Chiefs director was 1988. Tied with Whit as the longest serving director in Marching Chiefs history up to that time (if one discounts his two years spent in Columbus), Shellahamer was appointed assistant dean at the School of Music, a job that enabled him after a dozen years finally to recover his autumn Saturdays. Having given devoted and unwavering service following a disastrous collapse of pride and morale, Shellahamer will always be recognized as the man who restored—in remarkably short order—excellence and tradition to a now-venerable organization. As Madsen put it, "Bentley was a modern-day savior."[43]

Drum major Rodney Dorsey salutes the fans at Doak Campbell Stadium, circa 1986. His mother, Mable Dorsey, is situated off his left elbow. She never missed a home game (courtesy of Bob O'Lary/Olary.com).

"We played the 'War Chant' non-stop"

The director of the Marching Chiefs following Shellahamer's distinguished tenure was Robert Sheldon, a highly-regarded high school band director and a nationally known composer of music for winds. Besides his possession of a resume unlike that of any previous director, there was something particularly unusual about Sheldon compared to

7. Football Rising (1976–1990)

his predecessors: he received his bachelor's degree in music education from the University of Miami, and he earned a master's degree in conducting at the University of Florida. Following graduation at UF, Sheldon taught at P. K. Yonge Developmental Research School in Gainesville before moving to Bradenton to take over the respected Southeast High School program, where he remained from 1983 until 1989. Sheldon credits FSU music education professor Clifford K. Madsen for initial encouragement to apply for the Chiefs director job, which he began in 1989.[44]

Sheldon had a healthy respect for Marching Chiefs tradition, and from the start he was careful not to cause upset. "The Chiefs are a very tradition-oriented organization," he realized, "and, when you have someone come in from outside, you have to be careful. The last thing I was going to do was to throw stuff [i.e., traditions] out."[45]

In fact, under Sheldon's leadership surprisingly little changed. He continued to employ picture formations while also incorporating drum corps influences, although, Sheldon says, "It's hard to do real corps style with that many people."[46] Sheldon's shows were wonderfully accessible to both the fans and the Chiefs. His first show was based on the music of George Gershwin; it included the hit "Strike up the Band," from Gershwin's show of the same name. Sheldon followed with many other popular shows—a patriotic show ("If not always loved by the Chiefs, they always got the best ovations"); a superheroes show, for which Sheldon provided the arrangements himself; and a Beach Boys show, during which "We had someone on a surfboard and surfed them all the way across the field on a giant wave." And Sheldon did not neglect more serious strains of music. The 1989 Fiesta Bowl featured a Russian Classics show with selections that included Tchaikovsky's *1812 Overture* and Shostakovich's exuberant *Festive Overture*.

Naturally, Sheldon, whose own talents as an arranger are considerable, was careful not to encroach too far into Charlie Carter's territory. "My first year there," he reports, "I didn't do any more than three or four arrangements" so as not to make Charlie feel uncomfortable. Although initially Sheldon thought that working with Charlie "was a little awkward," it did not take too long for the duo to comprehend and appreciate each other's work habits. Sheldon notes that Charlie's arranging assignments "had to be very, very specific: there will be this many measures of this, in this key, and this many measures of that. And he would go ahead and work his magic."[47]

The workload associated with running a top-notch college band program has long been challenging for its directors. Time schedules were always very tight, and Charlie's delivery of the music seemed to be getting later as he advanced in age. As Sheldon remembers, "If we were lucky, we had the music on the first day we needed it." Like his predecessors, Sheldon manually created the drill after the music was completed, an excruciating exercise. "Basically it was 450 black dots on paper and trying to number everything by hand," an enormously time-consuming activity that was fraught with the possibility of error.[48]

It did not help that, as drill was being written, exhaustion seeped into the mix. Sheldon admitted that "I was pretty sleep-deprived the whole time, at least during the fall." He provided an excellent sketch of a typical day in the life of a Marching Chiefs director:

> You start your day at 8:00 a.m. in the office. You were lucky to get out of the university by 6:30 or 7:00 that evening, grab a quick dinner; go home and chart. And you'd try to get your charting done for the next day, and if you were lucky you'd get it done by 2 or 2:30 in the morning, and you'd run over to the university then, because it was the only time you could use the copy machine to run that many copies. You'd copy until about five in the morning, take the boxes and put them in your office; go home and sleep a couple of hours, and start all over again.[49]

Following a grueling season of rehearsal, half-time shows, and band travel, there was no small sense of relief when it was over: "I can remember my very last show of the season my first year, when I numbered that last dot on the last piece of paper; I can never remember feeling so liberated as when that was done."[50]

※ ※ ※

Early on Sheldon got an idea of how much the Chiefs meant to some people when it came to school spirit and the band's role in assuring football victories. He related one unpleasant incident that occurred following the 1989 loss to Clemson:

> On Monday morning I got this phone call, and I heard this absolutely wildly out of control person on the phone who was screaming at me—just screaming, I could barely understand him, he was screaming so loud—that it was my fault that the team lost because I didn't have the Chiefs play the "War Chant" enough. He was going on and on, and he was screaming at me over and over, "It's your fault, it's your fault," he told me over and over, and I finally said "We played the 'War Chant' non-stop!"[51]

When he hung up, Sheldon asked his assistant, who had forwarded the call, "Who was that crazy person on the phone?" As it turns out, it was

7. Football Rising (1976–1990)

a prominent politician—lots of name recognition—who will remain nameless here.

Sheldon continued as director of the Chiefs for just two years. His brief tenure did not allow for the incorporation of traditions of his own invention. "If there was anything that may have changed," he said, "it may have been in the interpretation of the music. If you changed a little bit—phrasing of the 'Fight Song,' or the interpretation of the "Hymn"—those are the kinds of things that may have lingered for a little while."[52]

*   *   *

Bowden and Sliger brought to FSU a renewed sense of purpose that had been missing through the tumult of the late-1960s and 1970s. As Coach began to field winning teams, bowl games became expected, and, with talk of finally joining a conference, most Seminole fans believed that championships could not be far away. Sliger was similarly visionary; he not only brought FSU back from its doldrums, but he also established, in partnership with FAMU, a top-notch College of Engineering; he recruited to campus the National High Magnetic Field Laboratory; and he oversaw huge gains in enrollment and distinction. He was also able to repair relations with the student body; Sliger could often be spotted strolling about campus wearing an informal guayabera shirt and conversing with his beloved students who returned the affection.

For Shellahamer's part, it would be massive understatement to say that he is respected and loved. Many positively revere him, and all comprehend that he restored tradition to the Marching Chiefs, even as he was willing to adopt latter-day marching techniques that had been associated with an unbeloved era in the band's history. Arrouet, with quiet dignity and good humor, proved an excellent steward of Chiefs tradition, while Sheldon's slight deviations from, and additions to, tradition occurred only at the margins. Throughout the changes in leadership, vision, and artistry, two men—Charlie Carter, of course, and David Westberry, as the public voice of the Chiefs—provided a welcome and necessary constant.

From the late 1970s and throughout the 1980s, football at FSU had definitely risen. In its wake, the excellence and reputation of the university surged, and the Marching Chiefs resumed their rightful place among the best marching bands in the nation.

8

A Marching Band for a New Era (1991 to Today)

Dunnigan and Plack

Patrick Dunnigan, the man who would become the longest serving director in Marching Chiefs history, was named Assistant Professor of Music in 1991. As we have seen, every era of the Marching Chiefs has encountered its opportunities and its challenges, and Dunnigan's term has been no different.

Born in Frankfort, Kentucky, Dunnigan learned to play the guitar when he received one as a gift. He later took up the tuba and joined the high school band. After earning a Bachelor of Music Education degree from the University of Kentucky, Dunnigan then received a master's degree in conducting from Northwestern University, Whit's alma mater. Following seven years of public school teaching, he spent five years as band director at Kalamazoo's Western Michigan University; from there, he came to Tallahassee.

Dunnigan left FSU for two academic years (1997–1998 and 1998–1999) to pursue a doctoral degree in music education at University of Texas, during which time Dr. John L. Baker served as acting director of the Chiefs. Dunnigan currently teaches band and orchestra conducting and sometimes arranging, conducts the symphonic band, runs the Chiefs, and is tasked with various administrative duties. Although not part of his FSU workload, he also conducts the Tallahassee Winds, the city's fine adult community band, and runs the Thursday Night Music Club, a big-band in which he plays guitar.

8. A Marching Band for a New Era (1991 to Today) 169

Director Pat Dunnigan (left) and David Westberry, the Voice of the Marching Chiefs (right), review a show at a Saturday morning rehearsal (2016) (photograph by the author).

As one scans the repertoire that has been performed by the Chiefs in the last twenty-five years, one immediately notices Dunnigan's love of diverse musics. His earliest shows, in fact, demonstrate the wide variety that marks the entirety of Chiefs history. When asked to identify his favorite shows of the 1990s, Dunnigan names the Olympic shows of 1992 and 1996. "Those two were really, really memorable, because that's just great music."[1] The earlier show paid tribute to the games that had just been held that summer in Barcelona, Spain. Besides a few Olympic fanfare favorites—including venerable selections by John Williams and Leo Arnaud—jazz legend Chick Corea's classic "Spain" was a nod to the host country, while "Georgia on My Mind" reminded listeners that the 1996 Olympics would be hosted in nearby Atlanta.

A "Tribute to Summertime" was performed in 1994. Gershwin's delectable "Summertime" from *Porgy and Bess* and Charlie Carter's swing-style arrangement of "We're Having a Heat Wave," excellent though they were, took a backseat to the formation on the field, NAT'L

CHAMPS, following the Noles' first NCAA National Championship the previous season.

Movie themes have long been a favorite topic. One 1996 show featured strains from *Robin Hood: Prince of Thieves*, the themes from *Mission Impossible* and *Back to the Future*, and the song "Danger Zone" from the movie *Top Gun*. *Star Wars*, a perennial favorite, merited an entire show in 1999.

The band has also given the audience a healthy dose of the classics over the last several decades. Shostakovich's *Festive Overture* was performed in 1992; selections from Bizet's *Carmen* were offered in 2003; Tchaikovsky's *1812 Overture* and two movements from Beethoven's Ninth Symphony were played in 2006. Bernstein's vibrant Overture to *Candide* was heard in 2008.

Patriotic shows are a reliable Marching Chiefs perennial, and the band has long appealed to the audience's love of country. The 1980 performance in the wake of the Iranian hostage crisis is still considered a patriotic milestone for the Chiefs, although the show following the attacks on September 11, 2001, was also deeply moving. One of its greatest moments was the playing of Bob Thurston's arrangement of "Amazing Grace." Crafted two years before in honor of Charlie Carter, the hallowed tune was particularly apropos for this moment in the nation's history.

The creation of drill changed in the early 1990s. Although Dunnigan started off writing drill for the Marching Chiefs manually, that would be short-lived, as charting by computer was just around the corner. "It really came of age in 1991, just in time for me to get here," he recalls. That innovation, of course, brought benefits in both creativity and time management.

Dunnigan's leadership style has been enjoyed by the Chiefs. Says one Chief, "He related to all of us well," and there was a general appreciation of his laid-back style.[2] Lesley Ray Zebrowitz recalls the restrictive formality of other bands compared to the Chiefs. For example, when the Chiefs met the Ohio State band at a rehearsal prior to the January 1, 1998, Sugar Bowl, the difference was stark. Zebrowitz remembers that, clothed in their practice uniforms and hats, "They're looking all formal," and, "I distinctly remember them looking at us like we were ... rogue children invading the Superdome."[3] But the Chiefs' informality completely comported with Dunnigan's personal style and with the relaxed vibe at FSU; it even harkens back to the reigns of Brownie and Mayo.

8. A Marching Band for a New Era (1991 to Today) 171

Awaiting instructions at a band practice on Chiefs Field in 1993. The well-trodden natural grass, now replaced by artificial turf, often gave way to dust or mud. Here and there one could even spot a pothole (courtesy of Kim Hadley).

Trusted partnerships among the leaders of the Marching Chiefs have been key to the band's success. For five decades, at least one of the partners was Charlie Carter. But in 2004, Dunnigan was joined by a new associate who would help him take on an increasingly unwieldy workload and add several new dimensions to FSU's band enterprise.

Dr. David Plack currently serves FSU as Director of Athletic Bands, but his first association with the Marching Chiefs was as a 1988 gunkie member of the baritone section. During his four years of marching, he had three band directors: Shellahamer for one year, Sheldon for two years, and Dunnigan for his senior season.

Plack had reservations about becoming a band director. Rather than pursuing a music education degree, he earned a Bachelor of Arts (BA) degree in music, which is essentially a liberal arts degree conferred by the College of Music. Although the BA offers the student wide latitude with respect to curriculum, it does not prepare the student with the specialized knowledge and skills necessary to be a credentialed music educator. Plack's eventual attraction to the band directing profession may be credited to the persistence of Professor James Croft, who offered him an assistantship for which Plack had not even applied. "My life would be drastically different," Plack insists, "if not for him."[4]

Plack went on to earn his master's and doctoral degrees in music education from FSU. First hired as instructional staff, he eventually rose to the post he now holds. Director of Athletic Bands is a relatively new position title at FSU, although it is not unique in the nation. It emerged on the heels of Croft's retirement, which provided an opportunity for a wholesale restructuring of FSU's band department. The band enterprise is now carried on by three men: in addition to his role with the Chiefs, Dunnigan conducts the symphonic and concert bands; Dr. Richard Clary, Director of Wind Ensemble Studies, conducts FSU's wind orchestra and graduate chamber winds; and Plack oversees all bands as they relate to the athletic department. The directors are also responsible for additional areas of teaching and related administrative duties.

Although Clary works independently, Dunnigan and Plack are co-directors of the Marching Chiefs. As directors have recognized for decades, managing the band is no small undertaking. Says Plack, "It's an incredibly massive job for one person to do."[5] Dunnigan agrees: "Football was just getting bigger, and bigger, and bigger," and "we wanted to expand the athletic bands into more areas."[6] But the job, as it was currently fashioned, was more than any one person could manage, never mind the prospect of doing even more. "My exhaustion level, prior to hiring David, was probably at its absolute peak. I just did not see how I was going to be able to go any farther and do anything else."[7] Although some college bands have a drill writer and an arranger, Dunnigan and Plack are actively engaged in both pursuits, and their efforts are supplemented by a team of graduate assistants. "As we have done this, and as we have done it together, that's been the key to this," Plack concludes. "Having someone to do it with is the key to this."[8]

"Zero tolerance"

The decade of the 1990s brought with it many changes in America's academic culture. Evolving social norms and heightened awareness of violence and fairness—to say nothing of vast increases in university liability—impacted every aspect of life at FSU (and most other colleges

8. A Marching Band for a New Era (1991 to Today)

Big 8 playing in the endzone at New Jersey's Giants Stadium in 1993. The Chiefs performed at FSU's season-opening game versus the University of Kansas. At the start of what would end up as their first National Championship season, the Noles destroyed the Jayhawks, 42–0 (courtesy of Kim Hadley).

and universities). As David Westberry put it, "The landscape has changed," and the changes could not but affect the Marching Chiefs.[9] "Dunnigan in his tenure has had to handle a lot of stuff," Westberry has observed. "There are a lot of changes that the Chiefs as an organization had to go through that made his job more challenging.... He eliminated a number of things that didn't need to be going on."[10]

One of them, of course, was hazing. Hazing has created headaches for many American institutions and their leaders over the past several decades, and the Marching Chiefs have been no exception. In September 1994 it was discovered that student leadership had taken part the month before in a hazing ritual that included marching while blindfolded, marching dangerously near traffic, a variety of silly and degrading activities—slurping gelatin through mouthpieces, bobbing for bananas in toilets, cracking eggs on tops of heads, etc.—and the far more objectionable coerced consumption of alcohol. The hazing abruptly ended when one student piled headlong into a brick wall, which resulted in injuries serious enough to require immediate medical attention. It was at that point that the School of Music "started the whole business of getting to the bottom of hazing," said Clifford K. Madsen; and the problem "was something I felt very strongly about."[11]

The hazing episode created a local firestorm—stoked in part by fraternities that wondered why the Chiefs escaped scrutiny, when they did not[12]—that soon caught the attention of media well beyond Tallahassee. And while an FSU Hazing Policy had already been crafted, one *FSView* writer admitted, "The truth is, no one will deny hazing takes place every day in almost every organization…. [Non-Greek] organizations might laugh you off, but when it gets down to it, the only response they can come up with honestly is 'it's all in fun,' or 'tradition.'"[13]

The matter was serious enough to require an investigation by the FSU Police Department. The School of Music also formed a committee to look into the matter. Headed by Madsen, its members deplored the hazing activities, which included "strongly demeaning, unsanitary and/or dangerous behavior" and "inappropriate and/or illegal alcohol consumption." The committee was especially disturbed by examples of "implied or encouraged competitive drinking where there is peer reinforcement."[14] The activities were not merely perilous, they were life-threatening.

Among the punishments meted out for the incident was at least one expulsion from the Chiefs—FSU's administration, citing student privacy, was remarkably tight-lipped about individual sanctions—and a three-year probation on the entire band. If at any time during the probationary period another incident were to occur, the consequences promised to be more severe. One additional School of Music remedy included the reclassification of the band from an extra-curricular activity—essentially a club for which credit was offered—to a regular class, which allowed for increased administrative oversight.[15]

For some, however, probation was far too lenient. South Florida's *Sun-Sentinel* newspaper complained that the Chiefs "got off far too lightly with a three-year probation. A violation of probation would lead only to another wrist-slap—all 426 band members would have to sit out one football game…. That's not good enough."[16]

Despite administrative best-efforts, a second hazing episode occurred in September 1999, just two years following the lapse of the band's earlier probation. At issue were the activities of the saxophone section, which forced members "to don certain apparel, carry certain equipment and/or food, and were subjected to 'name calling' that can certainly be viewed as demeaning...."[17] In a more egregious breach of hazing prohibitions, "certain second year members were paddled."[18]

The violations resulted in the permanent expulsion of two student leaders, including the fifth-year senior drum major; two other Chiefs were banned from band participation for a year; and approximately ten one-game suspensions were handed out. Another probation period—this time through January 2003—was established, but penalties for infractions would be a good deal harsher than previously; infringements would be met with a suspension of the entire Marching Chiefs organization for one game.

The School of Music's second ad hoc investigative committee, again led by Madsen, noted that the harsh punishments were intentional. "We're not as concerned here with retribution as we are with excising this kind of thing from the Chiefs. If we take it lightly, it's taken lightly by the students. A zero tolerance policy," Madsen declared, "must be that."[19]

※ ※ ※

"For every generation there are major changes. The generational change for this group, from the '90s and even from the 2000s," according to Plack, "is the culture change with social media and hazing; that's this generation's big change." Plack's reference to social media is of course related to the pervasiveness and immediacy of modern communications; everything said, done, and experienced can be—and often is—instantly documented for the ages.

But there have been other manifestations of change since the 1990s, some of which have not sat well with Marching Chiefs alumni. In a time when the culture is more sensitive to potentially hurtful language, "gunkie"—a term formerly applied to freshman band members, which originally implied that these new members "gunked up the works" of a smooth-running machine—was interpreted more pejoratively over the years. When the word was disallowed in 1995, it naturally took a while to abandon. "They tried very hard to make us not to call people gunkies the next year," recalls Lesley Ray Zebrowitz, "but of course that was the big joke.... 'We'll call you what we're supposed to call you but what you really are is a gunkie.'"[20]

Before filing into their seats at home games, the Chiefs snake their way through the underbelly of Doak Campbell Stadium to the noisy delight of fans (courtesy of Kim Hadley).

In addition, the band's unofficial "newspaper," *The Chieftain* was discontinued. Although a longstanding tradition that had been established during Whit's time, over the years it morphed from an organ that actually conveyed news of student and band activities to one that lampooned every aspect of life in the Marching Chiefs. Often it was critical of individual members and even approached bullying. In an era when student safety and university liability are an ongoing concern, information is transmitted quickly, and positive public relations is paramount, steps had to be taken to ensure that the Chiefs represented FSU in the best light. Very often, *The Chieftain* failed to meet that standard.

Some of the reforms were inevitable, but, as Westberry notes, the Marching Chiefs have gotten through yet another era of seismic change with remarkable success. "The band survived," he said. "They've gotten bigger; they've gotten better; they've gotten stronger."[21]

Exit Charlie

Charlie Carter retired in 1996. He died in December 1999. Toward the end, his various health challenges prevented him from taking a fully active role with the Chiefs. He attended games regularly, although he was seldom seen at rehearsals. As far as Saturdays at Doak Campbell Stadium, Dunnigan remembers that "He went to every game, unless he was ill. Only when he would call me and tell me he was not feeling well would he not come to the games."[22] As a younger man, Charlie was a frequent sight at Chiefs field. In the last decade of the twentieth century not only was his absence increasingly noticeable, but his sonic contributions to the Chiefs were noticeably dwindling.

But if Charlie's on-field presence had diminished, his legend and legacy continued to grow. Besides the power of his original compositions and his masterful arrangements, Charlie has left an enviable record as a teacher. He inaugurated arranging classes in 1966 as a summertime occupation. Camp Kirkland, an FSU drum major and then graduate assistant, was a student in Charlie's first class, which included about twenty-five others. Kirkland relates that, although the class was advertised as a general arranging class, Charlie emphasized traditional marching band scoring, making it in effect a course in arranging for the marching band. Kirkland loved Carter and the class. "He was great because he knew exactly what he did, and he knew exactly how he did it."[23] The class paid off for Kirkland when the always-generous Brownie programmed one of his arrangements, an armed services medley. Pre-1953 arrangements notwithstanding, to Kirkland's knowledge the medley comprised "the first notes that had ever been played by Chiefs other than by Charlie Carter."[24]

Marching Chief Gene Crowe also took Charlie's arranging class as a graduate student in the summers of 1968 and 1969. He remembers that Charlie had his students over for a cookout every year, during which time he would play Chiefs recordings from the 1950s and early 1960s. Charlie "would put the record on," Crowe remembers, "and he had such a memory that he could tell you exactly what the formation was at that point, and what they were doing in the show."[25]

Charlie was a generous and caring teacher, but as a rule his students and others did not contribute much in the way of arrangements to the Chiefs until the 1980s. Shellahamer produced an arrangement of Don Menza's "Groovin' Hard," which was used as a stands cheer following its premiere in a 1979 jazz-themed half-time show. And in 1980 Marching Chiefs trumpeter and student arranger Ed Hogan contributed a fine version of Joe Zawinul's "Birdland." But it was not until the arrival of Andre Arrouet that one particularly talented student was asked to arrange the music for an entire show.

"I'm not sure what prompted Andre to let me write a whole show," said Bob Thurston, "other than that he wanted to give me some experience."[26] Not that Thurston was a complete novice; with Shellahamer's hearty endorsement he had recently written three fine arrangements for the Chiefs—George Benson's great "On Broadway" and the James Bond favorite, "For Your Eyes Only," in 1981, and the fusion band Spyro Gyra's hit "Heliopolis" in 1982. Thurston also contributed a peppy original Latin tune, "Brio," in 1981. "If Charlie was uneasy about it, he never let it show—he was very supportive and helpful," Thurston reports.[27] Thurston's full show was *Songs of the South*, an amalgamation that included the Walt Disney tune "Zip-a-Dee-Doo-Dah," a gospel medley ("Swing Low, Sweet Chariot," "Will the Circle Be Unbroken," and "Amazing Grace"), and a crowd-pleasing favorite, "Old Man River."

When it came to perceived musical intrusions by young arrangers, things did not always proceed smoothly. In 1980, Thurston had just been named section leader of Big 8. A knowledgeable percussionist, he knew that the drum section could provide more than the standard boom-chick patterns that were common at that time. He asked Charlie if he could arrange some of the percussion parts to make them more interesting. "I was taking Charlie's arranging course that semester," Thurston relates, "so he knew who I was, and he liked me enough that I felt confident in asking. Charlie was agreeable, if perhaps cautiously. He told me he generally approached percussion as an afterthought—

8. A Marching Band for a New Era (1991 to Today) 179

even considered it a nuisance (his words). He scored the same way for marching band as he did for concert band—percussion was there only for rhythmic and dynamic reinforcement, not [tonal] color for its own sake."[28]

Charlie experienced difficulty accepting the new emphasis on the percussion section after the rise of drum corps style. Drum corps gave a prominence to the percussion section that it had not formerly enjoyed. Gone were the simple accompaniments that simply punctuated the wind passages; modern percussion parts were complex, busy, and—depending upon your point of view—intrusive. Charlie was growing impatient. When Shellahamer left for his doctoral sabbatical in Ohio following the 1981 season, he told Thurston, "You need to talk to Charlie about the drum parts. He hates 'em."[29]

According to Thurston, Charlie regarded the increasingly kinetic Marching Chiefs drum arrangements as a sort of musical vandalism, a noisy infringement that obscured the band's rich sound and often failed to mesh with his own stylistic interpretations. Charlie's thoughts on the matter are not unreasonable coming from an arranger who had been producing his own far less complicated and perfectly serviceable parts for decades. It is hard to believe that Charlie, despite his accommodating demeanor, was not beginning to feel as though upstart arrangers were beginning to intrude on his turf. "I feel like the drummers just want to take over the whole band!," Charlie complained. "The trumpets don't get to write their own parts, the clarinets don't. Why should the drums?"[30] For a time, at least, Charlie resumed writing the parts for Big 8.

For the duration of Shellahamer's tenure as Chiefs director, Carter's arrangements were supplemented by contributions from students—including Thurston, whose relationship with the arranger warmed considerably and resulted in Thurston's fine biography of Charlie—and graduate assistants. Sometimes the Chiefs even played arrangements that had been written for other college bands.[31] Sheldon and Dunnigan continued to rely on Charlie, but more frequently they took on the duties themselves or hired outsiders. As Thurston has written,

> In Dunnigan's case, this was a necessity, as Carter's health problems—including a bout with stomach cancer in early 1991—forced him to curtail his writing and teaching activities. Carter wrote only four new arrangements for the 1991 season; eight old arrangements were revived in different shows; the remainder

were written by various other arrangers. As of July 1992 ... Carter had completed several new arrangements for the coming Marching Chiefs' season, and had conferred with Dunnigan on several others.[32]

Asked if the band's sound has changed since Charlie left the scene, Dunnigan replies, "I don't think the basic sound has changed much at all. Our cadre of arrangers all knew, studied with, or were influenced by Charlie. Bob Thurston, Larry Clark, Tom Singletary, Kimberly Archer, David Plack, and me." But among the things that have changed, says Dunnigan, "are the technical abilities of the students in Chiefs. Today's kids are much better players than when I first got here (and they were pretty damn good in 1991, for sure)."[33] As for Charlie's arrangements, they still crop up on half-time shows from time to time; of course, his pre-game tunes and stands cheers are in constant use.

Dunnigan, an accomplished arranger himself, was familiar with Charlie and his large reputation, and at first he was tentative about working with him. "That was scary for me," Dunnigan says. "I would show him some of the charts that I had done, and got some feedback from him." The prospect of meeting and working with Charlie "was

Several members of the Chiefs Flutes perform for the crowd at a Skull Session at Mike Martin Field (2016) (photograph by the author).

8. A Marching Band for a New Era (1991 to Today)

more nerve-racking than walking into Doak for the first time.... Because of all his expertise and fame, and [he] just never wrote a note that wasn't absolutely perfect."[34] The Marching Chiefs continue to use Charlie's arrangements when possible.

It has not been lost on many of Charlie's admirers that his final Chiefs arrangement was the farcical song, "What Would Brian Boitano Do?," from the 1999 animated feature, *South Park: Bigger, Longer & Uncut*. Although Charlie's instrumentation is characteristically crisp, the tune does not lend itself to several of the strokes—harmonies and countermelodies, especially—for which Charlie is best known. And one wonders what he thought of *South Park*. "It's a perfectly good arrangement," says Thurston, "but the source material doesn't exactly scream Charlie's name. Then again, who knows. With his cartooning talents and sense of humor, Charlie might have totally gotten it."[35]

Charlie has deservedly won heaps of praise by his colleagues, legions of Marching Chiefs, and the alumni. He was inducted onto the Marching Chiefs Alumni Wall of Fame in 1996. But perhaps the most touching tribute occurred in 1992, when a half-time show was dedicated to him in honor of his forty years of faithful service. The

Charlie Carter poses with clarinetist Kim Hadley in 1993. By this time, Charlie had been writing arrangements for the Marching Chiefs for exactly forty years. Throughout the decades he was a beloved presence among students (courtesy of Kim Hadley).

show paid homage to various of his arrangements throughout the decades and ended with an endzone-to-endzone script CHARLIE.

World Renowned ... Still

Recent Marching Chiefs half-time shows have a wide-ranging appeal and draw upon sources that have proven popular over the decades. Latin shows have remained front-and-center in the Chiefs' repertoire, with selections by Chick Corea and Chuck Mangione; classic tunes such as "Malagueña" (2009), "Malaga" (2012), and a "Spanish Fantasy" (2011) have been heard now and then, as has "El Toro Caliente" (2009 and 2016); and Dunnigan's own original composition, "La Danza del Fuega" (Fire Dance), has appeared on the gridiron at least twice (2008 and 2014).

Movie and television themes also remain standard fare. 2013's *James Bond* show gave highlights of Bond tunes over the decades. *Star Wars* reappeared in 2014, along with selections from *Ghostbusters* (1984) and *Beetlejuice* (1988). *Hawaii Five-0* (2011) is evergreen for marching bands, and the theme from *Game of Thrones* (2012) may be considered a new classic.

As has been true throughout Chiefs history, pop music is also regularly on the menu. A blockbuster show titled "Music from the Days of Disco" was created for Parents' Weekend in 2010. Hits such as Barry Manilow's "Copacabana," the Bee Gees' "Stayin' Alive," and Donna Summer's "Last Dance," were enjoyed by the crowd, but it was Wild Cherry's great "Play That Funky Music (White Boy)," complete with the dancing Marching Chiefs, that brought the house down. (Although the Chiefs have danced off and on since at least 1981, in recent years it has become a popular annual addition to the band's repertoire.)

Songs from Motown were highlighted in a 2013 show that included The Temptations' "Get Ready," Otis Redding's "My Girl" (which is also closely identified with The Temptations), and "Ain't No Mountain High Enough," made famous by Marvin Gaye and later Diana Ross.

Pop diva Beyoncé was recognized in a 2014 tribute that included "Survivor," a song that became famous during her time in the group, Destiny's Child. 2003's "Crazy in Love" was featured, and "Single Ladies," included another full-band dance routine. The drill featured

8. A Marching Band for a New Era (1991 to Today) 183

a football-field-sized script spelling of BEYONCE. The Beyoncé show gained a good deal of social media traction; it was also performed at that season's Rose Bowl.

In the era of the internet and social media, marching bands have to be careful to obtain permissions to arrange music for their purposes. Although permission is most often granted, it is sometimes denied. A case in point for FSU: during the period when FSU's track & field team won NCAA National Championships in consecutive years (2006, 2007,[36] 2008), Plack got the clever idea to produce a show based on Bruce Springsteen's "Born to Run." Permission was not forthcoming. Reasons generally range from failure to pay for past permissions to the artist's (or the manager's) reluctance to relinquish artistic control, as occurred with the Springsteen song.[37]

✢ ✢ ✢

In 1972 Title IX of the federal Education Amendments was signed into law. Title IX provided that "No person in the United States shall, on the basis of sex, be excluded from participation in, be denied the benefits of, or be subjected to discrimination under any education program or activity receiving Federal financial assistance." The law aimed to provide "equivalent treatment, benefits and opportunities" to girls and women.[38]

Although Title IX covers a broad spectrum of activities related to females, it has perhaps generated the most notoriety in the world of athletics. As attention and money flowed into men's sports, especially football, basketball, and baseball, it was not difficult to see the disparities suffered by the women's teams. Getting to Title IX took a good deal of time and effort. As one writer put it, "These changes were propelled by women and men who, in the spirit of the early seventies, demanded that the benefits of athletics and sports be extended to everyone. It began with small steps; parents scrimped to pay for coaching or equipment for daughters who competed in swim meets or track and field, girls and women trained as never before, and college women started rowing, throwing, swimming and running."[39]

As a result of Title IX, FSU's band program was compelled to engage in many additional activities beyond its traditional role on the football gridiron or as a basketball pep band. A more formalized pep band, the "Seminole Sound," comprises 120 total members divided into two bands, one garnet and the other gold. These two groups "cover everything outside of football."[40]

In the decades prior to the pep band's new structure, members of the Marching Chiefs were often simply requested to show up at basketball games, which, at least in the 1980s, were run by a graduate assistant and the Chiefs assistant drum major. Now the Seminole Sound is a College of Music-sanctioned ensemble class, with expected attendance, uniforms (students wear the same warm-up attire as the players), and dedicated graduate students.

The Seminole Sound plays at a variety of women's sports contests, including soccer, tennis, beach volleyball, softball, basketball, and volleyball (Plack quips, "We probably have the country's largest volleyball pep band!"[41]) Unlike football and basketball events, the band does not always remain for the entire game. Most often, "we show up at the start of the match and play the "Fight Song" and the National Anthem. We try to do at least one appearance for every team."[42] The members of the Seminole Sound are buoyed by the fact that, for their part, the women's teams are very appreciative.

❧ ❧ ❧

David Plack has been a presence at FSU since 1988. Here he leads the Seminole Sound, the athletic pep band that bolsters Seminole dominance in sports other than football (photograph by Steve Chase/Chase-photography.com).

8. A Marching Band for a New Era (1991 to Today)   185

Despite the new emphasis on women's sports and the Chiefs' involvement with them via the Seminole Sound, football at FSU has remained paramount. Since joining the Atlantic Coast Conference in 1992, and as of this writing, the Noles have won fifteen conference championships and taken three National Championships, in 1993, 1999, and 2013.

The credit for much of FSU's success is rightly attributed to head coach Bobby Bowden, who led his last season in 2009. Retirement was foisted upon him, and for several years his relationship with the university was strained. But time has healed some of the wounds, and Bowden has again embraced the city, the school, and the fans who have loved him for the better part of five decades. The Marching Chiefs demonstrated their affection with a salute to Bowden in October 2013. The show included Lynyrd Skynyrd's "Sweet Home Alabama," a reference to Bowden's home state. The band formed the iconic word DADGUM on the field. John Denver's "Country Roads" paid tribute to the Country Boy. And "My Way," a song most closely identified with Frank Sinatra, was played as the Chiefs formed BOBBY.

Bowden was succeeded in the 2010 season by Jimbo Fisher, an up-and-coming coach who had actually been given the title "head coach-in waiting" in 2007. Relations between Fisher and the Bowdens are thick. Fisher was born in West Virginia; Bowden coached at West Virginia University. Fisher played for Bowden's son, Terry, at Salem College (West Virginia), and transferred to Samford University (Birmingham), when Terry Bowden took a job there. Later he assisted at Auburn University for Terry, who was then the school's head coach. Immediately prior to accepting his position at FSU, Fisher coached at LSU, where he became especially well regarded for his ability to develop quarterbacks.

FSU's winning ways have continued under Fisher. Since he became the head coach the team has competed in seven bowls, compiling a 5–2 record, including its 2013 National Championship. The Marching Chiefs have played no small role in the team's gridiron achievements, as Fisher acknowledges. Like Bowden, he is an enthusiastic advocate for the band, as attested by his 2016 annual welcome back speech at Chiefs Field:

> And I mean it from the bottom of my heart, everybody talks about the games and all that, but y'all are such a huge part of creating the energy, the vibe, and what Florida State football is all about.... There's a tremendous appreciation for what you do, I'm tellin' you.[43]

✦ ✦ ✦

In 1997—twenty-three years after its first international foray—the Marching Chiefs traveled abroad again, this time to England. The trip was occasioned by an invitation to perform during half-time at a London Monarchs game. The Monarchs were one of nine teams affiliated with the World League of American Football (WLAF; later called NFL Europe). The game versus the Barcelona Dragons was set for Sunday, May 4, at the historic Chelsea Stadium.

The World League, the brainchild of the National Football League, was desperately trying to sell its product in Europe. In their effort to introduce Europeans to American football—no small task in a part of the world devoted to soccer—organizers also sought to make the experience as wholesomely authentic as possible. As Dunnigan put it, "They were looking to bring a college band over to perform at half-time, because you can't have American-style football without a marching band."[44]

The offer was too good for the Chiefs to pass up; although the band's fame on the national stage had been buoyed by fifteen years of annual appearances at post-season bowl games, in recent years it had not enjoyed international acclaim. Besides that, the WLAF offered a generous financial subsidy to band members. For just over a week, the Chiefs would reside at Royal Holloway, a college affiliated with the University of London system, located about twenty miles outside London. In addition, local transportation, various guided tours (to Windsor Castle and other landmarks), and two meals per day were provided. The cost per student? $600 for airfare. "Looking back on that now," Dunnigan says, "the subsidy really helped."[45]

Band students were not required to attend, of course. Many couldn't, for a variety of reasons, one of which was the late spring date. That situation resulted in a truncated version of the Chiefs; approximately 150 students made the journey. Had the band fallen below that number, which Dunnigan believes is the minimum number required to adequately represent the university and the Marching Chiefs, he likely would have rejected the offer.[46]

Once in London, the Chiefs settled into their residences, held a couple of rehearsals, and participated in promotional activities that attempted to bring much-needed attention to the WLAF. Although the half-time show had been learned in Tallahassee, the rehearsals turned out to be a good idea, given the WLAF gridiron. Lesley Ray Zebrowitz recalls that "We were all completely confused because the marks on

8. A Marching Band for a New Era (1991 to Today)   187

the field for the European American football [league] are different than either the pro football here or the college football here."[47] Not unlike the 1974 Chiefs performances in the Middle East, the drill could only suffer slightly because of the layout.

The Chiefs' pep rallies for the WLAF were a valiant attempt to spread the gospel of American football to a skeptical British audience. When the Chiefs finally got on the field for their half-time performance, it is estimated that the crowd numbered less than 15,000.[48] They were the only band that day, although there were other attractions. "Performance artists" strolled about the stadium, and, following the Chiefs, the beloved Roly Polys dance troupe—a corps of older ladies of marked rotundity—also performed a routine.

As we have seen, the mighty Big 8 bass drums have long helped to spread the word of the Marching Chiefs and the Seminole Nation (photograph by Melina Myers/Melinasphotography.com).

The Chiefs performed several American favorites that were likely known to some extent by the Brits. Sammie Nestico's big band favorite "Ya Gotta Try" (1970) was made famous by the Count Basie Orchestra and the Buddy Rich Band. Chuck Mangione's "The Legend of the One-Eyed Sailor," from his 1973 *Land of Make Believe* album, showed the Chiefs in a more contemporary vein. And "Let It Be Me," a perennial made popular by legions of American singers—the Everly Brothers, Elvis Presley, Willie Nelson, and others—was the closer.

American football has never really taken off in Great Britain or Europe, but the effort by the NFL to export the game continues. Several times each autumn a pair of American teams are sent abroad to compete with one another. That strategy probably provides to the uninitiated a better version of the sport talent-wise than was previously available via the WLAF. But there is still scant evidence that football is flowering on another continent. As for the Monarchs, they lost to the Barcelona Dragons 32–37 and went 4–6 in 1997, making it entirely possible that the Marching Chiefs were the highlight of the game. It would not have been the first time.

It is undeniable that the Marching Chiefs' London trip lacked the hefty political moment of the band's 1974 adventure. Unlike with Syria and Jordan, there were no deep diplomatic chasms that had to be bridged. And London, for all its charms, cannot match many attributes—the utter cultural distinctiveness, the exoticism, and even a thrilling whiff of danger—that marked the trip to the Middle East. It nevertheless furnished the Chiefs several meaningful benefits: a chance to perform for a second time on the world's stage; another chance to act as musical ambassadors on behalf of the University, the State of Florida, and the nation.

And another chance to lay claim to the title "World Renowned."

Post-Game
"Here's a hymn..."

In 1970, one *Flambeau* journalist flatly claimed that, "the *Alma Mater* just doesn't make it." In an overall grim assessment, he further lamented that FSU's school song is "musically dead."[1] That was not a particularly new sentiment at the university. More than twenty years earlier, in anticipation of the 1959 football season, the *Flambeau* published a headline that pleaded, "Let's Swap Alma Mater for One We Can Sing." According to the writer, "Our *Alma Mater*"—an embarrassing creation, he judged—"is not singable for mixed voices." Moreover, "The exuberant 'FSU' at song's end is too often a mighty whisper, or in small groups, dead silence."[2] If the alma mater perhaps stimulated nostalgia, apparently it did not inspire participation.

It is not true that FSU's official alma mater, Johnny Lawrence's 1947 "High O'er the Towering Pines," is an unappreciated song. Both time and tradition have been kind to it. Composed by an FSU student, it provides a sort of mawkish solemnity that is prized in tunes of this variety. It conjures familiar images of a beautiful and beloved campus; at just four phrases, it is brief; its melody is easily remembered; it is relatively smooth, devoid of harsh or difficult leaps, and therefore it is easy to sing; and it ends with a resounding affirmation of school pride: "F.S.U." But these commendable qualities aside, there is a reason why it took so long to be confirmed as the university's official alma mater: its rhythmic and melodic simplicity result in a composition that is neither musically arresting nor emotionally wrenching.

One of the alma mater's critics compared it to another beloved school song, and concluded that, "We've listened to the music that goes with both songs also ... the 'Hymn' is vibrant and alive." The writer especially commended the "Hymn'"s instrumental arrangement as "exciting and moving," and observed that the alma mater was even being ignored by the university: "No mention is made in the *Pow Wow* [FSU's student handbook] denoting the existence of an *Alma Mater*. Much less the words."[3] This even though the texts to two other beloved songs, the "Fight Song" and the "Hymn," were included.

"We like the 'Hymn,'" the writer admitted. "It does what an *Alma Mater* is supposed to do—portray the spirit of the university it represents. There has been some talk around Student Government about changing the official university song to the 'Hymn.' Let's do it."[4]

※ ※ ※

The "Hymn" referred to above is, of course, J. Dayton Smith's magnificent "Hymn to the Garnet and Gold." If "High O'er the Towering Pines" has remained FSU's official alma mater, the "Hymn" has become the anthem of the Marching Chiefs. Played and sung from the stands following every home football game, it symbolizes the band's teamwork, esprit de corps, and camaraderie. Besides that, it is a beautiful composition, and its arrange-

Uniforms have varied through the decades: simple skirts and jerkins sufficed until they gave way to bright gold uniforms in the late 1940s. Whit favored military-style black uniforms, which lasted through the 1960s. By the early 1970s, garnet uniforms emblazoned with gold amplified school spirit. Here trombonist Adam Faucett wears a contemporary hybrid, part military, part pageantry (photograph by Melina Myers/Melinasphotography.com).

ment for band is replete with flourishes, harmonies, and sentiments that mark it as fully reflective of the FSU experience and Marching Chiefs tradition.

The "Hymn"'s composer was an enormous credit to FSU. Smith, a tenor vocalist, received his bachelor's degree from faraway St. Olaf College in Northfield, Minnesota. A former professor of music at the University of Nebraska, he arrived in Tallahassee in 1950 to pursue his doctoral degree at FSU.[5] As a graduate student, he led the Men's Glee Club, sang in the university's Choral Union, taught theory and other classes, and later was hired by Dean Kuersteiner to be his administrative assistant.[6] Smith's musical and managerial talents did not go unrewarded; he later became a successful Dean of Music at San Diego State University, where the 300-seat J. Dayton Smith Recital Hall is named in his honor.

J. Dayton Smith, composer of "Hymn to the Garnet and the Gold," was a respected teacher, administrator, and early Marching Chiefs announcer (from *Tally Ho*, 1955. Courtesy of Heritage Protocol & University Archives, Florida State University Libraries).

Smith's "Hymn to the Garnet and Gold" was premiered by the Men's Glee Club (which would soon be renamed the Collegians) at FSU's 1950 Pow Wow.[7] The "Hymn"'s text reads:

> Here's a hymn to the Garnet and the Gold, ringing to the sky.
> Here's a song for the men and women bold. Sing with heads held high.
> Striving e're to seek to know, fight for victory.
> Alma mater, this our song to you. Echoes F. S. U.

Immediately after the Pow Wow, the Collegians—a forty-voice ensemble—initiated "their first serenading tour of the campus," during which "they will stroll beneath the 'towering pines'" on Saturday nights to sing popular songs of the day. "The Collegians will also combine four-part harmony on the new 'Hymn to the Garnet and the Gold.'"[8] Over the next several years, Smith and his choruses relentlessly performed the "Hymn" at the university and elsewhere.

✤ ✤ ✤

The "Hymn" came into the orbit of the Marching Chiefs in 1958, when, according to Charlie Carter, "[Manley Whitcomb] asked me to think of something for an ending to a Homecoming show. He didn't say what. And I remembered that song; I loved it because of the parallel sixths in there, that was unusual. The bridge was kind of static, so I changed the harmony [there]."[9] Charlie perhaps saw something of his own style in Smith's clever progressions.

Shortly after Charlie arranged the "Hymn," it was taken up in rehearsal. One Chief remembers that as the session started, "Whit said, 'Charlie has just finished up a little piece here. It's on your stand, so let's give it a go.'" Following that first revelatory read-through by the Marching Chiefs, "There wasn't a dry eye in the house."[10] Charlie's gorgeous arrangement, thick and luxuriant in its harmonies and countermelodies, made its public premiere—at which it was considered "a salute to the future"[11]—at Homecoming on November 1, 1958.

There are alternate accounts of the "Hymn"'s origins. Some 1950s-era band members insist that the "Hymn" was played the throughout the entire decade, although it seems more probable that those memories are recalling the Collegians' ubiquitous performances of the vocal version. Another report suggests that Charlie in fact arranged the piece for FSU's Air Force Reserve Officer Training Corps (AFROTC) band in 1955, just ahead of scheduled performances in New Orleans.[12] The AFROTC band—whose membership included a number of Chiefs—was featured at the February 1956 Krewe of Carrollton parade, the first of twenty-two parades that kicked-off that season's Mardi Gras celebration.[13] The band also performed in concert at the Krewe's formal ball, where a version of the "Hymn" was purportedly rendered, but documentation of the repertoire has so far proven elusive.

The "Hymn," which is almost certainly Charlie's most oft-performed arrangement, was perhaps his discovery, but it was not his creation.[14] He steadfastly refused to lay claim to any more than a small slice of the credit. Sara Pankaskie has recollected, "…always, when anyone tried to say 'Oh, Charlie, that's such a great song' he would say, 'I didn't write it. J. Dayton Smith wrote it. I arranged it.'" Says Pankaskie, "He always made very clear that distinction."[15] It helped, of course, that the two were friends: "Charlie adored J. Dayton Smith."[16]

Not long after it was crafted, the Chiefs appropriated and appended to the "Hymn" a standard university cheer for themselves. "FSU one time. FSU two times. FSU three times. FSU All the Damned Time!" had been used to enliven school spirit since at least the early-1950s.[17] The Chiefs replaced "FSU" with "Marching Chiefs" and have used the huzzah as an invocation of unity after each performance of the "Hymn."

There was one brief and unhappy episode in the lustrous history of the "Hymn." Raxsdale jettisoned the song from the band's repertoire in 1976. "From the beginning of his tenure as director," one Chief recalled, "we were not allowed to sing the "Hymn." We were not allowed to play the "Hymn." He ruled that out right off."[18] The director's motives for banning the song that was by then inseparably bound to the Marching Chiefs remain unclear.

※ ※ ※

It has taken decades for the traditions of the Marching Chiefs to accumulate. The playing of the "Hymn" is just one—and one of the most important—among countless rituals that have burgeoned over what is now a long and venerable history. In 1992, Charlie said of his and Whit's adventure to Tallahassee, "The reason we had it made down here is because [FSU] didn't have any traditions. So everything we did was okay. Anybody comes along now, he has a rough time—you gotta put up with all these traditions!"[19]

Charlie overstated it a bit. When the duo from Ohio State arrived, the Marching Chiefs was not void of traditions. Some of them—the amplification of college spirit, the emphasis on pageantry and entertainment, the quest for military-like precision and uniformity—had been installed by Hughes, Sellers, Sykora, and Smith. And, of course, Brownie's early years saw excellent progress in the band's sound, a continuation of its strong desire to forge campus unity, and the acquisition of its very name. Whit landed in Tallahassee with dreams of developing a formidable band program, and he significantly increased its discipline and artistry. He was also able to marshal university resources unlike any of his predecessors. Charlie, of course, aided the band's sound with his exquisite arrangements. But they were not forced to start from scratch. They simply hoisted a substantial roof onto an existing sturdy foundation.

Brownie's second term as director featured distinguished and unprecedented artistic gains, and Mayo expanded upon that creativity to give the band a contemporary sound and appearance to match a modern outlook. Raxsdale must be given his due for additions related to the drums-corps style of marching that were retained. And following a year that saw performance quality and morale plummet, Shellahamer returned the band to its former glory. Excellence accrued under Arrouet and Sheldon, and it continues to do so today under the leadership of Dunnagin and Plack, who oversee one of America's most highly acclaimed marching bands.

※ ※ ※

If the history of the Marching Chiefs demonstrates anything, it demonstrates that change is relentless, ongoing, inevitable. Band directors, students, and audiences come and go. So do musical imperatives, marching techniques, and other elements of the show. All that has really remained true is the enthusiasm that attends gridiron performances on steamy Tallahassee afternoons and evenings every autumn. And, despite the fluctuations, upsets, and reorganizations, more than a century of devoted faculty leadership and loyal student participation have combined to forge a Marching Chiefs that brims with history and tradition.

The art of the marching band is ephemeral. While, as institutions, marching bands may stand for generations, their pre-game and half-time shows, like music itself, exist only in the moment. The magical energy of a performance lingers briefly and then dissipates into memory. We can capture its essence via technology. Recordings—LPs, cassette tapes, and CDs—are treasured by many of us; more than a few are piled on shelves, tucked away in drawers, or perhaps stowed more permanently. A few films and videos lie hidden in institutional and personal archives. Shows of recent vintage, and a few older ones, may be viewed online. But these reproductions of on-field efforts are naturally a pale shadow of an actual, live performance by the Marching Chiefs. Other artifacts help us cling to our hallowed past. Photographs, drill charts, *Chieftains*, marching manuals, and a variety of miscellany remove us to an earlier, perhaps happier time.

Memory remains for many us an important avenue for reliving our college band days. Marching Chiefs from all eras share common memories and unique traditions. We recall our leaders—the women

History. Pageantry. Excellent performances of artfully arranged music. The thrill of the home crowd in Doak Campbell Stadium. These are the World Renowned Marching Chiefs (photograph by Melina Myers/Melinas photography.com).

and men who founded, built, and re-built the organization—with tales and monuments that maintain their legend. We have emblazoned their names on revered sites and enshrined many on our Wall of Fame. As the decades pass, we can expect to honor more individuals who have dedicated to the Marching Chiefs a fair part of their lives. We owe them all our gratitude.

This book opened with a recitation of memories that we share by way of our personal involvement as Marching Chiefs. Shows, music, gamedays, and thousands of others come to mind with one degree of clarity or another. Often the embers of our memories flare in our alumni years, when we joyfully relive pieces of our own journey at rehearsals, Skull Sessions, and football contests. These are rejuvenating bridges to our cherished past.

But a crucial element—perhaps *the* crucial element—of membership in the Marching Chiefs lies in the relationships that we forged with one another. Shared stresses and shared triumphs led to sturdy bonds. Friendships blossomed; loyalties could not wither. Many remain as stalwart as they were decades ago. And in many cases, the shared Chiefs experience resulted in love and even marriage.

The legions of FSU Seminoles who directed, played, marched, drum-majored, twirled, and glue-crewed, have forged and maintained customs—not mere activities, but ways of thinking and being—that are and will remain constants in our lives. Our history, our traditions, and our relationships, have in no small part made us who we are:

"Marching Chiefs All the Damn Time!"

Chapter Notes

Preface

1. "College Tradition" [Letter to the Editor], *Florida Flambeau* (April 1, 1916): 2.

Chapter 1

1. Although the word "seminary" is today often used to reference religious education, it actually refers to any upper-level schooling (colleges, universities, etc.).
2. Dodd, "Early Education" [Part 1], 27.
3. *Ibid.*, 22–23.
4. *Ibid.*, [Part 2], 160.
5. Sellers, "Femina Perfecta," 6.
6. *Ibid.*, 6.
7. Thompson, *A Tallahassee Girl*, 7–8.
8. "Florida State College," *Argo* [Florida State College yearbook], vol. 2 (1901–02): 89.
9. An observation of Ella Scoble Opperman cited in Swingle, "A History," 8.
10. A. Clyde Evans, "West Florida Seminary" [a poem], *Argo* [West Florida Seminary yearbook] (1901): 45.
11. F. A. Hathaway in *Argo* [Florida State College yearbook], vol. 2 (1901–02): 17.
12. "Florida State College," *Argo* [Florida State College yearbook], vol. 2 (1901–02): 115–116.
13. The letter from Winthrop to Bainbridge officials is reprinted in *The Search Light* [Bainbridge, GA] (November 14, 1902): 1.
14. Notice in *The Search Light* [Bainbridge, GA] (November 28, 1902): 8. The standards for scoring in college football have changed since this game took place.
15. "The Bainbridge Game," *Argo* [Florida State College yearbook], vol. 3 (1903): 95.
16. See *The Search Light* [Bainbridge, GA] (December 5, 1902): 7.
17. *Ibid.*
18. Buckman's efforts are treated thoroughly in Sellers, "Femina Perfecta," 10–12.
19. Sellers, "Femina Perfecta," 13.
20. *Ibid.*, 25–26.
21. *Ibid.*, 26.
22. See Swingle, "A History," 11; and Sellers, "Femina Perfecta," 46–47.
23. Avant, *My Tallahassee*, 26.
24. *Ibid.*, 79.
25. *Ibid.*, 79–81.
26. *Ibid.*, 65.
27. *Ibid.*, 75.
28. Sellers, "Femina Perfecta," 39.
29. "History of the Florida State College for Women," *Flastocowo* (1910): 4.
30. "F.S.C.W.," *Florida Flambeau* (February 27, 1927): 4.
31. Ludwig Kotelmann, *School Hygiene* (trans. by John A. Bergström and Edward Conradi). Syracuse: C. W. Bardeen, 1899.
32. "Fight Against Liquor Traffic Begun in Tallahassee," *Florida Flambeau* (March 13, 1915): 1.
33. "The New Telephone Proves a Great

Success," *Florida Flambeau* (October 21, 1916): 4.
34. By now, the reader must have noticed the close connection that FSU and its predecessors have, especially in the musical arena, to the State of Ohio.
35. Swingle, "A History," 13.
36. *Ibid.*, 15.
37. Campbell, *University in Transition*, 82.
38. See "Orchestra Organized," *Florida Flambeau* (February 24, 1917): 1.
39. "F.S.C. Orchestra to Make Its Debut Tuesday Nite, May 12," *Florida Flambeau* (May 9, 1925): 1.
40. "College Orchestra Has Successful Debut," *Florida Flambeau* (May 16, 1925): 1.
41. "Florida State College Organizes Both Band and Orchestra," *Florida Flambeau* (November 13, 1926): 5.
42. "First Appearance of Florida State Band," *Florida Flambeau* (November 27, 1926): 1.
43. Opperman cited in Swingle, "A History," 19.

Chapter 2

1. "Concert Given by the University of Florida Band," *Florida Flambeau* (March 4, 1922): 1.
2. "Many Floridians Support Gators in Fla-Tech Game," *Florida Flambeau* (October 24, 1925): 1.
3. "Go Get 'Em, Gators," *Florida Flambeau* (October 16, 1926): 5.
4. "Gator Band Arrives Today for Concert," *Florida Flambeau* (March 10, 1939): 1.
5. "Corps Formed on the Campus," *Florida Flambeau* (October 7, 1938): 3.
6. "Tally Troupers Pick 39 Girls," *Florida Flambeau* (November 4, 1938): 3.
7. Mark Twain, *Life on the Mississippi* (New York: P. F. Collier & Son, 1917): 357–358.
8. See "Drilling" [caption and photo]. *Florida Flambeau* (May 5, 1917): 1.
9. "Department of Physical Education," *Flastacowo* (1939): 34.
10. "Troupers Hold Last Try-Outs," *Florida Flambeau* (October 21, 1938): 3.
11. "Parents' Day Climaxed by Thanksgiving Festivities," *Florida Flambeau* (November 25, 1938): 2.
12. "Troupers Head Pep Parade," *Florida Flambeau* (November 25, 1938): 8.
13. *Ibid.*
14. "Fifty New Tally Troopers Added," *Florida Flambeau* (October 20, 1939): 3.
15. From an interview with Richard (Dick) Mayo (April 19, 1993), cited in Sellers, "Femina Perfecta," 278.
16. "Let's Face the Facts" [Letter to the Editor], *Florida Flambeau* (March 10, 1939): 4.
17. "New Band to Play at Holiday Games," *Florida Flambeau* (November 24, 1939): 3.
18. Paul, "A History," 10.
19. George Corradino interview, April 20, 2016.
20. *Ibid.*
21. "Sellers Studies in Rochester for Master's in Music," *Florida Flambeau* (August 18, 1939): 1.
22. "New Band to Play at Holiday Games," *Florida Flambeau* (November 24, 1939): 3.
23. "Color Rush Will Be Lead [sic] by Band," *Florida Flambeau* (November 7, 1941): 1. See also, "FSC Band Celebrates Spring Anniversary," *Florida Flambeau* (May 12, 1944): 1.
24. "Present Odd-Even Demonstrations Originated Back in 1910 When Classes First Took Sides," *Florida Flambeau* (December 1, 1939): 6.
25. "Odd-Even Rivalry Has Been Changed Since '25," *Florida Flambeau* (November 24, 1944): 2.
26. "The Garnet and the Gold," *Florida Flambeau* (November 23, 1928): 3.
27. "There've Been Some Changes Made," *Florida Flambeau* (December 3, 1948): 6.
28. "Memory Doors—'Odds' vs. 'Evens,'" *Florida Flambeau* (October 15, 1963): 3.
29. "Sellers Organizes Band for College," *Florida Flambeau* (December 6, 1940): 1.
30. "College Band Begins Career Under Sellers," *Florida Flambeau* (December 13, 1940): 1.
31. "Florida State College Band Plays"

Chapter Notes—2

[photo caption], *Florida Flambeau* (May 2, 1941): 6.

32. "Tally Troopers Hear Chiotakis," *Florida Flambeau* (March 7, 1941): 2.

33. "Sellers Announces Progress of the Band," *Florida Flambeau* (March 28, 1941): 3. The Sturchio march was "Dedicated to [and likely commissioned by] the United States Sugar Corporation."

34. *Ibid.*

35. Sellers quoted in Swingle, "A History," 30.

36. "Heinlein to Talk to Musical Group," *Florida Flambeau* (April 18, 1941): 1.

37. *Ibid.*

38. "Band to Make First Public Appearance," *Florida Flambeau* (April 4, 1941): 3.

39. "Join the Band Campaign Opens with Parading," *Florida Flambeau* (October 3, 1941): 1.

40. "Tally Troopers Will Organize," *Florida Flambeau* (January 10, 1941): 3.

41. Virginia Dunn, "Musically Speaking," *Florida Flambeau* (February 20, 1942): 5. The ellipses are found in Dunn's text.

42. Righter, *Gridiron Pageantry*, 29.

43. *Ibid.*

44. *Ibid.*, 54.

45. *Ibid.*, 30.

46. Wright, "Marching Maneuvers," 8.

47. "Campbell Warns FSCW Students of Coming Trials," *Florida Flambeau* (December 12, 1941): 1–2.

48. *Ibid.*

49. Righter, *Gridiron Pageantry*, 61.

50. Lamar K. McCarrell, "The Impact of World War II Upon the College Band," *Journal of Band Research* 10/1 (Fall 1973): 3.

51. *Ibid.*, 4.

52. Righter, *Gridiron Pageantry*, 38.

53. *Ibid.*

54. William Revelli, "How Music Can Help Win the War," *Etude* (November 1942): 741 and 779.

55. *Ibid.*

56. "Band to Stage 3 Appearances," *Florida Flambeau* (November 20, 1942): 6.

57. William Revelli, "School Bands in Wartime," *Etude* (December 1943): 791.

58. "Former Member of FSC Faculty to Appear Here with Symphony," *Florida Flambeau* (February 22, 1946): 6.

59. "Sykora, Music Professor, is Native Russian," *Florida Flambeau* (February 12, 1943): 2.

60. "Music: Soviet Overture," *Time Magazine* 34/22 (November 27, 1939): 60.

61. "Former Member of FSC Faculty to Appear Here with Symphony," *Florida Flambeau* (February 22, 1946): 6.

62. "Sykora to Give Cello Recital," *Florida Flambeau* (March 26, 1943): 1, 6.

63. "Band Will Play at Dale Mabry," *Florida Flambeau* (October 15, 1943): 1.

64. "Band Participates in Inauguration," *Florida Flambeau* (February 23, 1945): 3.

65. "FSC Band to Go to Gordon Johnson," *Florida Flambeau* (April 13, 1945): 4.

66. "Sykora Leads Band Concert on V-E Day," *Florida Flambeau* (May 11, 1945): 1.

67. *Ibid.*

68. "Former Member of FSC Faculty to Appear Here with Symphony," *Florida Flambeau* (February 22, 1946): 6; "FSCW Plans Concert, Drill," *Florida Flambeau* (November 5, 1943): 3.

69. "College Swingsters Make Dance Debut," *Florida Flambeau* (November 12, 1943): 1.

70. "Band Tryouts to be Held Immediately," *Florida Flambeau* (September 29, 1944): 2.

71. Ella Scoble Opperman, letter to "the Officers and Members of the Florida State College Band," December 6, 1943. My thanks to Bentley Shellahamer for bringing this letter to my attention and for sharing his copy with me.

72. "Dr. Heinlein Congratulates Professor Sykora and Band," *Florida Flambeau* (March 23, 1945): 3.

73. *Ibid.* Emphasis mine.

74. *Ibid.*

75. *Ibid.*

76. "New Band Students Are Entertained," *Florida Flambeau* (November 9, 1945): 3.

77. "Concert to be Next Thursday in Westcott," *Florida Flambeau* (February 8, 1946): 1.

78. "Two College Deans Retire from Service," *Florida Flambeau* (May 12,

1944): 1–2. The other retiree was William G. Dodd, Dean of the School of Arts and Sciences.
 79. Paul, "A History," 4; see also *FSCW Bulletin* 1945–1946 (Winter Quarter): 12.
 80. "FSC Adds 101 New Members to the Faculty This Quarter," *Florida Flambeau* (October 5, 1946): 1–2.
 81. "Sellers Leads Winter Band Performances," *Florida Flambeau* (February 15, 1946): 1.
 82. Paul, "A History," 14.

Chapter 3

 1. "FSC Expands as Veterans Overflow from Florida U Is Housed at Dale Mabry," *Florida Flambeau* (October 5, 1946): 1.
 2. "Trial Run" [editorial], *Florida Flambeau* (October 4, 1946): 4.
 3. "Choral Group Holds Tryouts this Week" and "College Orchestra Consists of Coeds," both in *Florida Flambeau* (October 5, 1946): 1.
 4. William Revelli, "When G. I. Joe Comes Marching Back to College," *Etude* 64 (May 1946): 259.
 5. Swingle, "A History," 39.
 6. Campbell, *University in Transition*, 32.
 7. Doak Campbell quoted in Swingle, "A History," 45.
 8. Campbell, *University in Transition*, 32.
 9. *Ibid.*, 34.
 10. "Plans of Music Building Call for Early Completion," *Florida Flambeau* (October 8, 1948): 2.
 11. Campbell, *University in Transition*, 52.
 12. "FSC Expands as Veterans Overflow from Florida U Is Housed at Dale Mabry," *Florida Flambeau* (October 5, 1946): 1.
 13. "Milestone" [editorial], *Florida Flambeau* (October 4, 1946): 4.
 14. "Students to Name FSU Athletic Teams," *Florida Flambeau* (November 7, 1947): 1.
 15. "Seminoles Clash with Cumberland Tonight," *Florida Flambeau* (November 14, 1947): 3.
 16. "Alma Mater Selected," *Florida Flambeau* (November 21, 1947): 1.
 17. Diane Godin, "Wrong Lyrics Sung for Years," *Florida Flambeau* (October 14, 1958): 4.
 18. *Ibid.*
 19. "Alma Mater Selected," *Florida Flambeau* (November 21, 1947): 1.
 20. See Lawrence photo caption in *Florida Flambeau* (December 5, 1947): 1.
 21. "Make Our Song Official," *Florida Flambeau* (December 3, 1948): 6. See also, Davis, "What's in a Song?" *Illuminations* [FSU online magazine] (September 22, 2015).
 22. "Marching Band Sports New Uniforms," *Florida Flambeau* (October 15, 1948): 1.
 23. "University Band to Make Debut," *Florida Flambeau* (October 17, 1947): 3.
 24. George Corradino interview, April 20, 2016.
 25. "University Band to Make Debut," *Florida Flambeau* (October 17, 1947): 3.
 26. "FSU's Debut on the Gridiron Delights Pigskin Spectators," *Florida Flambeau* (October 24, 1947): 1–2.
 27. "Band Performs at FSU Game," *Florida Flambeau* (December 5, 1947): 3.
 28. *Ibid.*
 29. "Marching Band Sports New Uniforms," *Florida Flambeau* (October 15, 1948): 1.
 30. "Band Members Try, Music Sheets Fly, Drum Major Cries," *Florida Flambeau* (November 19, 1948): 8.
 31. "FSU Marching Band to Emphasize Drill for the Rest of the Term," *Florida Flambeau* (October 22, 1948): 1. Robert Smith the band director is not the same Robert Smith who would later teach music history at FSU's School of Music.
 32. George Corradino interview, April 20, 2016.
 33. *Ibid.*
 34. "FSU Marching Band to Emphasize Drill for the Rest of the Term," *Florida Flambeau* (October 22, 1948): 1.
 35. "Band Is Colorful Attraction at Florida State University," *Florida Flambeau* (November 11, 1949): 2.
 36. "Braunagel Will Present Recital," *Florida Flambeau* (December 5, 1947): 1.
 37. "Band Is Colorful Attraction at

Florida State University," *Florida Flambeau* (November 11, 1949): 2.
38. George Corradino interview, April 20, 2016.
39. See *Bulletin*, 1950 (Winter Quarter): 31.
40. "Twirlers Add Color to Marching Band," *Florida Flambeau* (November 29, 1949): 2.
41. *Ibid.*
42. George Corradino interview, April 20, 2016.
43. *Ibid.*
44. "Seminoles Reject Bid to Play in Cigar Bowl," *Florida Flambeau* (December 1, 1950): 3.
45. "FSU Band Gives Cigar Bowl Finale," *Florida Flambeau* (January 10, 1950): 4.
46. "Contest Continues for Band Entries," *Florida Flambeau* (October 6, 1950): 1.
47. "19 Names Entered for Band Contest," *Florida Flambeau* (October 17, 1950): 1.
48. "Jett Munroe Reigns Over Homecoming," *Florida Flambeau* (October 31, 1950): 1.
49. Doug Alley, "Poetically Yours," *Florida Flambeau* (October 6, 1950): 3. I have removed several of Alley's textual ellipses from this paragraph.
50. "College Songs," *Florida Flambeau* (November 19, 1927): 4.
51. "Good Seminoles Sing Fight Song," *Florida Flambeau* (September 25, 1951): 5.
52. George Corradino interview, April 20, 2016.
53. Doug Alley, "Poetically Yours," *Florida Flambeau* (October 6, 1950): 3. I have removed several of Alley's textual ellipses from this paragraph.
54. Bracketed words denote later additions and changes to the song.
55. Joel P. Smith, "Campus Carousel," *Florida Flambeau* (October 31, 1950): 2.
56. "Good Seminoles Sing Fight Song," *Florida Flambeau* (September 25, 1951): 5.
57. "Wright Composes Fight Song Music," *Florida Flambeau* (October 10, 1950): 1.
58. See "FSU Fight Song," *Florida Flambeau* (October 27, 1950): 21.
59. "Wright Composes Fight Song Music," *Florida Flambeau* (October 10, 1950): 1.
60. "U of F Afraid?" *Florida Flambeau* (October 12, 1951): 2.
61. "Seminoles Clamor for Gator Game," *Florida Flambeau* (October 16, 1951): 1.
62. "Band Announces Season's Outline for Ball Games," *Florida Flambeau* (September 23, 1952): 1.
63. "300 Indians Cheer Team On at 1st Rally," *Florida Flambeau* (October 2, 1951): 1.
64. "Chiefs Head Band Parade," *Florida Flambeau* (October 18, 1957): 1.
65. "Massed Bands to Play Here," *Tallahassee Democrat* (October 19, 1951): 4.
66. "Twenty-One Bands Perform at Game," *Florida Flambeau* (November 13, 1951): 1.
67. Al Pierce, "Band Performance Thrills Spectators at Louisville Game," *Florida Flambeau* (October 7, 1951): 1.
68. *Ibid.*
69. *Ibid.*
70. "College Spirit of the '20s Reborn on Campus," *Florida Flambeau* (October 14, 1952): 2.
71. "Football Coaches Played for Indiana University," *Florida Flambeau* (October 8, 1948): 4.
72. Bentley Shellahamer interview, December 5, 2015.
73. Florence Helen Ashby interview, May 22, 2016.

Chapter 4

1. "Band Director from Ohio State May Replace Braunagel," *Florida Flambeau* (April 24, 1953): 1.
2. Interview with Manley R. Whitcomb, March 26, 1970; in McCarrell, "Historical Review," 263.
3. Interview with Manley R. Whitcomb, March 26, 1970; in McCarrell, "Historical Review," 264.
4. *Ibid.*, 264–5.
5. See Bonner, "Eugene J. Weigel," 23. Bonner states that Weigel "created a high step of marching which consisted of eight steps ... for every five yards."

6. One writer was still advocating the use of the 6-to-5 step as late as 1952. See Julian E. Opsahl, "What About That Halftime Show," *The Instrumentalist* (September 1952): 12.

7. Interview with Manley R. Whitcomb, March 26, 1970; in McCarrell, "Historical Review," 266.

8. "Weigel Made Director," *The Lantern* (November 18, 1940): 4.

9. Although he remained at OSU, Whit was replaced by Jack O. Evans, acting director of the marching band, in 1952. See "Workout for Bandsmen to Continue till Game," *The Lantern* (September 24, 1952): 1.

10. "Band Director from Ohio State May Replace Braunagel," *Florida Flambeau* (April 24, 1953): 1.

11. "Spirit, Precision Typify Band," *The Lantern* (October 23, 1951): 7.

12. See "Team, Band Written Up in New *Life*," *The Lantern* (October 28, 1948): 2.

13. Whitcomb quoted in Zirkle, "Manley R. Whitcomb," 26.

14. "Band Director from Ohio State May Replace Braunagel," *Florida Flambeau* (April 24, 1953): 1.

15. George Corradino interview, April 20, 2016.

16. Bob Mitchell, "Marching Chiefs Come No Better," *Florida Flambeau* (November 15, 1963): 8.

17. Johnny M. Clark interview, November 22, 2016. Chicago, as a major manufacturing city and a rail hub, could have provided instruments from Holton, Olds, or even Conn or Buescher, whose companies were situated in the nearby town of Elkhart, Indiana.

18. Florence Helen Ashby interview, May 22, 2016.

19. "FSU Students Asked to Join Marching Band," *Tallahassee Democrat* (August 13, 1953): 13.

20. Florence Helen Ashby interview, May 22, 2016.

21. See Whitcomb, "Your Band CAN Entertain," 62–66. For a comprehensive listing of Whitcomb's half-time shows see Zirkle, "Manley R. Whitcomb" (Appendix D), 76–106.

22. "Marching Chiefs Hail Frosh in 1957 Debut," *Florida Flambeau* (September 23, 1957): 1.

23. "Bands 'Halftime' Dedicated to All," *Florida Flambeau* (October 31, 1958): 5.

24. "Jazz Jumpin' at Halftime," *Florida Flambeau* (October 25, 1957): 1.

25. "Band Day Uses 'Civil War' Show," *Florida Flambeau* (October 20, 1961): 1.

26. "Marching Chiefs Band Performs in Miami," *Florida Flambeau* (September 25, 1953): 3. The Ohio State marching band had performed a very similar show in 1952; see "Marching Band Will Repeat Wisconsin Show at Illinois," *The Lantern* (November 14, 1952): 1.

27. "Marching Chiefs to Perform at Freshman Game Tomorrow," *Florida Flambeau* (October 12, 1962): 3.

28. "Marching Chiefs featured in Saturday Performance," *Florida Flambeau* (October 30, 1953): 6.

29. "Marching Chiefs to Salute All Armed Forces Personnel," *Florida Flambeau* (November 10, 1961): 1.

30. "Band's Show Fetes Florida," *Florida Flambeau* (October 26, 1962): 5.

31. The quote is taken from the show script on the annual recording. My thanks to Paul A. Ort for sharing his copy with me.

32. Whitcomb, "Your Band CAN Entertain," 65–66.

33. *Tally-Ho* (FSU yearbook), 1955, dedication.

34. "Half-time Show Featured Band, Majorettes," *Florida Flambeau* (September 24, 1954): 4. Georgia has two fight songs, the official "Hail to Georgia," and the unofficial but more popular "Glory, Glory." The Chiefs probably played the latter.

35. Florence Helen Ashby interview, May 22, 2016.

36. Casavant, *Precision Drill*, 12.

37. See Zirkle, "Manley R. Whitcomb," 21 and 32–33.

38. Carter quoted in Thurston, "Charles Carter," 36.

39. *Ibid*.

40. Bowles, "Marching Band Trends," 37–38.

41. *Ibid.*, 38.

42. Ellen Taafe Zwilich interview, April 25, 2016.

43. Johnny M. Clark interview, November 22, 2016.
44. John Garrett interview, January 29, 2017.
45. Charles Bauerle interview, November 30, 2016.
46. Johnny M. Clark interview, November 22, 2016.
47. See Shin, "Okay, Seminoles," 110–111.
48. Jon D. Gilbert interview, November 29, 2016.
49. John Garrett interview, January 29, 2017.
50. Bentley Shellahamer interview, March 17, 1988; quoted in Paul, "A History," 50.
51. Bentley Shellahamer interview, December 5, 2015.
52. *Ibid.*
53. "Tradition Overthrown—Women Take Place," *The Lantern* (January 9, 1942): 2.
54. George Corradino interview, April 20, 2016.
55. Florence Helen Ashby interview, May 22, 2016.
56. See "Spirit at Game was Incomparable" [Letter to the Editor], *Florida Flambeau* (October 15, 1957): 2.
57. Florence Helen Ashby interview, May 22, 2016.
58. Gary J. Campbell, "Flying Seminoles Franklin, Puckett featured with Band Performance," *Florida Flambeau* (October 30, 1953): 3.
59. Richard (Dick) L. Puckett interview, August 12, 2016.
60. See *Tally-Ho* (1956): 303. Although Parsons appears in several photos captioned "Flying Seminoles," she was independent from that duo.
61. *Ibid.*
62. Several of Lipscomb's press releases from 1960 may be found in FSU's College of Music Band Archive.
63. Warren Gerard, "'Flying Seminoles' Novel Tradition," *Florida Flambeau* (November 8, 1957): 6.
64. See "Chiefs Give Bowl Show in Mobile," *Florida Flambeau* (December 19, 1961): 1. See also "Marching Chiefs Perform at Game," *Florida Flambeau* (September 29, 1961): 6.

65. Irvin Lipscomb, "Garnet & Gold Girls Beverly Calvert & Janice Freeman" [Marching Chiefs press release] (November 1, 1960), in College of Music Band Archive.
66. *Ibid.*
67. Mark Austin, "Plains Indians or Seminoles?" *Florida Flambeau* (October 14, 1958): 2.
68. Shin, "Okay, Seminoles," 105.
69. Zirkle, "Manley R. Whitcomb," 31–32; see also Thurston, "Charles Carter," 24.
70. Bennett Shelfer interview, January 26, 2016.
71. George Corradino interview, April 20, 2016.
72. "Marching Chiefs See Band Show Movies," *Florida Flambeau* (December 15, 1953): 5.
73. Tony Swain interview, January 22, 2017.
74. Florence Helen Ashby interview, May 22, 2016.
75. Charlet Poitevint, "'Flying High to Appear on TV Monday Morning," *Florida Flambeau* (October 26, 1956): 6.
76. "Chiefs Stay—So Does Acclaim for FSU" [editorial], *Florida Flambeau* (September 24, 1957): 2.
77. The Chiefs' Sun Bowl appearance was filmed in its entirety and titled "Marching Chiefs at the Sun Bowl" (photography by Bob Mouldin). See "Marching Chiefs in Bowl Films," *Florida Flambeau* (May 10, 1955): 1.
78. Dick Victory, "Second Period Decisive in El Paso Sun Bowl Duel," *Florida Flambeau* (January 7, 1955): 3.
79. Paul A. Ort interview, November 23, 2016.
80. Lil Classen interview, November 18, 2016.
81. Paul A. Ort interview, November 23, 2016.
82. *Ibid.*
83. "Chiefs Give Bowl Show in Mobile," *Florida Flambeau* (December 19, 1961): 1.
84. "Band Spoils Record," *Florida Flambeau* (October 18, 1955): 1.
85. Jim Ed Glass "Defends Chiefs" [Letter to the Editor], *Florida Flambeau* (October 21, 1955): 2.

86. *Ibid.*
87. Wiljohn, "Answers to This Week's Gripes," *Florida Flambeau* (October 21, 1955): 2.
88. Wiljohn, "Have the Chiefs Declared War?" *Florida Flambeau* (October 25, 1955): 2.
89. *Ibid.*
90. "Senate Lauds FSU's 'Chiefs,'" *Florida Flambeau* (October 28, 1955): 6.
91. Jack Murphy, "FSU-UF Athletic Question May Be Officially Raised," *Florida Flambeau* (February 10, 1950): 1.
92. *Ibid.*
93. Don Bacon, "Florida State Is Still Whimpering" [reprinted from *The Alligator*], *Florida Flambeau* (October 11, 1955): 2.
94. "U of F Won't Play Football with FSU Declares Woodruff," *Florida Flambeau* (January 7, 1955): 3; see also Fred Burrall, "Florida Coach Always Against Gridiron Test," *Florida Flambeau* (November 21, 1958): 1.
95. Campbell, *University in Transition*, 107.
96. *Ibid.*, 109.
97. Fred Burrall, "Florida Coach Always Against Gridiron Test," *Florida Flambeau* (November 21, 1958): 1, 6.
98. Bennett Shelfer interview, January 26, 2016.
99. Penny MacArthur Janowski interview, October 4, 2016.
100. Bennett Shelfer interview, January 26, 2016.
101. Jack Peacock, "FSU 'Frozen' 15–6 in Bowl; First Classic May Be Last," *Florida Flambeau* (December 16, 1958): 3.
102. "State Agencies Furnish Funds for the Marching Chiefs," *Florida Flambeau* (December 12, 1958): 1.
103. Bennett Shelfer interview, January 26, 2016.
104. *Ibid.*
105. Charles E. Beutel interview, June 27, 2016.
106. Sara Pankaskie interview, June 4, 2016.
107. Bentley Shellahamer interview, December 5, 2015.
108. "Bands Prepare Christmas Show," *Florida Flambeau* (December 6, 1955): 4.
109. Whitcomb, "The Future of the College Band," 85–7.
110. *Ibid.*, 86.
111. *Ibid.*, 87.

Chapter 5

1. My treatment of Carter's biography relies in part on Bob Thurston's excellent thesis, "The Life and Music of Charles Carter" (1992).
2. Andy Lindstrom, "Marching Chiefs' Music Man," *Tallahassee Democrat* (November 16, 1984): 5C.
3. Thanks to Bob Thurston for his clarification of Charlie's army experiences; email communication to the author, September 11, 2016.
4. Charlie Carter quoted in Zirkle, "Manley R. Whitcomb," 28; also in Thurston, "Charles Carter," 19.
5. For more on these various performing units, see Paul, "A History," 21.
6. Jack Haskins to Marjorie Nell Fogarty (April 12, 1949) in FSU Special Collections and Archives.
7. Clifford K. Madsen quoted in Paul, "A History," 20.
8. Robert (Bob) S. Thurston, email communication to the author, October 13, 2015.
9. George Allen, "Here Come the Chiefs and A & M's 100," *Tallahassee Democrat* (November 17, 1963): 31.
10. Interview with Charles Carter (October 1986) in Zirkle, "Manley R. Whitcomb," 31.
11. Johnny E. Clark interview, November 22, 2016.
12. Hugh Stanford, "Seminole Marching Chiefs Plan a Big Homecoming," *Florida Flambeau* (November 13, 1970): 2.
13. Sara Pankaskie interview, June 4, 2016.
14. Robert Sheldon interview, April 5, 2016.
15. *Ibid.*
16. Sara Pankaskie interview, June 4, 2016.
17. I experienced this once myself when talking to him in the early 1980s.
18. Curtis E. Falany interview, June 25, 2016.

19. Charles E. Beutel interview, June 27, 2016.
20. *Ibid.*
21. Curtis E. Falany interview, June 25, 2016.
22. Sara Pankaskie interview, June 4, 2016.
23. Ellen Taafe Zwilich interview, April 25, 2016.
24. Robert Sheldon interview, April 5, 2016.
25. Clifford K. Madsen interview at "Cliff Madsen—FBA Legacy Project (part 2)," Florida Music Educators Association (December 10, 2015). Accessed on August 1, 2016, at www.fba.flmusiced.org/legacy-project.
26. Clifford K. Madsen interview, August 24, 2016; Bentley Shellahamer interview, December 5, 2015.
27. "Marching Seminoles Get New Chief," *Florida Flambeau* (May 7, 1963): 1; Bentley Shellahamer interview, December 5, 2015.
28. Bob Mitchell, "Chiefs Boast New Sound," *Florida Flambeau* (September 17, 1963): 2.
29. Sara Pankaskie interview, June 4, 2016.
30. Clifford K. Madsen interview at "Cliff Madsen—FBA Legacy Project (part 2)," Florida Music Educators Association (December 10, 2015). Video accessed on August 1, 2016, at fba.flmusiced.org/legacy-project.
31. Curtis E. Falany interview, June 25, 2016.
32. J. Michael Pate interview, August 22, 2016.
33. *Ibid.*
34. Bob Mitchell, "Chiefs Boast New Sound," *Florida Flambeau* (September 17, 1963): 2.
35. *Ibid.*
36. Tommie Wright quoted in Manahan, "Musician Memoirs" (blog).
37. Clifford K. Madsen interview, August 24, 2016.
38. *Ibid.*
39. *Ibid.*
40. "Flair Added to Football Game," *Florida Flambeau* (October 1, 1964): 3.
41. "Marching Chiefs Entertain 'Bama," *Florida Flambeau* (October 22, 1965): 7.
42. "Chiefs Feature Political Theme," *Florida Flambeau* (October 29, 1964): 3.
43. "Band to Do Review," *Florida Flambeau* (October 9, 1964): 7.
44. *Ibid.*
45. "Bands March for Houston," *Florida Flambeau* (September 16, 1966): 1.
46. "Got a Groovy Thing Going," *Florida Flambeau* (September 23, 1970): 6.
47. "Chiefs Will Boost Seminoles in Miami," *Florida Flambeau* (October 29, 1970): 16.
48. "Chiefs Have Spirit," *Florida Flambeau* (November 4, 1963): 2.
49. Bob Mitchell, "FSU Marching Chiefs Defeather Miami Mascott [*sic*]," *Florida Flambeau* (September 25, 1963): 1.
50. See a photo of the marquee at *Florida Flambeau* (September 25, 1963): 4. My thanks to members of the 60s list, especially Al Krombach, Mike Pate, and Gene Crowe, for directing my attention to the precise wording.
51. Gene S. Crowe interview, August 2, 2016.
52. Charles E. Beutel interview, June 27, 2016.
53. *Ibid.*
54. J. Michael Pate interview, August 22, 2016.
55. *Ibid.*
56. Hugh Stanford, "Seminole Marching Chiefs Plan a Big Homecoming," *Florida Flambeau* (November 13, 1970): 2; and J. Michael Pate interview, August 22, 2016.
57. J. Michael Pate interview, August 22, 2016.
58. *Ibid.*
59. *Ibid.*
60. W. Alan Smith, email communication to the author, November 11, 2016.
61. "Marching Chiefs Win Again," *Tally Ho* 16 (1963): 216–217.
62. Bob Mitchell, "Chiefs Boast New Sound," *Florida Flambeau* (September 17, 1963): 2.
63. W. Alan Smith interview, June 26, 2016.
64. Alan Bailey, "Marching Chiefs Winners in Tampa Half-Time Show," *Florida Flambeau* (December 1, 1970): 1.
65. See photo and caption in the *Tallahassee Democrat* (November 27, 1970): 1.

66. Alan Bailey, "Marching Chiefs Winners in Tampa Half-Time Show," *Florida Flambeau* (December 1, 1970): 1.
67. Bob Mitchell, "Boda's 'Ballet for Band' to Be Half-Time Show," *Florida Flambeau* (November 14, 1963): 1.
68. I had the privilege of taking classes with Boda in the 1980s and '90s. Not only was he a universally beloved man, but he was also a highly respected teacher; his "Masterworks" classes were virtuoso lectures in music history and literature.
69. Untitled, undated press release in "Braunagel 1962–70, Chiefs" [file folder] at the College of Music Band Archive.
70. Ibid.
71. Paul Basler, email communication to the author, September 20, 2015.
72. Bob Mitchell, "Boda's 'Ballet for Band' to Be Half-Time Show," *Florida Flambeau* (November 14, 1963): 1.
73. *Tallahassee Democrat* (November 18, 1963): 4
74. Ibid.; also quoted in Paul, "A History," 24–25.
75. *Tallahassee Democrat* (November 18, 1963): 4
76. Clifford K. Madsen interview, August 24, 2016.
77. "Chiefs to Play Carter Original Half[time]-Show," *Florida Flambeau* (November 20, 1964): 3.
78. "42,500 Expected at UF Contest," *Florida Flambeau* (November 18, 1964): 1.
79. "Chiefs to Play Carter Original Half[time]-Show," *Florida Flambeau* (November 20, 1964): 3.
80. *Music at Half-time, FSU vs. Florida, November 21, 1964* [show script] in "Braunagel 1962–70, Chiefs" [file folder] at the College of Music Band Archive.
81. Gene S. Crowe interview, August 2, 2016.
82. "Chiefs Offer Something Special," *Florida Flambeau* (October 24, 1969): 1.
83. W. Alan Smith interview, June 26, 2016.
84. Ibid.
85. "FSU Band Disgusted" [Letter to the Editor from a group of Marching Chiefs], *Florida Flambeau* (October 14, 1964): 2.
86. Thomas E. McCrea, "Boos [Pow Wow]" [Letter to the Editor], *Florida Flambeau* (October 14, 1964): 2.
87. William H. Grimm, "Condemns Pow Wow" [Letter to the Editor], *Florida Flambeau* (October 14, 1964): 2, 3.
88. Curtis E. Falany interview, June 25, 2016.
89. Ila Rubel, "FSU Women's Rules Too Restrictive," *Florida Flambeau* (January 21, 1964): 2.
90. Curtis E. Falany interview, June 25, 2016.
91. Steven L. Sparkman interview, August 30, 2016.
92. Gene S. Crowe interview, August 2, 2016.
93. Sam Miller, "Champion Answers Blacks' Resolutions," *Florida Flambeau* (October, 18, 1968): 1.
94. Marshall, *Tumultuous Sixties*, 104–105.
95. White, "From Desegregation to Integration," 495 and 479.
96. Jennifer Rutland, "Indians Upset Over Name of Spirit Chief," *Florida Flambeau* (October 12, 1970): 6.
97. "Basketball Chief Chooses Yahola as Indian Name" [Letter to the Editor], *Florida Flambeau* (October 14, 1970): 4.
98. "Agrees with SG Pres.," *Florida Flambeau* (October 16, 1964): 2.
99. [Name Withheld], "Blasts Unjust Charges" [Letter to the Editor], *Florida Flambeau* (October 16, 1964): 3.
100. "Student Support Can Send FSU's Chiefs to Sun Bowl," *Florida Flambeau* (December 2, 1966 [page one incorrectly dated December 1]): 1.
101. "Send State's Marching Chiefs to Sun Bowl," *Florida Flambeau* (December 2, 1966): 8–9.
102. Gonzalez quoted in "Student Support Can Send FSU's Chiefs to Sun Bowl," *Florida Flambeau* (December 2, 1966 [page one is incorrectly dated December 1]): 1.
103. "FSU's Chiefs Go to Bowl," *Florida Flambeau* (January 6, 1967): 3.
104. "Student Boosters Praise Chiefs" [Letter to the Editor], *Florida Flambeau* (January 10, 1967): 4.
105. J. Michael Pate, email communication to the author, January 19, 2017.

106. "Chiefs Give Finale," *Florida Flambeau* (December 1, 1967): 10.
107. Bennett Shelfer interview, January 26, 2016.
108. Kim Rogers, "A Full-time Halftime Show," *Florida Flambeau* (October 7, 1970): 16.
109. Chris Haughee interview, May 10, 2016.

Chapter 6

1. Richard (Dick) L. Puckett interview, August 12, 2016; George R. Corradino interview, January 28, 2017.
2. Florence Helen Ashby interview, May 22, 2016.
3. Some of this information comes from Dick Mayo himself; see "Reunion: F.S.U. Marching Chiefs; Individual Bios." (April 12, 2007). My thanks to Paul Ort for sharing this recording with me.
4. William (Bill) J. Hinkle interview, May 25, 2016.
5. See *Tally-Ho* (1957): 254.
6. Press release, FSU Office of Information Services (April 29, 1971), in FSU Heritage Protocol & University Archives, "Music-1972" file.
7. "Marching Chiefs Practice for New Season," *Florida Flambeau* (September 13, 1971): D-18.
8. See "FSU Adds Programs in Band and Music Education Areas," *Florida Music Director* 24 (January 1971): 23.
9. Kim Rogers, "Mayo Introduces Modern Courses," *Florida Flambeau* (January 11, 1971): 7.
10. George Corradino interview, April 20, 2016.
11. Sara Pankaskie interview, June 4, 2016.
12. *Ibid.*
13. *Florida State vs. Memphis State, November 15, 1969* [show script] in "Braunagel 1962–70, Chiefs" [file folder] at the College of Music Band Archive.
14. W. Alan Smith interview, June 26, 2016.
15. My thanks to Robert (Bob) S. Thurston for clarifying this in an email communication to the author, January 23, 2017. The tonal bass drums arrived in 1979.
16. Betty Reid, "Marching Chiefs: Backbone of Spirit," *Florida Flambeau* (October 8, 1971): C1.
17. W. Alan Smith interview, June 26, 2016.
18. George Rosete, email communication to the author, January 24, 2017.
19. *Ibid.*
20. William (Bill) J. Hinkle interview, May 25, 2016.
21. Ray Reynolds, "Chiefs Add Musical Virtuosity to Homecoming," *Florida Flambeau* (October 19, 1973): 7.
22. *Ibid.* This is the first mention in the *Flambeau* of the Glue Crew.
23. Betty Reid, "Marching Chiefs: Backbone of Spirit," *Florida Flambeau* (October 8, 1971): C1.
24. Mayo quoted in Thurston, "Charles Carter," 43.
25. Sara Pankaskie interview, June 4, 2016.
26. John Carmichael interview, October 18, 2016.
27. Sara Pankaskie interview, June 4, 2016.
28. John Carmichael interview, October 18, 2016.
29. Chris Haughee interview, May 10, 2016.
30. W. Alan Smith interview, June 26, 2016.
31. *Ibid.*
32. William (Bill) J. Hinkle interview, May 25, 2016.
33. See Thurston, "Charles Carter," 37–38.
34. Interview with Bentley Shellahamer, December 5, 2015.
35. "News You Can Use," *Florida Flambeau* (July 14, 1975): 7.
36. Bill Haggard interview, November 8, 2016.
37. *Ibid.*
38. Timothy G. Wise interview, September 22, 2016.
39. *Ibid.*
40. Bill Haggard interview, November 8, 2016.
41. Sid Smith, "Band Uniforms Cost SG $18,000," *Florida Flambeau* (September 29, 1972): 1.

42. "Sports Financing Undermines Library" [Letter to the Editor], *Florida Flambeau* (October 20, 1972): 4.
43. "Anti-Football Views Clarified" [Letter to the Editor], *Florida Flambeau* (October 20, 1972): 4.
44. "Football Now Uses Entertainment Approach," *Florida Flambeau* (October 4, 1974): 7.
45. *Ibid.*
46. Davis Whitman, "New Thrills Needed for Half-Time," *Florida Flambeau* (October 9, 1974): 4.
47. "FSU Band" [Letter to the Editor], *Florida Flambeau* (October 5, 1973): 5.
48. "A Chief Replies" [Letter to the Editor], *Florida Flambeau* (October 9, 1973): 4.
49. "Another Chief" [Letter to the Editor], *Florida Flambeau* (October 10, 1973): 5.
50. "Marching Chiefs" [Letter to the Editor], *Florida Flambeau* (October 23, 1973): 4.
51. Robin Sexner, "Marching Band" [Letter to the Editor], *Florida Flambeau* (October 25, 1974): 4.
52. For an overview of these events, see Marshall, *Tumultuous Sixties*, 21–27.
53. For details on the "Night of the Bayonets," see Parr, "The Forgotten Radicals," 1–2.
54. Thomas E. Drick interview, December 15, 2016.
55. David Morrill, "FSU Football: An Autopsy," *Florida Flambeau* (December 6, 1973): 5.
56. For details see Bruce Raben and Davis Whiteman, "Report Clears Coach Jones," *Florida Flambeau* (October 26, 1973): 1.
57. Prior to the Syria trip, the Chiefs had been called "The Greatest Band in the Land" (as had many other bands) and other names. See, for example, "Marching Chiefs Drum Major Is a Miami Music Ed. Student," *Florida Flambeau* (September 27, 1957): 4.
58. Marshall, *The Tumultuous Sixties*, 211.
59. See Thurston, "Charles Carter," 46.
60. Leesa Brown, "Marching Chiefs Excel in Skill, Precision," *Florida Flambeau* (October 17, 1974): 6.
61. "Bands Heading to Syria," *Florida Flambeau* (August 2, 1974): 3
62. Harry E. Price interview, November 21, 2016.
63. William (Bill) J. Hinkle interview, May 25, 2016.
64. Robert Duke interview, October 21, 2015.
65. John Carmichael interview, October 18, 2016.
66. "FSU Musicians Conclude Tour," *Florida Flambeau* (September 23, 1974): 3.
67. Richard Mayo, trip memo and itinerary [undated]. My thanks to Sara Pankaskie for providing this document.
68. Marshall, *The Tumultuous Sixties*, 212.
69. *Ibid.*
70. John Carmichael interview, October 18, 2016.
71. "FSU Musicians Conclude Tour," *Florida Flambeau* (September 23, 1974): 3.
72. See Paul, "A History," 41.
73. Mike Osinski, "Marching Chiefs Step Out Again," *Florida Flambeau* (September 15, 1975): 62. If one actually does the math, one concludes that Mayo was exaggerating to make a point.
74. Leesa Brown, "Marching Chiefs Excel in Skill, Precision," *Florida Flambeau* (October 17, 1974): 6.
75. Vanessa Williams, "Chiefs' Music Most Important," *Florida Flambeau* (November 14, 1975): 20.
76. "Mudra's Job in the Balance," *Florida Flambeau* (September 15, 1975): 32.
77. Nancy Haughee interview, May 10, 2016.
78. "Marshall Raised Mudra Funds," *Florida Flambeau* (January 12, 1976): 1.
79. Michael Crawford [Letter to the Editor], "Marshall Another Richard Nixon," *Florida Flambeau* (November 1, 1974): 4.
80. Creston Nelson, "Marshall Calls It Quits," *Florida Flambeau* (March 9, 1976): 1.
81. "Mayo Quits FSU Band," *Florida Flambeau* (April 5, 1976): 1.
82. Interview with Robert Duke, October 21, 2015.
83. William (Bill) J. Hinkle interview, May 25, 2016.
84. Alan Jenkins, "Protest Shows FSU

Music School Unrest," *Tallahassee Democrat* (November 26, 1978).
85. William (Bill) J. Hinkle interview, May 25, 2016.
86. Richard Mayo quoted in Paul, "A History," 44.
87. *Ibid.*
88. Bill Haggard interview, November 8, 2016.
89. Clifford K. Madsen interview, August 24, 2016.
90. Harry E. Price interview, November 21, 2016.
91. W. Alan Smith interview, June 26, 2016. Mayo's three-piece suits were generally worn indoors; outdoors he can frequently be seen wearing just a tie. I have yet to discover a photo of him tie-less.
92. William (Bill) J. Hinkle interview, May 25, 2016.
93. Clifford K. Madsen interview, August 24, 2016.
94. George Corradino interview, April 20, 2016.
95. Bill Haggard interview, November 8, 2016.
96. *Ibid.*
97. Bentley Shellahamer has said that most of the Chiefs section names, "except for Big 8, which has always been Big 8," originated in the Mayo era (Bentley Shellahamer interview, December 5, 2015). Also, the 1970 movie "Five Easy Pieces"—a name used by the clarinet section—was first shown on campus in October 1973.
98. Robert Duke interview, October 21, 2015.
99. My thanks to Christian Dickinson for pointing this out. The replacements were Carl Bjerregaard (symphonic bands and wind ensembles), William Raxsdale (Marching Chiefs), and Bill Kennedy (jazz).
100. "8 Join FSU Music Faculty," *Tallahassee Democrat* (August 29, 1976): 12E.
101. Raxsdale quoted in Thurston, "Charles Carter," 47.
102. There is some dispute about how many new shows were performed that year. Some members recollect that there was just a single show; others recall that three shows were given.
103. Clifford K. Madsen, quoted in Paul, "A History," 48–49.
104. Robert Duke interview, October 21, 2015.
105. Sara Pankaskie interview, June 4, 2016.
106. Nancy Haughee interview, May 10, 2016.
107. Christian Dickinson interview, December 13, 2016.
108. Samuel T. Anderson, "Chiefs' Quality Dwindling" [Letter to the Editor], *Florida Flambeau* (October 29, 1976): 5.

Chapter 7

1. David Bedingfield, "Bowden Named New FSU Head Coach," *Florida Flambeau* (January 13: 1976): 8.
2. Robert Mashburn, "Bowden Promises Enthusiasm," *Florida Flambeau* (September 13, 1976): 76.
3. Godwin Kelly, "Seminole Fans Should Not Get Their Hopes Up Too High This Fall," *Florida Flambeau* (August 25, 1977): 8.
4. Mary Tebo, "What About Monday's Heroes?," *Florida Flambeau* (September 15, 1980): 83.
5. Andy Kanengiser, "Sliger's Chances Revived," *Florida Flambeau* (August 23, 1976): 1.
6. *Ibid.*
7. *Ibid.*
8. Bentley Shellahamer interview, December 5, 2015.
9. *Ibid.*
10. *Ibid.*
11. *Ibid.*
12. *Ibid.*
13. Bennett Shelfer interview, January 26, 2016.
14. Bentley Shellahamer interview, December 5, 2015.
15. "Thanks, Marching Chiefs," *Tallahassee Democrat* (September 23, 1980): 4-A.
16. Bentley Shellahamer interview, June 16, 2016.
17. Bentley Shellahamer interview, December 5, 2015.
18. *Ibid.*
19. Fred Blosser, "Praising the Marching Chiefs" [Letter to the Editor], *Florida Flambeau* (November 12, 1981): 6.

20. Bentley Shellahamer interview, June 16, 2016.
21. Bentley Shellahamer interview, June 16, 2016.
22. Bentley Shellahamer quoted in Paul, "A History," 73.
23. "Chiefs Get New Chief," *Tallahassee Democrat* (April 19, 1982): 2B.
24. David F. Westberry interview, April 20, 2016
25. *Ibid.*
26. Andre Arrouet interview, August 6, 2016.
27. *Ibid.*
28. Heinz Kluetmeier, "All Horns Up!!!," *Sports Illustrated* 57 (December 6, 1982): 44–51.
29. *Ibid.*
30. *Ibid.*
31. See Gerald D. Poe, "The Making of a Super Band for Super Bowl XVIII," *Florida Music Director* 37 (April 1984): 10–11.
32. Andre Arrouet interview, August 6, 2016.
33. *Ibid.*
34. See Gerald D. Poe, "The Making of a Super Band for Super Bowl XVIII," *Florida Music Director* 37 (April 1984): 10–11.
35. See "FSU Marching Chiefs" [Photo with caption], *Florida Flambeau* (November 25, 1958): 1.
36. David F. Westberry interview, April 20, 2016.
37. *Ibid.*
38. *Ibid.*
39. Interview with Bentley Shellahamer, December 5, 2015.
40. From the script to "A Seminole Saga" (1988). Accessed at www.youtube.com/watch?v=e0_aHZmz0is on August 3, 2016.
41. *Ibid.*
42. Carter P. Vaverek interview, January 8, 2016.
43. Clifford K. Madsen interview, August 24, 2016.
44. Robert Sheldon interview, April 5, 2016.
45. *Ibid.*
46. *Ibid.*
47. *Ibid.*
48. *Ibid.*
49. *Ibid.*
50. *Ibid.*
51. *Ibid.*
52. *Ibid.*

Chapter 8

1. Patrick Dunnigan interview, October 20, 2016.
2. Lesley Ray Zebrowitz interview, November 6, 2016.
3. *Ibid.*
4. David Plack interview, July 12, 2016.
5. *Ibid.*
6. Patrick Dunnigan interview, October 20, 2016.
7. *Ibid.*
8. David Plack interview, July 12, 2016.
9. David F. Westberry interview, April 20, 2016.
10. *Ibid.*
11. Clifford K. Madsen interview, December 6, 2016.
12. Lesley Ray Zebrowitz interview, November 6, 2016.
13. Kelly Korey, "Does FSU Enforce the University's Hazing Policy?," *FSView and Florida Flambeau* (September 8, 1994).
14. Letter to the Marching Chiefs, from the School of Music ad hoc disciplinary committee (September 27, 1994): 2.
15. Thomas B. Pfankuch, "FAMU Band Hazing Goes Way Back, Reports Say," *Florida Times-Union* (November 19, 2011).
16. "Hazing Deserves Harsher Penalty" (editorial), *South Florida Sun Sentinel* (October 8, 1994).
17. Letter to Dr. Jon Piersol, Dean of the FSU School of Music, from the School's ad hoc disciplinary committee (September 2, 1999): 2.
18. *Ibid.*
19. Melanie Yeager, "Chiefs Drum Major Barred for Hazing," *Tallahassee Democrat* (September 9, 1999).
20. Lesley Ray Zebrowitz interview, November 6, 2016.
21. David F. Westberry interview, April 20, 2016.
22. Patrick Dunnigan interview, October 20, 2016.
23. Camp Kirkland interview, July 6, 2016.

24. *Ibid.*
25. Gene S. Crowe interview, August 2, 2016.
26. Robert (Bob) S. Thurston, email communication to the author, August 24, 2016.
27. *Ibid.*
28. *Ibid.*
29. *Ibid.*
30. Charlie Carter as told to Robert (Bob) S. Thurston, e-mail communication to the author, August 24, 2016.
31. Thurston, "The Life and Music of Charles Carter," 62.
32. *Ibid.*
33. Patrick Dunnigan, email communication to the author, January 5, 2017.
34. Patrick Dunnigan interview, October 20, 2016.
35. Robert (Bob) S. Thurston, email communication to the author, August 7, 2016.
36. FSU won the 2007 Track & Field championship, although, owing to an academic scandal that rocked the athletic department, the NCAA vacated that crown in 2010. None of the members of the track & field team were actually involved in the scandal.
37. David Plack interview, July 12, 2016.
38. See U.S. Department of Education, Office of Civil Rights, "Title IX and Sex Discrimination" at www2.ed.gov/about/offices/list/ocr/docs/tix_dis.html (accessed September 26, 2016).
39. Hanson, et al., *More Than Title IX*, 166.
40. David Plack interview, July 12, 2016.
41. *Ibid.*
42. *Ibid.*
43. Jimbo Fisher, 2016 address to the Marching Chiefs (August 25, 2016) found at www.youtube.com/watch?v=19qJu4tWsDw (accessed October 30, 2016).
44. Patrick Dunnigan interview, October 20, 2016.
45. *Ibid.*
46. *Ibid.*
47. Lesley Ray Zebrowitz interview, November 6, 2016.
48. *Ibid.*

Post-Game

1. "Alma Mater," [editorial], *Florida Flambeau* (November 11, 1970): 4
2. "Let's Swap Alma Mater for One We Can Sing," *Florida Flambeau* (September 18, 1959): 2. The opposite occurs these days, of course, as the "FSU" portion is commonly roared, while the first part of the lyrics are largely whispered, if that.
3. "Alma Mater," [editorial], *Florida Flambeau* (November 11, 1970): 4.
4. *Ibid.*
5. Anne Marie Gregory, "Three-Part Musical Show Presented by Collegians," *Florida Flambeau* (December 8, 1950): 1.
6. Swingle, "A History," 53–4.
7. "Jett Munroe Reigns Over Homecoming," *Florida Flambeau* (October 31, 1950): 1.
8. "Male Chorus Group Collegians Serenade Campus Tonight," *Florida Flambeau* (November 17, 1950): 1.
9. Charlie Carter quoted in Thurston, "The Life and Music of Charles Carter," 77.
10. Bennet Shelfer interview, January 26, 2016.
11. "Band's 'Halftime' Dedicated to All," *Florida Flambeau* (October 31, 1958): 5.
12. This account, penned by Paul A. Ort, is found on two identical plaques that were presented to the College of Music and FSU's ROTC in 2007 (Paul A. Ort, email communication to the author, January 18, 2017).
13. See Walter Goodstein, "Parades Will Open Carnival Pageant Season," *Times-Picayune* (February 5, 1956): 1.
14. Charlie's "discovery," according to the plaque, may have been aided by others.
15. Sara Pankaskie interview, June 4, 2016.
16. *Ibid.*
17. Lilian Classen interview, November 18, 2016.
18. Nancy Haughee interview, May 10, 2016.
19. Charlie Carter quoted in Thurston, "The Life and Music of Charles Carter," 25–26.

Bibliography

Interviews and/or Email Correspondence

Frances E. Adams
Andre Arrouet
Florence Helen Ashby
Paul Basler
Charles Bauerle
Charles E. Beutel
John C. Carmichael
Johnny M. Clark
Lilian O. Classen
George R. Corradino
Gene S. Crowe
Christian Dickinson
Thomas E. Drick
Robert A. Duke
Patrick Dunnagin
Curtis E. Falany
John Garrett
Jon D. Gilbert
William (Bill) K. Haggard
Chris Haughee
Nancy Spencer Haughee
William (Bill) J. Hinkle
Penny MacArthur Janowski
Camp Kirkland
Clifford K. Madsen
Paul A. Ort
Sara C. Pankaskie
J. Michael Pate
David Plack
Harry E. Price
Richard (Dick) L. Puckett
George Rosete
Robert Sheldon
Bennett Shelfer
Bentley Shellahamer
W. Alan Smith
Steven L. Sparkman
Tony Swain
Robert (Bob) S. Thurston
Carter P. Vaverek
David F. Westberry
Timothy G. Wise
Lesley Ray Zebrowitz
Ellen Taafe Zwilich

Archival Resources

College of Music Band Archive. Florida State University. Tallahassee.
Heritage Protocol & University Archives. Robert M. Strozier Library. Florida State University. Tallahassee.
State Library and Archives of Florida. Division of Library and Information Services. Florida Department of State. Tallahassee.

Books, Dissertations, Theses and Articles

Avant, Fenton Garnett Davis. *My Tallahassee*. Tallahassee, FL: L'Avant Studios, 1983.
Bayless, A. J. "Showtime Stigma versus Precision Magic." *The Instrumentalist* (November/December 1952): 20–21.
Bonner, John Brian. "Eugene Weigel: Major Contributions to the Music Program of The Ohio State University." M.A. thesis, Ohio State University, 1972.
Bowden, Bobby, with Mark Schlabach. *What it Means to Be a Seminole*. Chicago: Triumph Books, 2007.
____ (with Steve Ellis). *Bobby Bowden's Tales from the Seminoles Sidelines*. Champaign, IL: Sports Publishing, 2004.
Bowles, Richard. "Marching Band Trends in the Southeast." *Instrumentalist* (August 1963): 37–38.
Braunagel, Robert T. "The Marching Band: A New Direction." *Instrumentalist* (December 1964): 76–77.
Campbell, Doak S. *University in Transition*. Tallahassee: Florida State University, 1964.
Casavant, A. R. *Precision Drill*. Chattanooga, TN: ARC Publishing Company, 1957.
Cornell, George A. *A Manual of Marching*. Springfield, MA: Seminar Publishing Company, 1906.
Davis, Hannah Wiatt. "What's in a Song? The Many Melodies of FSU." *Illuminations* [the online magazine/newsletter of Florida State University Special Collections and Archives Division] (September 22, 2015).
Dodd, William G. "Early Education in Tallahassee and the West Florida Seminary, Now Florida State University" [Part 1]. *Florida Historical Quarterly* 27/1 (July 1948): 1–27.
____. "Early Education in Tallahassee and the West Florida Seminary, Now Florida State University" [Part 2]. *Florida Historical Quarterly* 27/2 (October 1948): 157–180.
Grabel, Victor. "College Football Bands." *Etude* 55 (November 1937): 717.
Groene, Bertram H. *Ante-Bellum Tallahassee*. Tallahassee, FL: Florida Heritage Foundation, 1971.
Hanson, Katherine, Vivian Guilfoy, and Sarita Pillai. *More Than Title IX: How Equity in Education Has Shaped the Nation*. Lanham, MD: Rowman & Littlefield, 2009.
Hare, Julianne. *Tallahassee: A Capital City History*. Charleston, SC: Arcadia Publishing, 2002.
Jones, James P. *F.S.U. One Time! A History of Seminole Football*. Tallahassee, FL: Sentry Press, 1973.
Kluetmeier, Heinz. "All Horns Up!!!" *Sports Illustrated* 57 (December 6, 1982): 44–51.
Manahan, Theresa. "Musician Memoirs: Tommie Wright." ESPN (blog), December 31, 2012. Retrieved from http://espn.go.com/blog/playbook/fandom/post/_/id/16208/undefined.
Marshall, J. Stanley. *The Tumultuous Sixties: Campus Unrest and Student Life at a Southern University*. Tallahassee, FL: Sentry Press, 2006.
Mayo, Richard D., producer/director. *FSU Bands: Proud Heritage, Bright Future* [audiovisual material/documentary]. Tallahassee, FL: Seminole Productions, 1993.
McCarrell, Lamar Keith. "A Historical Review of the College Band Movement from 1875–1969." Ph.D. dissertation, Florida State University, Tallahassee, 1971.
____. "The Impact of World War II Upon the College Band." *Journal of Band Research* 10/1 (Fall 1973): 3–8.
Opsahl, Julian E. "What About that Half-time Show?" *The Instrumentalist* (September 1952): 12–13.
Parr, Stephen Eugene. "The Forgotten Radicals: The New Left in the Deep South, Florida State University, 1960–1972." Ph.D. dissertation, Florida State University, Tallahassee, 2000.

Paul, Timothy Allan. "A History of the Band Program at Florida State University, 1969–1987." M.M.E. thesis, Florida State University, Tallahassee, 1989.
Piersol, Frank A. "The Future of the College Marching Band." *The Instrumentalist* (June 1965): 89–90.
Revelli, William D. "The Gridiron Marching Band." *Instrumentalist* (September 1966): 44–46.
———. "When G. I. Joe Comes Marching Back to College." *Etude* 64 (May 1946): 259.
Righter, Charles B. *Gridiron Pageantry.* New York: Carl Fischer, 1941.
———. "How to Kill the Marching Band." *The Instrumentalist* (May-June 1950): 8–9.
Roberts, Diane. *Tribal: College Football and the Secret Heart of America.* New York: Harper, 2015.
Sellers, Robin Jeanne. "*Femina Perfecta*: A History of Florida State College for Women, 1905–1947." Ph.D. dissertation, Florida State University, Tallahassee, 1995.
Shin, Dong Hyuk. "Okay, Seminoles, Take Over from Here: Native American Mascot as Organization Builders at Florida State University." Ph.D. dissertation, University of Iowa, Iowa City, 2015.
Sieradzki, Amanda. "Conductor Patrick Dunnigan Explores the Spatial Element of Music." *Tallahassee Democrat* (December 4, 2015). Accessed online.
Sousa, John Phillip. "Why the World Needs Bands." *Etude* 48 (September 1930): 613–614.
Swingle, Marilyn Ruth. "A History of the Florida State University School of Music." Ph.D. dissertation, Florida State University, Tallahassee, 1974.
Thompson, Maurice. *A Tallahassee Girl.* Boston: James R. Osgood & Co., 1882.
Thurston, Robert Samuel. "The Life and Music of Charles Carter." M.M.E. thesis, Florida State University, Tallahassee, 1992.
Whitcomb, Manley R. "The College Band Director and Contemporary Music." *Instrumentalist* (June 1964): 64–65.
———. "Controversy and Dialogue." *The Instrumentalist* (September 1963): 32.
———. "The Future of the College Band." *School Musician* 39 (November 1967): 85–87.
———. "The World of Change and the School Band." *The School Musician Director and Teacher* 41 (August/September 1969): 68–73.
———. "Your Band CAN Entertain." *The Instrumentalist* (November 1956): 62–66.
White, Derrick E. "From Desegregation to Integration: Race, Football, and 'Dixie' at the University of Florida." *Florida Historical Quarterly* 88/4 (Spring 2010): 469–96.
Woodward, Eddie. *Florida State University.* Charleston, SC: Arcadia Publishing (The Campus History Series), 2012.
Wright, Al G. "Marching Maneuvers 'That All May See.'" *The Instrumentalist* (September-October 1949): 8–11.
Yoder, Paul. *Haskell's Rascals: Snare Drum Trio with Band.* Chicago: Neil A. Kjos, 1954.
Zirkle, Dean Lester. "The Contributions of Manley R. Whitcomb: Music Educator, Band Director." M.M.E. thesis, Florida State University, Tallahassee, 1987.

Periodicals

Etude
Florida Flambeau
Florida Historical Quarterly
Florida Music Director
Florida Times-Union (Jacksonville)
FSView and Florida Flambeau
The Instrumentalist
Journal of Band Research
The Lantern (Ohio State University)
Miami Herald
School Musician
Search Light (Bainbridge, Georgia)
South Florida Sun Sentinel
Sports Illustrated
Tallahassee Democrat
Time Magazine
Times-Picayune (New Orleans)

Index

Numbers in **_bold italics_** indicate pages with photographs

Abraxas 125–126
academic culture 172–173
academic programs 14–15
Adderley, Cannonball 123
African-American 79
Afro-American Student Union 114–115
AFROTC *see* Air Force Reserve Officer Training Corps
Air Force, U.S. 62–63, 72
Air Force Reserve Officer Training Corps (AFROTC) 192
Alabama Technical High School 34
Allen, George 95
Allen, Susan ***122***
Alley, Doug 56–58
The Alligator 86
Alma Mater see "High O'er the Towering Pines"
Alumni Band 106–107
"America the Beautiful" 6
An American in Paris 71
Anderson, Leroy 70
announcers 159–160
Appalachian State University 154–155
Argento, Dominick 93
Armstrong, Louis 123
Army, U.S. 92
Arnaud, Leo 169
arrangements 165; by Braunagel 58, 99; by Carter 169–170, 177–182, 192; classic 170; by Dunnigan 180–181; by Shellahamer 178–180
Arranger in Residence 97
Arrouet, Andre 154–159, 178

Artist Series 84–85
Arts & Props Committee "Glue Crew" 127–128
Ashby, Florence 68–69
Askew, Rube 55
athletics 86; *see also* football; track & field
Atlanta Braves 77
Atlantic Coast Conference 185
Auburn University 185
auditions 23, 27, 160
Austin Symphony Orchestra 52
Avant, Fenton Garnett Davis 15
"Ave Maria" 71

Bacon, Don 86
Bainbridge, GA 13
"The Bainbridge Game" 13
Bainum, Glenn C. 65–66
Baker, John L. 168
Ballet for Band 109–112
Ballet for Band No. 2 112
Baltimore Symphony Orchestra 39
band budgets 67
band camp 69, ***143***
Band Day 60–62, ***62***, 102–103, ***157***
band formations 31–32, ***46***, 49, ***70***, 102–107, 128–129, 150, ***162***, 163
band pageantry 30–34, 79
bands 1, 3, 23, 28, 45, 90–91; development 40, 95–97; evolution 194–196; at FSCW 19–22, ***29***, ***37–38***, ***41***, ***51***
Barfield, Tommy 159
Barlow, Wayne 93

215

Index

basketball 184
Basler, Paul 110
bassoon *61*
Battle of Natural Bridge 11
Belafonte, Harry 162
Belton, Carrie 5
Bernstein, Leonard 121, 140
Beutel, Charles E. "Chuck" 89, 97, 105
Beyoncé *see* Knowles, Beyoncé
Big 8 75–76, 126, *173*, 178, *187*
Billock, Mildred 19
Blood, Sweat & Tears 125
Blosser, Fred 153
Bluegrass Bowl 88
Board of Control 86–87
Board of Regents 147
Board of Student Publications 133
Boda, John 109–111, 206n68
Boston College 83
Boulevard Drive- In Theatre 104–105
Bowden, Bobby 146–147, 167, 185
Bowden, Terry 185
Bowl Committee 116
Bowles, Richard 75
Braunagel, Robert "Brownie" 1, *56*; arrangements 58, 99; career 52–60, 65, 97–101, *98*, 118–120, 193–194; style 63–64, 81–82, 99–103, 109–112
Briggs, Robert 55
Brigham Young University 98
Broadway shows 126
Broomstick Brigade *22*
Brown, Lee 109
Bruce, Jim *151*, 157
Brussels World's Fair 102
Buckman, H.H. 14
Buckman Bill 14
budgets 85, 117–118, 130–131, 153; *see also* band budgets; fund raising
Bulletin 53
Burton, Karen 136–137
Butler University 58

cadence 126
Cahn, Sammy 71
Caldwell, Millard F. 36, 42
Calvert, Beverly 80
Camp Gordon Johnston 36, 39
Campbell, Doak S.: career 28–29, 79–80, 86–87; leadership 32–34, 39–40, 43, 60
campus culture 102
capitalism 17
career: of Braunagel 52–60, 65, 97–101, *98*, 118–120, 193–194; of Campbell 28–29, 79–80, 86–87; of Carter 74–77, 83, 91–97, 100–101, 111–112, 126–127, 157; of Dunnigan 168–172, 177–179, 194; of Opperman 17–19, 23, 33, 37–78, 43; of Sellers 24–28, 30, 52, 193; of Shellahamer 78, 89–90, 148–156, 179–180; of Whitcomb, M. 65–69, 74–75, 78–80
Carlton, William 27
Carmichael, John 127, 136–137
Carroll, Wesley B. "B" 80
Carter, Charlie 6, *92*, *181*; arrangements 169–170, 177–182, 192; career 74–77, 83, 91–97, 100–101, 111–112, 126–127, 157; childhood 91–92; retirement 177–182; style 162, 165–166
CBDNA *see* College Band Directors National Association
cello 24–25
Centennial Exhibition 102
Champion, John E. 113–115, 133
Chase, Bill 125
cheerleaders 57
cheers 28
Chicago Philharmonic 35
Chief step 143–144
Chief Yahola 115
Chiefs Field 5
The Chieftain 176–177
Choral Union 191
church 15
Cigar Bowl 55, 59
Cincinnati Conservatory of Music 15, 17, 24, 52–53
Cincinnati Symphony 35
Cinderella 72
Citrus Commission 117–118
civil rights 130–131
Civil War 11, 71
Clark, Johnny E. 76–77, 96
Clark University 16–17
Clary, Richard 172
Cleveland Orchestra 109–110
Cliburn, Van 73
Cline, Martha May 15
Coca-Cola 32, 73
"Coed Four" 76
coed universities 42–48
co-education 133
Cole, Nat King 70
College Band Directors National Association (CBDNA) 90, 142

College-Conservatory *see* Cincinnati Conservatory
College of Music Band Archive 2
College Orchestra 19
College Swing Band 36
Collins, Leroy 134
Columbia University 122
"Come-On and Go" 77–78
Como, Perry 83
competitions 26–27, 61, 107–109
composers 92–93, 96
Connor, James E. 87
Conradi, Edward 16, 36
convocation 32
Cooper, Charlotte 27–28, 39
Corea, Chick 169, 182
Corradino, George 52–54, 67, 79, 81, 141
Cougar Marching Band 98
Cramer, William 153
Crimson Tide Band 115
Crockett, Davy 69
Croft, James 171–172
Crowe, Gene 104–105, 178
culture 32
Cumberland University 48

Dale Mabry Army Air Force Field 36, 44
Danford, Howard 86
Daniel, Ted 80
DCI *see* Drum Corps International
death 13, 177
Dick Howser Stadium 155–156
Dickinson, Chris 144
discipline 63–64, 116–119, 146–147, 174; *see also* hazing
discrimination 17, 33, 114; *see also* integration
Disney, Walt 71, 72
Ditto Corporation 66
"Ditto machine" 66
"Dixie" 114–115, 133
Dixie Conference 55
"Dixieland Jubilee" 71
Doak Campbell Stadium 56, 77, 99–100, 110, *176*, *195*
Dobert, Earl 55
Dominican Republic 79
"Don't Cry for Me Argentina" 153–154
Dorsey, Mable *164*
Dorsey, Rodney *164*
Drick, Tom 134, *134*
drill charts 66–67

drill corps 28
drill design 142
Droste, Paul 153
drum corps 142–143
Drum Corps International (DCI) 142
drums 23, 50, 77–78, 179
Duke, Bob 136–137
Dunn, Virginia 29
Dunnigan, Patrick 2, **169**, 186; arrangements 180–181; career 168–172, 177–179, 194
Dylan, Bob 131

East Florida Seminary 9–10
Eastman School of Music 93
education 13, 123
Education Amendments 183
Edwards, Karl 85
enrollment 42–43
ensemble participation 18
entertainment 125
Everglades Sugar March (Sturchio) 27
Evita 154
expulsion 174–175

Falany, Curtis 106, 114
Falany, Jo Ellen 106
family 26
"Fanfare" 151–153
Ferris, George 101–102
FFC *see* Florida Female College
Fiesta Bowl 165
"Fight Song" 5, 56–58, 106–107, 157, 167, 190
Fighting Gator Band 87
Fighting Seminoles 57
Finlayson, Walter A. 49
Fisher, Jimbo 185
Flastacowo **25**, 45
Florida Female College (FFC) 14–20; *see also* Florida State College for Women
Florida Flambeau 2, 19, 21–27, 35–36, 45, 85–86, 110–111, 116–117, 130–131
Florida Institute 9–10
Florida Legislature 58–59
Florida Military and Collegiate Institute 11
Florida Normal 14
Florida State College (FSC) 12–13; *see also* Florida Female College
Florida State College for Women (FSCW) 18; band 19–22, **29**, **37–38**, **41**, **51**; *see also* School of Music

218 Index

Florida State University (FSU) *see specific topics*
Floyd, Carlisle 102, 139, 148
"Flush" *see* Royal Flush
"Flush the Field" 105–106
flutes *180*
Flying High Circus 53
Flying High Circus Band 94
Flying Seminoles 5, 63, 80, 147
The Focus 129–130
Fogarty, Marjorie Nell *see* Lee, Marjorie Fogarty
football 5–6, 13, 44, 59–64; anti- 130–135; losses 166–167; popularity 13, 31
Formula Shows 69
Fort Lauderdale Beach 4
Foster, William P. 79, 109, 123
Fowler, Nancy 153
Franklin, Ed 79–80
Freeman, Janice 80
Friendship Ambassadors Foundation 141
FSC *see* Florida State College
FSCW *see* Florida State College for Women
FSCW Artist Series 19
"FSU Victory March" 100
FSView & Florida Flambeau see Florida Flambeau
fund raising 139–140
future 90–91

Gallows Hill 9
"Garnet and Gold" 36
Garroway, Dave 82–83
Gasparilla Parade 82
Gator Band 21–22, 63, 159
Gator Bowl 116, 118
gender 14, 21–22, 43, 86
Georgia Tech 60
Gershwin, George 70, 165
Gilbert, Jon 78
Glass, Jim Ed 84
Glee Club 12, 36, 42, 191
Glière, Reinhold 35
Go Cadence 74, *119*, 126
Godspell 126
Goldwater, Barry 102
Gonzalez, Larry 117
graduate degrees 43
Great Britain 188
Great Depression 17, 91–92
Great War *see* World War I
Greek system 79

Gridiron Pageantry (Righter) 31, 33
Grundman, Clare 66
Gunnoe, Pat 56

Hadley, Kim *181*
Haggard, Bill 129, 138, 141
Haigh, Joanne 5
Hair 126
half-time shows 48–52, 69, 101–109, 157
Hamlisch, Marvin 144
Hammerstein, Oscar, II 70, 72
Haskell's Rascals 77–78
Haskins, Jack 94
Haughee, Chris 119–120
Haughee, Nancy 144
hazing 173–175
Hazing Policy 174
Heinlein, Christian P. 38–39
"Hell-Raisers" 76
Henderson, Jennie 12
Heritage Protocol & University Archives 2
"High O'er the Towering Pines" 189–190
high schools 33
Hinkle, Bill 140
Hirt, Al 52–53
history 1–3
Hogan, Ed 178
Holling, Spessard I. 28
Holst, Gustav 162
Homecoming *70*, 81
Homecoming Pow Wow 113–114
Housewright, Wiley 135
Hughes, Frances M. *25*, 25–27, 193
"Hymn to the Garnet and Gold" (hymn) 4, 190–193

Ibis 104
Idea Theme Shows 69–70
idealism 32
Indiana University 58, 62–63
Industrial College for Negroes 14
Institute for the Blind, Deaf, and Dumb 14
The Instrumentalist 31–32, 69, 75
instruments 18, 19, 40–41
integration 133
investigations 134

J. Dayton Smith Recital Hall 191
Janowski, Penny MacArthur 88
Jayhawks 123
Jazz Lab Band 135–136

Index 219

jazz music 123
J.M. Smucker Company 153
Jones, Larry 133
Jones, Spike 52
Jordan 135–138
Jordan, Jimmy 147
Jordanian Army Band 137

Kansas City Chiefs 77
Kansas City Philharmonic 35
Keipp, Madeleine 15
Keith, Denton 137
Kellum, J.G. 17
Kelly, Godwin 147
Kluetmeier, Heinz 156
Knight, Frank 159
Knowles, Beyoncé 182–183
Kotelmann, Ludwig 16–17
Kuersteiner, Karl 43, 47, 63, 191
Kuperberg, Mike 6
Kyser, Kay 92

labor movement 17
Ladd, Helen L. 19
Landis Green 36, 79
Langford, Gary 159
Langley, Dubby 48
Langley, Jack 48
Latin influence 182
Latin percussion 125–126
Lawrence, John (Johnny) C. 45–48, *47*, 189
Lawton, Robert O. 94
Lecuona, Ernesto 73
Lee, Jack 109
Lee, Marjorie Fogarty *49*, 94
legacies 27
legislation 42
Leon Female Academy 10–11
Leon High School 34, 36
liberal organizations 24
Life 67
Life on the Mississippi (Twain) 22–23
Lipscomb, Irvin 80
Lockhart, Dawn 5
Louisiana State University (LSU) 109, 132

Mabry, Dale 44
MacDill Air Force Base 55
Madsen, Clifford K. 94, 98–101, 143–144, 164–165, 174
majorettes *51*, 53–54, *54*, *59*, *124*, *161*; see also Marching Maidens

management 63
Mancini, Henry 102
Mangione, Chuck 182, 187–188
Manley R. Whitcomb Band Complex 90
March Militaire (Schubert) 27
marching bands *see specific topics*
Marching Chiefs 56, *59*, 68, *82*, 98, 101, 103, 108, 117, 119, 128, 151, 161, 162, 171, 173, 176, 180, 187, 195; *see also specific topics*
Marching Chiefs Alumni Wall of Fame 181
Marching Chiefs Fantasia 111–112, 162
Marching Maidens 72, 80
Marine Corps, U.S. 72
Marshall, J. Stanley 114, 133–136, 139–140
Martin, Mike 155–156
mascots 57, 81, 104
mass entertainment 72
Mayberry, Hilda Gay 61
Mayer, Betty 22
Mayo, Richard "Dick" 1, 79–84, *82*, 121–130, *122*, 137–141, *138*
McBride, William 92
McCarrell, Lamar K. 33
Meisburg, Steve 163
Mercer, Johnny *51*
Miami Jackson High School 79
Middle East 135–138, 187
military, U.S. 30, 36–37
Miller, Glen 102
Minear, Doug 159
Miscellaneous Legislation Committee 87
Mississippi Southern College 84
Mitchell, Bob 104
Moffit, Bill 108–109
Monroe, Amanda 4
Moore, Claudia 23
morale 20, 150
Motown music 182
movie themes 72, 170, 182
Mudra, Darrell 134–135, 139
Murphree, Albert Alexander 11–12, 14–16
Murphy, Kathleen 5
music 1, 7, 19, 20, 90, 128–129
music education 31–32, 92, 122, 154, 160, 172
musical theme shows 69, 71–72
musical vandalism 179
My Tallahassee (Avant) 15

Index

national acclaim 156
National Anthem 153, 160
National Association of Schools of Music 20
National Championships 185
National Collegiate Athletic Association (NCAA) 107–108, 183
National Defense Educational Act (NDEA) 149
National Football League (NFL) 186–188
National High Magnetic Field Laboratory 167
Native Americans 55–56, 80–81, 115, *154*
NCAA *see* National Collegiate Athletic Association
NDEA *see* National Defense Educational Act
Nestico, Sammy 187
New York Philharmonic 121
NFL *see* National Football League
North Carolina State 60
Northwestern University 65, 168
Nugent, Tom 63, 87

obsessive-compulsive disorder (OCD) 96
odd-even games 23, 25, 26–27, 44, 57, 198*n*24
Odum, Andy 77–78
Ohio State University 65–66, 78, 92–93, 152–153
Ohio State University Marching Band 93–94, 95–96
Oklahoma Sooners 4–5
Oklahoma State University 107
"Old Folks at Home" 159
Opperman, Ella Scoble *18*, 199*n*71; career 17–19, 23, 33, 37–38, 43
Opperman Music Hall 99, 155
Orange Bowl 4
organ 15
Ort, Paul 83
Owen F. Sellers Music Amphitheatre 52

"Pageant Idea" 31–32
Pankaskie, Sara 96, 125–127, 192–193
Parker, Fess 69
Parsons, Paula 80
Pate, Judy 106
Pate, Mike 106–107, 118
paternalism 17

patriotism 34, 72
Peach Bowl 118
Pearl Harbor 32
percussion placement 99
Peterson, Bill 133, 146
The Phantom of the Opera 163–164
piano 16, 76–77
Picoult, Jodi 2
Pinocchio 71
P.K. Yonge Developmental Research School 165
Plack, David 2, 171–172, 175, ***184***, 194
Plains Indian Rain Dance 81
Poe, Gerald D. 158–159
police 104–105
Police Department, FSU 174
politics 100, 102, 130–131, 135
popular culture 102, 122–123, 182–183
Porter, Cole 72–73
post-game parties 107
Prague Conservatory 35
precision drill 21–22, 163
Price, Harry E. ***122***, 140
public criticism 132–133
public relations 176–177
publicity 73
Puckett, Dick 79–80
Purdy, William T. 49
Pythian Bowl 55

race 79, 80–81, 114; *see also* African-American; Native Americans
Raiders of the Lost Ark 153–154
Raxsdale, William 142–145
recruitment *see* rehearsals
Refrigerator Bowl 55
rehearsals 66–67, 68, 137–138, 160
religion 136–137
Reserve Officer Training Corps (ROTC) 65
Revelli, William 33–34, 42–43
Reynolds, Bookie 112
Rice, Tim 153–154
Rich, Buddy 123
Richardson, Ann 36, ***41***
Righter, Charles B. 30–31, 33
rivalries 85–86
Robinson, Sue 23
rock and roll music 123
Rocky 150
Rodgers, Richard 70, 73
Rogers, Bernard 93
Roly Polys 187
Rosete, George 126

Index

ROTC *see* Reserve Officer Training Corps
Royal Flush 105–106, 129, *156*
Rozelle, Pete 158
Russia 35
Russian Imperial Army 35–36
Russian Tchaikovsky Piano Competition 73

salaries 139
"Salute to the Spirit of the Southland" 71
"Salute to the Trimester System" 71
Salzburg Mozarteum 40
Samford University 185
"Sammy Seminole" 81
San Diego State University 191
Santana, Carlos 125–126
Santana, Ed 55
scandals 84–85, 113–116; *see also* hazing
scatter drills 75, 130, 150
Schmidt, Harry 153
School Hygiene (Kotelmann) 16–17
School of Music *18*, 18–20, 24–25, 43–44, *61*
school song 45–47, 189
school spirit 28, 30–31, 62, 166
Scotes, Thomas 137
Screech Squad 129
Script Shows 69
SDS *see* Students for a Democratic Society
Search Light 13
section names 129
sectionals 4
Sellers, Owen F. *40*, *41*; career 24–28, 30, 52, 193; return 39–41
seminary 197n1
A Seminole Saga 162–163
Seminole Sound 183–184, *184*
Seminole Tribe 115
Senior Bowl 84
Severinsen, Doc 109
SGA *see* Student Government Association
Sheldon, Robert 2, 96–97, 164–167
Shelfer, Bennett 89, *89*
Shellahamer, Bentley 1–2, 6, *149*; arrangements 178–180; career 78, 89–90, 148–156, 179–180; return 161–164
Sherwood Conservatory 15
"the show" 125
Skull Sessions 4, 155–156

slavery 15
Sliger, Bernard "Bernie" 147–148, 167
Smith, J. Dayton 60, 159, *191*, 192–193
Smith, Robert G. 40, 49, 52–53
Smith, Scott 5
Smith, W. Alan 107–108, 112, 128
Snow White and the Seven Dwarfs 71
social media 175, 183
socialism 17
Soloff, Lew 125
songs 28
The Sound of Music 72, 84
Sousa, John Philip 123
Sousa Band 72
South Park 181
Southern University 132
Sparkman, Steven L. 114, 159
Spielberg, Steven 153
sports 44
Sports Illustrated 156
Spradling, Robert 5
SSB *see* Student Seminole Boosters
stadiums 32
Stalin, Joseph 35
Stallone, Sylvester 150
Stanford University 109
State Department (Florida) 88
State Development Commission (Florida) 88
Steffen, Jean 23–24
Stetson 60
Strozier, Robert M. 70
Student Government Association (SGA) 131
student leadership 141
Student Seminole Boosters (SSB) 118
Students for a Democratic Society (SDS) 133
Sturchio, Frank G. (Pop) 27
Styne, Jules 71
Sullivan, Tom 131
Summer Twirling Camp 80
Sun Bowl 83–84, 116
"The Sunshine State" 73
Super Bowl XVIII 158
Susannah (Floyd, C.) 102
Swanson, Marian 25
Swingle, Marilyn Ruth 43
Switzer, Amanda 4–5
Swor, William F. 109
Sykora, Frank *35*, 35–39, 193
symphonic band 27, 77–78
Syria 135–138
Szell, George 109–110

Index

Tallahassee 9
Tallahassee Democrat 68, 95, 108, 110–111, 152
A Tallahassee Girl (Thompson, M.) 11
Tallahassee Winds 168
Tally-Ho 52, 73, 80–81, 107
Tally Troopers 23–24, 28
Tangerine Bowl 55, 147
Tau Beta Sigma (TBS) 79
teachers 36
Teaching Little Fingers to Play (Thompson, J.) 77
telephones 102
television 102
Texas Southern 132
Texas Western University 83
This Liberty Bell *51*
Thompson, John 77
Thompson, Maurice 11
315th Infantry Band 53
Thurston, Robert S. "Bob" 95, 157, 170, 178–179
Title IX 183
"Tomahawk Chop" 77
touring 135–138, 186–188
track & field 86, 211*n*36
traditions 88, 104–107, 129, 146–159, 165, 195–196
Trinity Church 16
Tripp, Ethel M. 19–20
trombone 92
Troy State Teachers College 48
trumpet 125
tuba 6, *156*
The Tumultuous Sixties (Marshall) 135
Twain, Mark 22–23
24th Corps Band 53

undergraduate degrees 43
uniforms 29, *68*, 78–79, 81, 131, ***190***
United States (U.S.) 135
university administration 130–131
university distinguished professor 102
University Executive Council 46–47
University Government Association 55
University of Alabama 109
University of Arkansas 109
University of Connecticut 107
University of East Carolina 152
University of Florida 85–87, 158
University of Georgia 74
University of Houston 108–109
University of Iowa 30–31
University of Kansas 40, 123
University of Kentucky 168
University of Louisville 61
University of Miami 60, 165
University of Michigan 33–34, 43
University of Nebraska 191
University of Richmond 71
University of South Florida 154–155
University of Southwestern Louisiana 142
University of Tampa 62
University of Tennessee 153
University of Texas 53, 168
University of the State of Florida 14
University of West Virginia 146, 185
University of Wyoming 116

Veller, Don 60, 62–63
Verhoeven, Daryl 4
veterans 42–43
"Victory Song" 5, 100–101
Vietnam War 114, 130–131
violence 175
Virginia Military Institute (VMI) 60, 63, 72
Vorce, Fred 159

Wagner, Richard 123
Walter, Bruno 40
war 10–11, 30–34, 36
"War Chant" 76–77
War Department, U.S. 33–34
"We Are the Girls from Old Florida" 28
Webber, Andrew Lloyd 153–154, 163–164
Weigel, Eugene 66–67, 74
Weingartner, Felix 40
Welker, Chris 78
West Florida Seminary 10–12
Westberry, David 155, 159–160, ***169***, 173
Westberry, Leonard L. 160
Westbrook, Don 159–160
Westcott, James D. 10
Westcott Building 100–101
Westcott Fountain 71
Western Michigan University 168
"When You Wish Upon a Star" 71
Whitcomb, Lea 79
Whitcomb, Manley R. "Whit" 1, *68*; career 65–69, 74–75, 78–80; style 85–91, 118–121
Wiggins, "Blind Tom" 15
Wiljohn 85
Williams, Clifton 93

Williams, Jerry 112
Williams, J.H. 50
Williams, John 153, 162, 169
Williams, Kenny 7, *154*
Williams, Vanessa 138
Willis, Mary Tarver *50*
Wilson, Woodrow 13
Winchester, Cookie 112
Wind Ensemble 135–136
Winthrop, Francis B. 13
Wise, Tim 129–130, 159
"The Wise Old Owl" 92
"With Spirits So Light" 28
WLAF *see* World League of American Football
Wofford 60
women 16, 21, 32–34, 40–41, 76, 102, 183; *see also* discrimination; Florida Female College; Florida State College for Women
women's liberation 114, 130–131
women's sports 185
women's suffrage 17
Woodham, Wally 147
Woodruff, Bob 86–87
woodwinds 95–96
World League of American Football (WLAF) 186–188
world trade fair 135–136
World War I (Great War) 17, 32
World War II 33–34, 41, 66, 100
Wright, Al G. 31–32
Wright, Thomas "Tommie" *58*, 58–59, 100

Yoder, Paul 77–78, 102–103

Zebrowitz, Lesley Ray 170, 175, 186–187
Zwilich, Ellen Taafe 75, 97

www.ingramcontent.com/pod-product-compliance
Ingram Content Group UK Ltd.
Pitfield, Milton Keynes, MK11 3LW, UK
UKHW041949140426
5217IPUK00014B/715